MARITIME SECURITY

MARITIME
SECURITY

BY KENNETH GALE HAWKES

CORNELL MARITIME PRESS

Centreville, Maryland

The reader should use good judgment and prudence in any involvement in matters relating to the subject of this work. Although the author and the publisher have diligently sought to offer correct and accurate information, no warranty or guarantee is expressed or implied that the text is in fact error free or that the recommendations herein are merchantable or appropriate for any particular purpose or situation. Neither the author, the publisher, nor their agents shall be in any way liable or responsible for any consequential, incidental, or exemplary loss or damage resulting from the use of this text.

Library of Congress Cataloging-in-Publication Data

Hawkes, Kenneth Gale
    Maritime security / by Kenneth Gale Hawkes.—1st ed.
      p. cm.
    Bibliography: p.
    Includes index.
    ISBN 0-87033-395-X
      1. Merchant marine—Security measures. 2. Harbors—Security measures. 3. Shipping—Security measures. I. Title.
VK203.H38 1989
387.5'028'9—dc20   88-43525
                                                       CIP

Manufactured in the United States of America
First edition

For my parents and my sons: my mortality and immortality,
each of our generations constituting
a small but significant step in the evolutionary ladder of humankind
and the progression toward a better and safer world.

CONTENTS

FOREWORD

A s we enter the latter part of the twentieth century, the business world, and society in general, reels to the torments of crime and terrorism. Indeed, fear for the security of one's own lifestyle, business, and sheer existence appears to be in the forefront of almost everyone's mind. So it is with the maritime industry, where concern is both intense and directed, as possibilities for huge losses in lives and profits exist. The maritime industry is characterized by numerous points of vulnerability—cruise and cargo ship pilferage, drug trafficking violence, dock theft, piracy, offshore production losses, LNG and oil tanker explosion, terrorism, war in neutral waters—the list appears unending.

Maritime Security is a timely text that is both comprehensive and analytical. It provides an all-inclusive, singular reference on security principles, tactical procedures, management techniques, and legal ramifications for addressing the topic of maritime security. The book is a well-organized compendium of both rational and economic considerations focusing on the prevention of losses and the management of security breaches.

Maritime Security recognizes the important principles involved in security planning, and thoroughly discusses the many types of programs and techniques that have been successful in reducing vulnerability to maritime loss. Also presented is a much needed discussion on the civil liabilities associated with the implementation of security measures. Further, this book offers the reader a series of extremely valuable appendices, important references to specific U.S. Codes and the *Code of Federal Regulations* addressing international maritime and port security; protection and security of vessels, harbors, and waterfront facilities; measures to prevent unlawful acts against passengers and crews on board ships; and drug abuse prevention on board vessels. In and by themselves, these appendices are a "must" for the maritime security manager.

Since man first went to sea, he has been plagued by those who would steal and plunder. Even in today's modern maritime commerce, piracy still runs rampant on the open waters of the world. Preventing crime and terrorism on the high seas should not be an unreachable possibility, but a reality. This book provides the first reasonable and pragmatic steps aimed at achieving this goal.

Robert W. Taylor, Ph. D.
Associate Professor, Department
of Social Sciences
The University of Texas at Tyler

ACKNOWLEDGMENTS

There have been many who have helped me gain the lifetime of knowledge and experience that was required before this book could be written or even contemplated, not all of whom can be mentioned and many of whom cannot now even be recalled. Others have helped or encouraged me in various ways in the development of the book itself. To those whom I fail to mention, but should, I apologize. To those whom I do mention, I do so with gratitude.

First and foremost I must thank my parents, Estes Gale Hawkes and Stevanie Joy Hawkes, for making me the person I am, for supporting me in every endeavor I can recall, and for being the role models they are. Both are truly exceptional individuals. My love affair with the sea began at an early age, and from scuba diving in the waters off Southern California at 13, to lifeguarding in the lakes of Washington State at 17, and commercial fishing in Alaska at 18, they supported me every inch of the way while developing grey hair in the process. I am sure I accelerated their aging process when I announced, in 1968, that I intended to join the Marine Corps. Yet they supported me in that decision as well. When I resigned my regular commission in 1976 to attend law school they supported my decision to do so, and when I decided to close my physically safe maritime trial practice in order to devote all my time and energies to writing and consulting they offered encouragement, even though offering myself as an international maritime security operations specialist might well place me again in harm's way.

Next to my parents, I owe a special debt of gratitude to the United States Marine Corps; without the training and experiences I received from serving in it I could not now be doing what I am. The world, unfortunately, is a dangerous place and it has been made even more so by the advent of twentieth-century terrorism. This book is about thwarting that terrorism and the potential for it within the maritime arena, and the knowledge of tactics, weapons, and weapons systems that has allowed me to argue my point of view was gained as a result of my service in the Corps.

Combat Marines are not generally given to analyzing legal issues, and I was no different. Law school was a completely new experience. So was learning to interact with lawyers and judges.

Three attorneys stand out as mentors in my training as a maritime trial lawyer. All three are military veterans, from different services and different wars, who each in his own way had a remarkable effect upon my legal development. They are David P. Karcher, Esq., and Laurence F. Valle, Esq., of Miami, and Dewey R. Villareal, Jr., Esq., of Tampa. All three are renowned maritime trial attorneys, and I owe them much.

I suppose it was inevitable that, after becoming a practicing maritime attorney in a law firm that represented primarily shipowners and their insurers, and after learning some of the ins and outs of the shipping business, I as a former Marine and ardent student of military history would draw the conclusions I have with regard to the terrorist threat and the potential legal liabilities now facing the maritime industry. Putting those conclusions on paper, however, was not something I could readily do. For one thing it would take a substantial amount of time, and young lawyers have a tendency not to have much of that commodity available. For another, a book-length writing project is not something that should be undertaken lightly or without considerable reflection, and a certain amount of encouragement is generally needed. I received much of that encouragement during the years I contemplated the idea from my brother, Dr. G. W. Hawkes, who teaches creative writing at the university level and who is an accomplished writer of fiction. I am indebted to him for his support and encouragement, not to mention professional advice.

Two special individuals deserve to be mentioned here. Dr. Robert W. Taylor of the University of Texas at Tyler teaches criminal justice and has been a friend and colleague in the security business for many years. We have worked side by side teaching S.W.A.T. tactics in the hot Yuma desert and providing security for sunken treasure expeditions in the waters of the Caribbean. I consider him a true comradein-arms in the fight against international terrorism, and I appreciate his comments and suggestions regarding both the concept of this book and the ultimate manuscript. I also owe much to Ninth Degree Grand Master Yung Ho Jun of Tampa. As my Kwan Jang Nim for over eight years in the Korean martial art of Tae Kwon Do, Master Jun has taught me invaluable hand-to-hand combat skills. When the "fortunes of war" required me to track down and locate a vessel suspected of having been secreted by drug smugglers in Haiti, he drilled me until he was satisfied I had at least a reasonable chance of facing an armed opponent bare-handed and surviving. I am grateful for his friendship and everything he has taught me.

Special thanks also go to Mark A. Buland of Sacramento, boyhood friend and former professional diver and North Sea oil field worker, for his information and advice.

MARITIME SECURITY

0730 hours in Boston Harbor. The city is beginning to accelerate. Slowly and cautiously, assisted by her tugs, one of the strangest ships ever built approaches her berth. With a length of 940 feet and a beam of 125 feet, she displaces over 940,000 deadweight tons. Rising from her main deck, and connected by pipes, valves, and catwalks, are five aluminum alloy spheres. Each sphere is 125 feet in diameter and weighs 750 tons. The five spheres together hold over 125,000 cubic meters of liquefied natural gas.

Waiting at the pier for the ship to dock is a man dressed in a conservative gray business suit. He has a raincoat draped casually over one arm and an attache case in his free hand. Inside his breast pocket is a card case containing business cards inscribed with the name of the ship's protection and indemnity association's Boston attorneys. By displaying one of these cards he has gained access to the dock upon which he now stands amidst line handlers, Customs officials, stevedore personnel, agents, and other people.

The mooring lines are manhandled ashore. The ship nestles into her berth. The gangway is lowered and the safety net rigged. Pilot and tugs depart and the ship is cleared for Customs quickly and routinely. Immediately thereafter the master is beset by agents, cargo-handling supervisors, Coast Guard inspectors, ship chandlers, and others, each with his own special problem and all requiring the master's full attention. The attorney walks aboard unnoticed. No one stops him. No one questions his right to be aboard. At this time in the morning the master has no way of verifying the attorney's employment, and wouldn't in any case once the attorney hands him one of his cards. The master cheerfully invites the man to have a seat and a cup of coffee while he waits to hear what he has to say. Dealing with P&I club attorneys at each port of call is routine and anticipated, although they usually do not come aboard so early in the morning.

The attorney places his attache case on the table. In it, however, are not the expected legal papers and notepads. No pens or pencils. No calculator. No legal tools of any kind. Contained instead is a 9mm machine pistol and a grenade. Under the raincoat is an American-made, self-contained 66mm rocket launcher, known as a LAW. The person who has so effortlessly seated himself next to the unsuspecting master of a ship that carries enough destructive potential to level a major portion of Boston, with a weapon capable of realizing that potential, is not an attorney at all but a terrorist. He plans extortion, destruction, and death; and he has just gained access to his objective.

Three thousand miles away, across the continent, it is half-past four in the morning in port facilities from San Diego to Seattle. The moon has set. The night is as dark, and cold, and quiet as it will get. A security guard nods sleepily at his desk. There has been no activity in his area of the port for hours, at least none of which he was aware. He has become bored with the night, bored with his job, and bored with the girlie magazine left by the guard he relieved hours before. His only concern, and that upon which he now focuses all of his attention, is staying awake until the end of his shift.

A hundred yards or so away, in a container storage area, the thieves are at work. They know the port. They come from the rank and file of the people who work there: the longshoremen, crane operators, truck drivers, warehousemen, agents, clerks, and security guards. Tonight there are three of them, and they are busily transferring cartons of radios from the container they have carefully broken into to another container that will be moved out of the port later in the day. The pilferage will go unnoticed for days, even weeks. The loss, when it is discovered, is insured against. It is considered a cost of doing business. The responsible underwriters may attempt to subrogate their loss by suing the stevedore or carrying vessel, if a case can be made against one or the other, but more than likely they won't. Pilferage is so widespread, and has continued for so long unchecked, that it is expected. It may be complained about, it may be litigated over, but it is not stopped.

In Singapore it is 8:30 P.M., 2030 hours for those aboard the oil tanker transiting the Phillip Channel. The night is overcast. The sea is dark. The lights of the city are barely visible off to port, and the mate on watch is just settling into his evening routine, having assumed his watch a little over half an hour ago. The ship's radar is functioning, but no one pays much attention to it. The only lookout posted is the able-bodied seaman on watch, and he is on the bridge with the mate. The ship is on automatic pilot and traveling at 12 knots. All is quiet. The engines throb hypnotically, and the watch promises to pass uneventfully.

All is not well, however. Unknown to the mate or anyone else on board, two high-speed boats are approaching from astern. They are manned by modern-day pirates who are armed with submachine guns, pistols, knives, and grappling hooks. Their intent is to board and loot the tanker, as they have done to similar vessels with impunity numerous times over the past decade. They are relaxed, even jubilant, knowing that no resistance whatever will come from their quarry. The ship, as virtually all others like her, carries no firearms and no security personnel. The master's instructions are to do nothing, in the event of a boarding, that might antagonize the captors. He is to let them have what they want and allow them to leave unmolested, even though he knows the boarding could be prevented and even though he knows members of his crew might be killed once the pirates come aboard.

On an oil rig in the North Sea between England and Scandinavia, it is lunchtime. The weather has been abominable for days, which is not unusual, and no one with any sense has stuck his nose outside. There wouldn't be much reason to do so in any case, since this platform is a production platform. Unlike exploration platforms, which require large numbers of personnel to accomplish their task, production rigs are manned by few people. The 24-hour, beehivelike activity that had engulfed crane operators, roustabouts, divers, welders, engineers, inspectors, boat crews, seismologists, food service personnel, and others ceased a long time ago. The job at hand now is to ensure the proper flow of oil from the wellhead hundreds of feet below the stormy waters through the interconnecting maze of subsurface pipelines to various shoreside facilities. The daily routine is mercilessly boring, the equipment automated, the pay good, and the likelihood of any unforeseen mishap remote.

Unbeknownst to the highly paid caretakers of this particular platform, however, their rig has been targeted by international terrorists bent on extortion. Their plan is to approach the platform under cover of bad weather and darkness, seize control, and demand a substantial ransom for the return of the installation and those on board. Their threat, aside from the obvious potential loss of lives, is the destruction of a $200 million platform and a blown wellhead that would cause environmental devastation and substantial economic loss.

The terrorists, pirates, and thieves in these scenarios would succeed. Indeed, some have been succeeding for years, for little or no effort is being made to stop them. Escalation from pilferage and bloodless piracy to hijacking, extortion, and mayhem is not only foreseeable but extremely likely in today's maritime security void. If the 1970s were the years international terrorists invaded the air, the 1990s will be the years they move offshore. It is reported that the Popular Front for the Liberation of Palestine has frogmen who have been trained in the use of underwater demolitions. Other reports indicate that another Palestinian group obtained four one-man submarines sometime in the early 1980s. In the now-famous *Achille Lauro* incident in October of 1985, four Arab terrorists hijacked a cruise ship and held its passengers and crew hostage for two days, ultimately killing an elderly passenger.

The *Achille Lauro* is not the first or last cruise ship to be hijacked, however. In January of 1961 maritime hijackers seized control of the Portuguese cruise ship *Santa Maria* and held the ship and her 560 passengers hostage for 11 days. In March 1973 another cruise ship, the *Sanya,* was sunk by a limpet mine in Beirut, and as recently as July of 1988 the cruise ship *City of Poros* was boarded and attacked by submachine gun–wielding terrorists who managed to kill 9 and injure 47 before escaping over the side. Other vessels besides cruise ships have been targeted. In February 1974 a Greek freighter was seized in Karachi, Pakistan, by terrorists who threatened to blow her up unless the Greek government freed two incarcerated terrorists. In February of 1981 Irish Republican Army terrorists boarded and sank the 1,100-ton coal ferry *Nellie M.*

These incidents are only slightly demonstrative of the myriad opportunities available within the maritime industry to international terrorists. Literally thousands of ships enter ports daily around the world carrying hazardous or valuable cargoes. At the present time virtually no nonmilitary ship, of any nationality, is prepared to meet a serious terrorist threat. Port facilities worldwide remain not only unprotected but oblivious to the danger.

Piracy in some corners of the world runs rampant. In some ports in western Africa, such as Lagos, pirates frequently board anchored vessels at night in substantial numbers. In the Far East tankers are boarded routinely. Between 1982 and 1985 pirates in the Gulf of Thailand killed 388 refugees, abducted 587, and raped 734. An additional 967 persons are missing and presumed dead.

The offshore petroleum industry has created hundreds of desirable targets. Drilling ships and rigs costing in the hundreds of millions of dollars apiece are wonderful targets for extortionists. Wellheads, pipelines, and storage facilities provide tremendous targets of opportunity upon which an attack could prove economically crippling or environmentally disastrous. There are over 500 supertankers of more than 175,000 deadweight tons plying the world's oceans. The potential for environmental destruction of just one of these vessels is enormous, as evidenced by the 250,000-ton oil spill in the *Amoco Cadiz* disaster of 1978.

Hundreds of other types of oceangoing vessels constitute targets for the opportunity-seeking terrorist. LNG tankers are, as the opening scenario suggests, likely and productive targets. Cruise ships have already proven their desirability. Cargo vessels of all kinds, traditionally unarmed and undermanned, are wonderful targets. Even an average-sized freighter with a modest cargo is worth millions and is capable of being sunk so that she blocks an important shipping channel.

Finally, in today's litigious world the civil liability for the lives of those aboard target vessels must be considered. The family of Leon Klinghoffer, the *Achille Lauro* passenger killed by terrorists, has filed a $1.5 billion lawsuit against the owners and operators of the cruise ship. Seamen injured aboard vessels attacked in the Persian Gulf, such as the *Sea Isle City,* have sued their employers for millions of dollars in damages. If it can be proven that a prudent shipowner should have recognized a security threat and taken responsible steps to protect his vessel, but failed to do so and thereby cost the lives of crew members or passengers, a judgment against the shipowner and possibly his insurance underwriters could well be in the millions of dollars. Since 1984 over 300 ships have been attacked in the Persian Gulf. More than 200 crewmen have been killed. These figures alone lend credibility to the claims of negligent security practices that allow attacks that other-wise could have been prevented or repelled.

The purpose of this book is to present, in one reference, the security principles, tactical procedures, management techniques, and legal considerations that all shipowners, offshore operators, and port facility administrators should utilize in designing and implementing programs that can provide adequate and reliable security. Some of the sugges-tions made may well be considered too extreme by many shipowners. Seamen's unions may object to the arming of vessels their members serve on. Port administrators may consider the recommendations too expensive or not cost-effective. Offshore operators may refuse to recognize any need whatever for security enhancement. All such ob-jections are foolhardy, head-in-the-sand viewpoints. All are deadly mistakes.

CHAPTER ONE

SECURITY GOALS AND PRINCIPLES

M ARITIME security can be defined as those measures employed by owners, operators, and administrators of vessels, port facilities, offshore installations, and other marine organizations or establishments to protect against seizure, sabotage, piracy, pilferage, annoyance, or surprise. It can also be considered as embracing all measures taken to prevent hostile interference with lawful operations. Proper maritime security creates a condition which establishes and maintains certain protective measures. These protective measures, while they may vary markedly from one organization to another depending upon its nature, must be capable in all instances of performing two absolutely imperative tasks. They must provide timely and accurate warning of an impending threat, and they must be capable of removing or neutralizing that threat by repelling, capturing, or killing those persons whose actions or intentions constitute it.

The two goals of maritime security are, therefore, adequate warning and timely reaction. Adequate warning is essential to timely reaction. Without such warning, a threat potentially becomes an attack and the ship or installation's ability to successfully repel that attack is substantially reduced. On the other hand, the ability to react in a timely manner to a security threat is just as important as the ability to provide adequate warning. Neither is more important than the other. Without adequate warning the best security force in the world may fail to protect its charge. Conversely, without the ability to effectively react, adequate warning is useless.

Managers and administrators must therefore continually keep in mind these two paramount objectives of maritime security. Both adequate warning and timely reaction are achieved through proper security indoctrination and training of personnel. Only those masters who have grasped the nature and magnitude of the terrorist threat, and who have carefully analyzed that threat as it pertains to their vessels, will be prepared to properly indoctrinate and train their crews and develop ships capable of thwarting an attack. Only those operators and administrators of port facilities and offshore installations who have taken the time and made the effort to understand the security ramifications of doing business within today's maritime industry are likely to do so unscathed.

ADEQUATE WARNING

The ability to provide adequate warning stems first and foremost from an awareness of security on the port of every person engaged in the particular maritime activity. In the shipping business this includes owners, managers, officers, and crews. In port and other support facilities it includes all personnel employed at the particular establishment. An acronym which can assist in developing this awareness and which should be thoroughly etched in the minds of all concerned is CARE. Each crew member must *care* about the safety and security of his ship. Each maritime employee must *care* about his installation and place of work, not to mention his own safety. CARE stands for:

C   Concentrate
A   Always
R   Remember
E   Enemies

By caring, by concentrating, by remembering at all times that the ship or installation is at risk and that there are enemies everywhere, the worker increases his awareness of security and his ability to give adequate warning of any suspicious activity or circumstance. Where necessary, he will also understand the reason for increased duties or security watches.

Awareness alone, however, is not enough. Each vessel, port facility, or installation must have a security plan that has been carefully and thoroughly prepared and analyzed. Security plans are discussed in chapter 3, but generally consist of security standing (or standard) operating procedures (SOPs), contingency plans, and personnel assignments that are all designed to meet the security threat applicable to that particular entity. All personnel must know and understand the security plan as it relates to their particular responsibilities. For instance, if a particular crewman's assignment on his ship's security bill calls for him to act as lookout, main deck forward, starboard side, he must know where he is to be, what he is to report, and how and under what circumstances he is to act. Awareness and knowledge can only be gained through proper indoctrination and training, which is a function of enlightened security management. Security management is discussed in chapter 6.

TIMELY REACTION

A ship's or installation's ability to react in a timely manner to any security threat is determined by its achieved level of preparedness. Preparedness is a function of awareness and planning, but even more so it is the result of proper training and indoctrination of personnel. A properly trained security force, whether it takes the form of additional full-time security personnel or regular personnel trained in additional security duties, provides the weapons needed to meet any given security threat. Without those weapons the ship or installation is defenseless. Without those weapons adequate warning is useless. Trained and indoctrinated security personnel are therefore paramount to the security of any maritime enterprise.

SECURITY IN DEPTH

Perfect, absolute security can never be fully realized, although it may well be the goal of those tasked with providing the necessary security. There exists no vessel, facility, or installation that is so well protected it cannot be seized, damaged, or destroyed. Consequently, the purpose of maritime security is to make access to the target so difficult as to discourage the attempt and, if the attempt is made, to minimize the damages and ensure the attempt remains an attempt. One way of doing this is to ensure that all security measures utilize the axiom that all security should be in depth. In-depth security establishes multiple security perimeters or lines of defense through which an attacker, saboteur, hijacker, or other criminal must penetrate. He is delayed at each perimeter, allowing for a higher likelihood of detection and additional reaction time for security personnel to respond. The classic security scenario calls for three lines of defense. For a land-based installation, the first security perimeter would be the fence, wall, or other barrier surrounding the property, and is usually referred to as the "outer perimeter." The second line of defense would be the exterior walls of the building or buildings that compose the installation, and is usually labelled the "secondary perimeter." Finally, the third security perimeter is established inside the installation itself in areas capable of being secured or defended and is known as the "inner perimeter."

Factors affecting the degree and type of security required by any ship or installation are her size, the nature and sensitivity of her cargo, the mission or types of services provided, the vulnerability of equipment, the geographical location or locations, the economic and political situations of the areas involved, the proximity of external support and the nature of that support, and the capabilities of potential attackers. An acronym useful in remembering to consider these security factors is ACTION. In order for a captain or manager to be prepared he must take *action.* ACTION stands for:

A   Always
C   Consider
T   The
I   Immediate
O   Obvious
N   Nightmare

Napoleon Bonaparte stated the same idea a little differently in his maxims when he wrote: "In forming a plan of a campaign, one must foresee everything the enemy may do and be prepared with the necessary means to counteract it."

Because of the cost of physical protective measures in terms of money and manpower, however, maximum security may not be achieved under all circumstances. The specific areas of vulnerability must therefore be determined and resources apportioned accordingly. Some of this is performed during the security planning stage prior to drafting the security plan. At other times those tasked with security decision-making must make judgment calls based upon the circumstances. In either case, however, the scope and character of the security program should be within the parameters already mentioned by an evaluation of the following criteria:

§ Vulnerability to potential hazards.
§ Effect of security measures on business, efficiency, and operations.
§ Practical limitations imposed by the physical characteristics of the vessel, facility, or installation.
§ Availability of funds.
§ Risk.
§ Alternative measures available.
§ Evaluation of the security capabilities of all available external resources.

Every manager, captain, or officer in charge must continually evaluate his security in light of the foregoing factors and employ security measures consistent with his evaluation. As is said in the infantry, "Security, like camouflage, is continuous." These factors will be considered more closely in the next chapters on security surveys and plans.

All of the awareness, planning, and preparedness a manager or master may bring to bear is of no value whatsoever if, when the chips are down, people fail to act. Timely reaction cannot exist, by definition, in the absence of action. In order for a crew to act it must be commanded by a master willing to be decisive, and it must have trained to the point where action is almost instinctive. The same can be said for port facilities and offshore installations. Someone must give the orders, and he must be prepared and willing to do so. Then the security forces, whatever their composition, must be prepared to act accordingly. The vehicle for such training is the time-honored technique of drilling. School children practice fire drills, community leaders practice natural disaster drills, hospitals practice triage drills, and the military practice battle drills. All serve the same purpose: to reduce panic to the lowest level and instill a "rote-ness" to the desired actions, which will help ensure their completeness under real conditions. Owners and masters can ensure adequate crew responses to terrorist threats by conducting regular security drills in conformance with their vessels' security SOPs. Managers of port facilities and offshore installations can do the same.

Maritime security must provide timely and accurate warning of an impending threat, and it must be capable of repelling or neutralizing any attack. These are its goals. Each goal is governed by two security principles. For the former, these principles are awareness and planning. For the latter, the principles are preparedness and action. Combined with the axiom that all security should be in depth, they form a blueprint for security which can be diagrammed as shown in figure 1.

Consider the tanker transiting the Phillip Channel at night off Singapore. Tankers and cargo vessels are routinely boarded, and have been for years. Piracy has been endemic in the region for centuries and now, with ever more deadly weapons—the war in Vietnam and its aftermath provided a glut of weapons and munitions that will keep that part of the world armed for years—and high-speed watercraft, modern piracy has become a very lucrative and relatively safe business.

The shipping industry is aware of the piracy threat, but refuses to meet it because of policy decisions made by short-sighted owners and managers who believe it better to peaceably succumb to a piratical act than to oppose it. The absolute ludicrousness of such policies will become clear, if it hasn't already, when legal liabilities are discussed in chapter 6.

For the moment, however, return to the bridge of the tanker. The mate on watch is alone at the conn. The only designated lookout serves more as an errand boy or watch companion than an early warning system and his attention, when it happens to be focused on looking-out, is forward, not aft. There is no after lookout posted and the radar, which might detect approaching small craft, is ignored. The navigational concern is one of collision and, although it is a dark night, it is a clear one—the lights of any approaching ships with collision potential will be seen. So the tanker proceeds on her course with virtually no warning of the impending pirate attack. Even if, through some fortuitous series of events, she did receive warning of the imminent boarding, it would serve little purpose other than to alert the crew to the certainty of a looting and the possibility of death. The ship is not, by policy, prepared to take any action against the pirates or to react in such a way as to prevent the boarding.

This vessel is absolutely devoid of shipboard security. What little awareness there may be of the security threat has not prompted any planning whatever, and the ship cannot provide adequate warning of the attack. Moreover, because she is not prepared to act on any such

FIG. 1.   Blueprint for maritime security

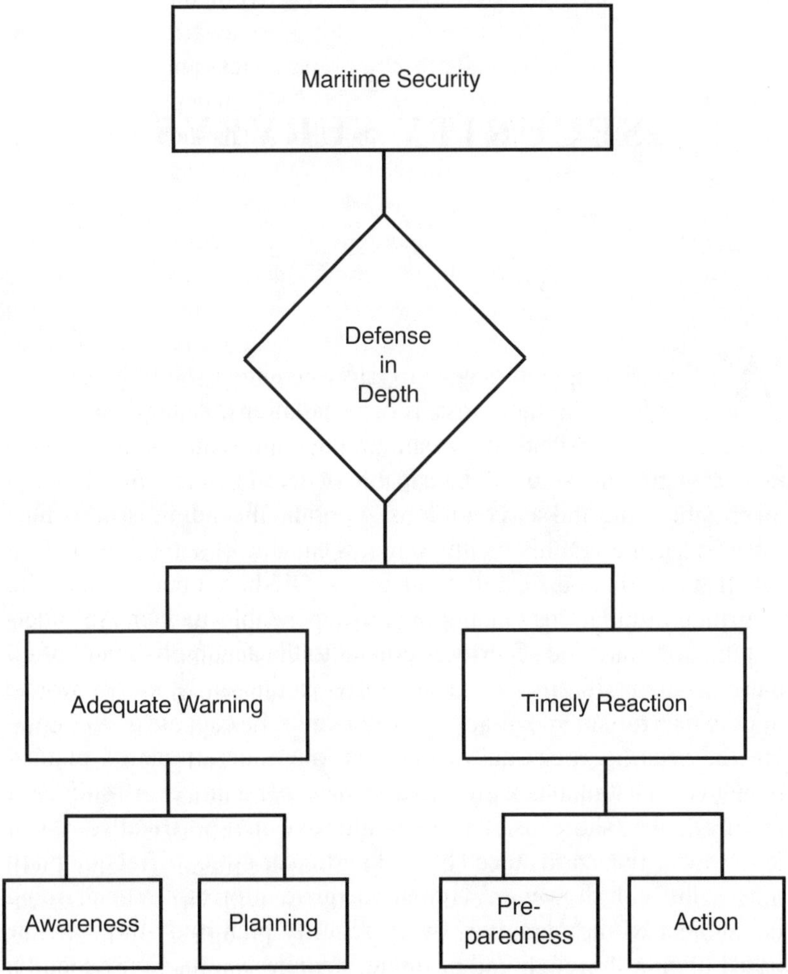

warning, if it were given, she cannot provide timely reaction to it. The
net result is that the two goals of maritime security, adequate warning
and timely reaction, have not been met and the security principles of
awareness, planning, preparedness, and action have been ignored. She,
and her crew, are at the mercy of whatever pirates or terrorists choose
to target her.

CHAPTER TWO

SECURITY SURVEYS

A LL marine operators need to know and understand the security hazards facing their vessels or installations. A ship's master is expected to understand the oceanographic and meteorologic conditions affecting his ship and be capable of steering her safely through all possible wind and sea conditions. A port facility administrator must likewise ensure that his facility remains capable of servicing the vessels that call there efficiently and safely. Offshore operators need to keep their installations functioning in a dependable manner. An understanding of maritime security is crucial to the accomplishment of all these missions. In order to successfully operate in the murky waters of global terrorism and piracy, operators must be capable of recognizing the security rocks and shoals, and have a formulated plan of maneuver. That plan is known as a *security plan,* and every ship, port facility, and offshore installation should have one specifically tailored to the security hazards faced by that particular entity. Effective planning is difficult, however, without adequate information concerning the subject of the planning. Every security plan must therefore be based upon a thorough and accurate *security survey.* Consequently, the first task in the process of establishing effective maritime security is to conduct a proper security survey.

The purpose of the security survey is to ascertain, to the fullest extent possible, the nature and measure of all foreseeable security threats. Because they are conducted with regard to a specific vessel, port facility, or offshore installation, the results of any two security surveys should never be alike. The methodology, however, of conducting the surveys should be the same. A survey should cover certain

16

aspects of the vessel or installation and its operation, and should be organized in such a way as to allow a complete and accurate analysis of all security weaknesses. That analysis is then presented in the subsequent *security survey report.*

The conducting of a proper security survey is no mean task. It is a time-consuming physical and mental exercise and the amount of information obtained can be substantial. It is essential, therefore, for the person conducting the survey to have at his disposal a logically organized and detailed procedure for performing it. This is best accomplished through the use of a form on which the various pieces of information can be entered. The form is the tool by which the raw security data can be collected, but it can also serve as the vehicle for the preparation of the security survey report itself. Once a security survey report has been generated, a security plan can be developed based upon the information and analysis contained in the report.

Examples of security survey report forms for vessels, port facilities, and offshore installations appear in this chapter and each shall be discussed at length. It should be noted at the outset, however, that there are two primary security concerns that must be analyzed during the security survey. The first involves the physical characteristics of the vessel, facility, or installation being surveyed. For a ship this would include such things as her measurements, location and number of accesses into her interior, construction and design, lights, locks, alarms, and so forth. The second concern involves the operational characteristics of the vessel, facility, or installation. Again, for a ship this would include such things as berthing, loading, and discharging, underway routines, personnel management, resupply, routing, and so on. It should also be noted that there is no magical format a security survey report form need have. The three examples discussed here are merely indicative of what can be devised, and are offered as models of the types of forms owners, operators, managers, or insurers might utilize in developing their security plans.

THE SHIP SECURITY SURVEY

In many ways the ship security survey is the most difficult of security surveys. By her very nature, a ship presents continually changing security environments while at the same time she is most likely to be unable to rely upon other sources of security assistance. The surveyor

must take as many possibilities as he can into account while performing his survey, and his security analysis must allow for virtually every
foreseeable maritime contingency. To do so he must have a realistic,
if not jaundiced, view of life and the world we live in, and he must
have a well-thought-out survey report form. Figure 2 is an example of
such a form.

The first section on the ship security survey report form contains
the ship's particulars. Obviously, the vessel's name identifies the object of the survey. The date provides a chronological record of the
security surveys performed for that vessel, as well as any date reference that might be needed with regard to correlation of vessel activities and events. For instance, if an insurer were to require a vessel
security survey prior to allowing insurance coverage to attach (which
none do at present), then the date of the survey would be significant.
Likewise, if an injured crew member sued as a result of injuries suffered during a security incident, and claimed negligent security on the
part of the vessel, the date of the last security survey prior to the incident would be significant. A record of the vessel's owners, charterers,
types of charters, and names and addresses of masters at particular
times in the ship's security history is equally important, especially
from a litigation standpoint. The ship's measurements are included
more as reference material than anything else, as is her age. Of course,
the age of a vessel might have a direct impact on her ability to remain
secure as a result of construction techniques, design, and maintenance.
The registry of the ship may have a direct influence on her manning
requirements and the nationalities of her officers and crew. Such
nationalities can be extremely significant when considering possible
crew involvement in security threats such as hijacking or sabotage.

Following the vessel's particulars, the survey report form is divided
into three parts: the preliminary assessment, the on-scene security survey, and the recommendations of the surveyor.

Part 1 contains information useful in assessing the risks faced by the
vessel. The first item to be ascertained by the security surveyor in this
section concerns the extent of company involvement in the vessel's
security on a managerial plane somewhere above that of the vessel. This
information is important for a number of reasons. First and foremost is
the fact that the finalized security survey report will, or should, form the
foundation for the vessel's security plan. A security plan can only be
prepared after security policy decisions have been made and dissemi-

FIG. 2.   Ship security survey report form

Vessel name_____ Date _____

Commanded by_____

Owners_____

Charterers _____

Charter party_____ Dated _____

LOA_____ Beam _____ Depth _____

Gross tonnage _____ Net tonnage _____

Year built _____ Place _____

Current registry_____

Part One: Preliminary Assessment

1. Company representatives (names, areas of responsibility, telephone numbers)

_____

_____

_____

_____

_____

2. Company crisis management team (if established)

_____

_____

3. Recent vessel activity history (types of cargo,
shipping routes, ports of call, frequency of employment, security incidents)

_____

_____

_____

_____

4. Previous security survey reports on file? Yes __ No __

5. Date of last security survey report found _____

6. Date of last security survey taken _____

7. Current threat intelligence for shipping route and ports of call

_____

_____

_____

_____

_____

_____

8. Threat intelligence source (FBI, USCG, local authorities)

_____

_____

_____

9. General layout of vessel

Construction material: Hull _____

Superstructure _____

Decks _____

Average draft (Light): Fwd _____ Aft _____

Average draft (Loaded): Fwd _____ Aft _____

Average freeboard (Light): Fwd ___ Midships ___ Aft ___

Average freeboard (Loaded): Fwd ___ Midships ___ Aft ___

Accesses (number, type, and location of all doors, hatches, and ports)

_____

_____

_____

_____

Accesses schematic

10. On-deck lighting (type, location, and wattage of
all fixtures)

_____

_____

_____

_____

_____

_____

11. Vessel manning: Ofc. _____ Crew _____

12. Current manning level: Ofc. _____ Crew _____

13. Existing security measures:

    A. Electronic surveillance equipment and alarms
      (including collision alarm radars)

_____

_____

_____

B. Interior security areas:

    Bridge: Yes ___ No___

    Engine room: Yes ___ No___

    Radio room: Yes ___ No___

    Ship's office: Yes ___ No___

    Master's safe: Yes ___ No___

    Other:_____

C. Firearms (number, type, stowage, and amount of ammunition on board)

_____

_____

_____

_____

D. Written security SOPs on board:

    Moored dockside: Yes ___ No ___ Date ___

    Moored dockside,
      cargo ops: Yes ___ No ___ Date ___

    At anchor: Yes ___ No ___ Date ___

    At anchor, cargo ops: Yes ___ No ___ Date ___

    Underway: Yes ___ No ___ Date ___

    Rendering assist.
      at sea   Yes ___ No ___ Date ___

    Docking/undocking: Yes ___ No ___ Date ___

    Rcvg/dschg pilots: Yes ___ No ___ Date ___

    Rcvg ship's stores: Yes ___ No ___ Date ___

    Bunkering: Yes ___ No ___ Date ___

    Rcvg official
      visitors: Yes ___ No ___ Date ___

    Changing crew: Yes ___ No ___ Date ___

E. Is there a security bill? Yes ____ No ____

Date of last revision _____

All crew members assigned station? Yes ___ No ___

Comments/recommendations regarding security bill

_____

_____

_____

Records maintained of security
drills?   Yes ___ No ___

Date of last security drill _____

Date of last crew security indoctrination_____

F. Permanent security personnel on
board?
                                           Yes ___ No ___

Number_____ Duties_____

Temporary security personnel on
board?
                                           Yes ___ No ___

Number _____ Duties_____

14. Equipment available for protection of passengers
and crew (description and location)

_____

_____

_____

Part Two: On-Scene Security Survey

1. Description and evaluation of access control:

   A. Inspection, control, and monitoring of
      visitors, passengers, and carry-on articles

_____

_____

_____

B. Pre-employment investigation of new or
   replacement crew members

_____

_____

_____

_____

_____

C. Inspection, control, and monitoring of cargo,
   ship's stores, and baggage

_____

_____

_____

_____

_____

D. Safeguarding of cargo, ship's stores, and
   baggage

_____

_____

_____

_____

_____

E. General comments regarding access control

_____

_____

_____

_____

_____

2. Evaluation of access points (as listed and shown
schematically in part 1)

_____

_____

_____

_____

_____

_____

3. Evaluation of existing security measures (including
SOPs)

_____

_____

_____

_____

_____

_____

_____

                  Part Three: Recommendations

_____

_____

_____

_____

_____

_____

_____   _____
     Date   Signature

nated. It is those managers in the company hierarchy tasked with security oversight and policy making who should be included here. Secondly, if the vessel is faced with a security incident the names and telephone numbers of those with authority to make life and death decisions should be documented. For this reason the form contains a place for naming the company's crisis management team, if one exists.

The vessel's recent history is very important to enable the security surveyor to get a feel for the ship and her security exposure. He needs to know the types of cargo carried, the various shipping routes and ports of call, the vessel's sailing history and frequency of employment, and of course any past security incidents. He might also want to note past drydocking and other yard periods, major overhauls, changes of ownership, changes of name, changes of flag, and any arrests or seizures. It is important to determine the date of the last security survey performed on the vessel as well as the results of that survey and any previous surveys.

Paragraphs 7 and 8 in the preliminary assessment (part 1) may be the most difficult portions of the survey to complete. That is because they deal with current security intelligence applicable to the geographical locations at which the vessel expects to find herself. Reliable intelligence is never easy to obtain, and foreign authorities may simply refuse to provide intelligence, assuming they have any to refuse.

Hopefully, the security surveyor will have sources of his own upon which he can draw. If not, a friendly chat with the appropriate authorities as well as some old-fashioned waterfront barhopping may prove useful. He should note the source of whatever information he decides to use, however, so that future assessments of that source as well as his final risk analysis can be made.

The next thing the security surveyor needs to ascertain is the general layout of the vessel. This includes her construction, her average draft both light and loaded, her freeboard, and most importantly her accesses. Ships are very complicated pieces of construction, and literally hundreds of items could conceivably be included. The object in preparing this section should be to include enough details to ensure that the drafter of the ship security plan is provided with adequate information, but not so much detail as to inundate him with useless information.

One of the first pieces of information the ship's security planner will need concerns the construction material used throughout the vessel. Is her hull made of steel, wood, fiberglass, aluminum, or carbon fiber? Is it of uniform thickness, or are there areas such as bulwarks or superstructures where construction is less heavy? Is the construction material uniform throughout? On some vessels the superstructures are not made of the same materials as the hulls. If the ship were ever to become embroiled in a firefight (a battle of small arms), it would be useful to know which portions of the vessel could provide cover (protection against bullet penetration) and which could not. The mode and design of construction is equally important. Is the steel hull welded or riveted? Is the stem reinforced? Does the ship have a double bottom? Where are the bunkers located? Are they protected?

Both the vessel's draft and freeboard are important. The former is of concern when considering the threat from underwater saboteurs, and the latter when contemplating the possibility of boarders. Both draft and freeboard vary with the vessel's loading, and both should be known by the master at any given instant.

The accesses into the ship's interior are of primary importance to her security. From a security standpoint, the fewer accesses a ship has, the better. Safety requirements, however, usually dictate just the opposite. The vessel's mission also determines her design and interior accessibility. Virtually no nonmilitary ships are presently being designed or built with security in mind. Consequently, the ship's security planner may well be faced with a great number of doors, hatches, scuttles, and ports which will require his attention and the attention of the officers and crew of the vessel. The first step to securing all of these accesses is to understand the location and function of each. Therefore, a description of each and every door, hatch, port, or other opening should be carefully given.

The surveyor should be gathering this information while keeping in mind its relevance to the security vulnerability of the ship. When he determines the freeboard of the vessel he should be mentally calculating the ease or difficulty one would have in boarding her at that location. When he describes the accesses into the vessel he should be considering the effort needed to breach them if secured. When he notes the construction of the hull or superstructure he should keep in mind its security-keeping qualities, or lack of them.

After describing the types and locations of all accesses, the surveyor should also sketch them, both in profile and from above, in the area provided on the survey report form. The same goes for the vessel's on-deck lighting. The on-deck lighting capabilities of the vessel are extremely important. With the advent of more and more personal injury lawsuits resulting from injury to crew members or others caused by inadequate deck lighting, ships are better lighted than 10 or 20 years ago. Lighting remains generally marginal, however, and this is particularly so from a security standpoint. Security lighting, for it to be effective, should cover every square foot of the vessel's topsides as well as her hull and surrounding area. There should be no shadows created in which a person could hide, either on deck or alongside. This is a tall order, and one that needs careful consideration by the security planner. So far as the security survey is concerned, however, the location of each light on deck should be described along with the type of lighting and the various fixtures' designed bulb wattage. A careful diagram should also be made in the space provided of the areas actually lighted at the time of the survey (for this reason part of the survey will need to be performed at night). Of the areas not lighted, it should be noted which are not lighted as a result of inoperative fixtures or burned-out bulbs, and which are not lighted as a result of inadequate arrangements.

The manning level of the vessel is crucial, and this is the next bit of information the surveyor should seek. The ship security plan, which encompasses her security bill and security SOPs, must be developed specifically with her manning levels in mind. Furthermore, if a vessel routinely operates at below her envisioned manning requirements, and her security plan was prepared with those manning requirements in mind, a new plan must be prepared. A vessel failing to have a workable security plan based upon reasonable manning requirements that suffers a security loss may leave herself, her owners, and her operators open to liability and possible denial of insurance coverage.

Paragraph 13 in part 1 of the ship security survey report form concerns existing security measures found aboard. The first of these involves electronic surveillance equipment and alarms. There is a growing number of electronic devices that can be suitably used aboard ship in either surveillance or alarm modes. Two of the most readily available types are the closed-circuit television (CCTV) systems and the new collision prevention alarm radars. While most commercial vessels do not presently carry such equipment, the security planner should be aware of their availability and the security enhancement they can provide. At this point in the survey, however, it is sufficient to simply note the presence or absence of any such devices.

Next to be mentioned on the survey report form are any interior security areas. These areas are important not only from a consideration of a security in-depth outlook, where they may well become the inner perimeter in a siege situation, but also from the standpoint of theft or sabotage prevention. In most commercial vessels today the only three secure areas inside the ship are the radio room, the ship's office, and the master's safe. Some masters secure the bridge or pilothouse when in port. Engine rooms are seldom secured, although they should be. If a ship carries firearms on board, the ship's armory or small arms locker should obviously be secured as well. In the event of a hijacking, one of the first areas aboard ship the terrorists will seek to control is the radio room and the vessel's communication capabilities. The radio room door can easily become an inner perimeter, therefore, which should be considered. Even a few minutes' delay could provide the time necessary to transmit the message which might save the ship.

No security survey could be complete without the mention of firearms, and the next section on the report form is devoted to them. Few commercial vessels presently carry weapons, but hopefully this will change. The security surveyor should note the number and type of weapons aboard, their location and manner of stowage, and the amount of ammunition available.

After firearms, but still within the paragraph on existing security measures, is the section on security SOPs. Security SOPs detail the security procedures that are to be followed during any particular shipboard evolution. They should be formulated in conjunction with the ship security plan, and should be in writing. If the ship security plan is changed, the security SOPs will more than likely need to be changed as well. There are generally a limited number of shipboard operations with which the ship's security planner needs to concern himself. There may be others depending upon the type of vessel and her purpose, but generally the operations are as follows:

§ Moored dockside.
§ Moored dockside, engaged in cargo operations.

§   At anchor.
§   At anchor, engaged in cargo operations.
§   Underway.
§   Rendering assistance at sea.
§   Docking and undocking.
§   Receiving and discharging pilots.
§   Receiving ship's stores.
§   Bunkering.
§   Receiving official visitors and guests.
§   Changing crew.

Some of these operations occur simultaneously. For instance, a vessel can be moored dockside, discharging cargo, and receiving ship's stores all at the same time. Likewise, she may be anchored yet receive official visitors or guests, and make a crew change. The ship is vulnerable, in one way or another, during all of these evolutions and it is the job of the security surveyor to indicate whether the ship security plan addresses such contingencies. He must therefore carefully view all of the vessel's security SOPs, if she has any, to determine their adequacy. A security SOP is obviously inadequate if it does not exist. If it does exist but is no longer valid due to the date it was promulgated and the changes that have occurred since, it is also inadequate. The security surveyor should indicate on the ship security survey report form which security SOPs exist, the date of their promulgation, and whether or not he believes them to be sufficient.

After he has studied the ship's security SOPs, the security surveyor should examine her security bill. This document should assign all crew members to a particular security station and task, just as the fire bill and abandon ship bill. It should be kept up to date and changed as crew changes occur. The status of the security bill should therefore be noted in the appropriate place on the survey report form. The existence of security drill records should also be noted, as well as the date of the last security drill and crew indoctrination. The ship security plan is absolutely useless if it contains all the necessary security SOPs and a properly maintained security bill but the crew has not been adequately trained and indoctrinated. The ship security plan should therefore provide for indoctrination of the crew as well as the routine conducting of security drills. These drills should be properly logged and documented so that a security history of the ship can be maintained. This is important not only for the safety of the vessel, but also to help owners avoid liability for a security-related loss. The security survey report form provides spaces for security history information.

Part 1 concludes with paragraph 14, which requires notation of all equipment aboard that can be used for the protection of passengers or crew. This can be anything from battle helmets and flak jackets to fire hoses. Whatever it is, if it can be used to protect passengers and crew during a security incident, it should be noted.

Part 2 of the ship security survey report form consists of the on-scene security survey. This is somewhat of a misnomer, since much of the information contained in part 1 must be gathered at the scene as well. What is really meant by "on-scene" is "operational." In this section the security surveyor is expected to observe, to the fullest extent possible, the operational characteristics of the vessel. He is also expected to evaluate those operational characteristics as they pertain to three specific areas: access control, access points, and existing security measures.

Access control is the key to the security of the vessel. Whether one is concerned with preventing pirate boarders in the South China Sea or a terrorist seizure at the dock, the security measure is one of access control. All of the ship's security SOPs are, or should be, designed with one thought in mind: access control. Consequently, paragraph 1 in part 2 of the security survey report form involves the description and evaluation of all matters related to access control of the vessel, and is divided into several subparts. The first concerns inspection, control, and monitoring of visitors, passengers, and carry-on articles. While such activity, if practiced, would normally occur dockside it should not be restricted to such. The concern is obviously to prevent persons bent on doing violence to the vessel from boarding, and from boarding with items that could be used to do violence, such as firearms and explosives. There are a number of ways persons routinely board vessels besides at the dock. They can board while the ship lies at anchor, they can be heli-lifted aboard while the ship is underway, pilots are picked up at sea just prior to entering port, and survivors can be rescued on the open ocean. The ship's security SOPs should cover all such contingencies. It should be noted that this subparagraph is not intended to include concerns of surreptitious boarding. Those concerns, while clearly involving access control, can be discussed during an evaluation of the ship's security SOPs and existing security measures. They can also be discussed in the general comments section regarding access control. This subparagraph is intended to define the procedures employed by the vessel in allowing persons to board who are not doing so in a clandestine manner. These procedures will differ depending on the nature of the vessel. Clearly, cruise ships, which board thousands of passengers a year and have the benefit of utilizing passenger terminals for baggage handling and passenger processing, will employ different procedures than general cargo vessels, which may carry only a very few passengers, or tankers or other ships, which carry no passengers at all. Whatever these procedures are, the security surveyor should observe the actual performance by the ship and her crew before determining from the master what procedures are supposed to be in effect. He should then describe the procedures as they are implemented, as they were observed being employed or not employed, and his evaluation of both.

Another way saboteurs and extortionists can gain access to a vessel is through employment on the vessel. They can come aboard posing as new crew members or can actually be crew members. Consequently, the ship needs to concern itself with both the pre-employment investigations of new or replacement crew members and the employment verification of new or replacement crew members. Usually, both can be handled by a competent and reputable crewing agency that will conduct the necessary background investigations, certify the good intentions of the prospective crew members, and escort them aboard. If the ship's owners use such an agency they are well ahead of the game. If they do not, they should consider doing so as soon as possible. Unfortunately, there is a real dearth in the industry of such agencies. The main reason is the market. Shipowners who have not yet grasped the security crisis within the industry are loathe to pay the substantial crewing agency fees required for such services. Increased negligent security litigation may change this viewpoint. In any event, the security surveyor needs to note and evaluate what security procedures are employed with regard to crewing.

The next section of the security survey report concerns the inspection, control, and monitoring of cargo, ship's stores, and baggage. Such procedures are important not only to prevent the introduction onboard of weapons or other dangerous devices, but to control or prevent pilfering as well. The best way to prevent pilferage is through effective, continuous observation of handling operations. This applies equally to cargo, baggage, and ship's stores. The concern for the ship is therefore twofold. It should ensure, through inspection, that no weapons or other dangerous items are introduced aboard and it should discourage pilferage by maintaining continuous observation of items being loaded or discharged. The procedures employed for such inspection and observation should be described and evaluated by the security surveyor.

The next section on the security survey report form is a logical extension of the preceding section. It involves the safeguarding of cargo, ship's stores, and baggage. While the two sections overlap somewhat in their concerns, the focus of this section is on the ultimate resting place or stowage area of the cargo, ship's stores, and baggage. The security surveyor needs to concern himself with the security procedures employed by the ship with regard to such stowage. Once the handling operations are concluded, are the stowage spaces secured? How are they secured? Who has access to them once they are secured? Are the accesses to the stowage spaces alarmed? Are they inspected regularly, and by whom?

The final section regarding access control on the security survey report form is a general comments section. Here the surveyor can remark on anything not already specifically covered concerning access control. He may choose to mention the ship's security SOPs again, or he may wish to comment generally on the vessel's overall security so far as controlling access is concerned.

Paragraph 2 at the end of the ship security survey report form is an evaluation of the access points found aboard the vessel. These should have been described previously in the report. Now, however, instead of concerning himself with the mere location and description of all the access points, the security surveyor needs to focus on the actual operational characteristics of such accesses. How are they used? When are they used? How are they secured? Are they alarmed? When are they inspected? Are they lighted?

The final paragraph in part 2 is an evaluation of the vessel's existing security measures. This includes an evaluation of everything previously reported in parts 1 and 2 that may need more comment. It can also serve as a summation by the surveyor of the general security condition of the vessel as he has found it. Finally, it is here the surveyor lays his foundation for part 3 of the ship security survey report form, his recommendations.

In detailing his recommendations, the security surveyor should be as specific as possible. By this time the reader of his report knows the security condition of the vessel. The report has, hopefully, pointed out the security problems that, in the opinion of the surveyor, exist. Now he wants to know what to do about them. He wants to know how much it will cost and how long it will take to correct the deficiencies. He wants to know his options. If he is smart, he wants to understand his potential exposure both to operational and legal liabilities. The security surveyor should make his recommendations clearly and succinctly.

The last thing the surveyor should do before submitting his report is date and sign it. The date the report is signed will most certainly not be the date the survey was conducted, and thus the date that appears on the first page of the report will not be the same as on the signature page.

Throughout the preparation of his security survey report, the security surveyor should keep in mind that it will presumably be his report upon which the ship's security planner relies in preparing the ship security plan. Of course, if the surveyor is an independent security consultant he may well be asked to prepare, or assist in the preparation of, the ship security plan. In any case, his report becomes an official document that may be read by many, many people. It should be prepared in a professional manner and treated with the importance it deserves. The security surveyor should remember that every word he places in his report may be questioned in a court of law, and that he may be called upon to defend his observations, conclusions, and recommendations.

THE PORT FACILITY SECURITY SURVEY

Port facilities, unlike ships, don't move. In most nations the ports were the first cities to be developed. They grew as their respective countries grew, and they are generally overcrowded and security-poor. Except for the very modern or recently revamped facilities, no thought whatever has been given to most port facilities' security needs. Consequently, a port facility presents a number of different security concerns not applicable to the vessels that call at the facility. Like all ships, however, every port facility must have a security plan if it has any hope of remaining even somewhat secure. The security plan should be based upon a competent, detailed security survey. The security surveyor needs to develop an appropriate port facility security survey report form in order to conduct the security survey. Figure 3 is an example.

As with the ship security survey report form, the port facility form consists of three parts: the preliminary assessment, the on-scene security survey, and the surveyor's security recommendations. The first paragraph in part 1 requires a listing of key port authority representatives, their areas of responsibility, and their telephone numbers. These are the persons with whom the security surveyor most likely will interact during his survey, and they are also the people tasked with the day-to-day operation of the port. In the absence of a crisis management team they are the ones who will make the necessary decisions. If the port facility has an established crisis management team, most if not all of these key personnel will be on it. Consequently, following the listing of the port authority representatives are spaces for the names of the crisis management team. In addition to the port authority key personnel, the crisis management team may contain high-level representatives from emergency external support agencies such as the Coast Guard, fire and police departments, and local FBI office. All members of the team should be listed, along with their respective office and emergency telephone numbers. The designated team leader should be indicated as well.

The last of the name lists appears in paragraph 3 following the naming of the crisis management team. This list consists of the representatives of the local emergency external support organizations, most of whom should be members of the port facility's crisis management team, if such a team has been designated. Again, both routine and emergency telephone numbers should be listed. It is also a good idea, when obtaining this information from the agencies involved, to ascertain the names and telephone numbers of backup representatives who are authorized to function in place of the designated representatives should they be unavailable.

Paragraph 4 requires a narrative history of recent shipping activity within the port. The port authority's traffic manager can supply most of this information. The security surveyor should note the different types of vessels that have called at the port, the cargoes loaded or discharged, the vessels' flags and the nationalities of their crews, the vessels' last ports of call prior to arriving and their destinations upon departure, and any security incidents involving the vessels at any time

FIG. 3.   Port facility security survey report form

Port _____ Date _____

City _____ State _____

Part One: Preliminary Assessment

1. Port authority representatives (names, areas of responsibility, telephone numbers)

_____

_____

_____

_____

_____

2. Crisis management team (if established)

_____

_____

3. Emergency external support representatives

USCG Captain of the port _____

Police Dept.   _____

Fire Dept.   _____

Sheriff's Dept.   _____

Local FBI office   _____

Other   _____

4. Recent shipping activity history

_____

_____

_____

_____

5. Recent port facility history (new construction, security incidents, new vendors, etc.)

_____

_____

_____

_____

6. Previous security survey reports on file? Yes __ No__

7. Date of last security report found _____

8. Date of last security survey taken_____

9. Current threat intelligence for locality

_____

_____

_____

_____

_____

_____

_____

_____

10. Threat intelligence source (FBI, USCG, local authorities)

_____

_____

_____

_____

_____

11. General layout of port facility

12. Areas and structures within vicinity of port
facility that should be noted (fuel depots, bridges,
locks, etc.)

_____

_____

_____

_____

13. Access points to port facility (also note in
paragraph 11)

_____

_____

_____

_____

14. External essential services (electricity, water,
telephones, etc.)

_____

_____

_____

_____

15. Internal emergency or routine essential services
(backup generators, water supplies, radio communications, etc.)

_____

_____

_____

_____

16. Port facility personnel (list functions and numbers of staff, permanent labor, and casual labor)

_____

_____

_____

_____

17. Emergency port facility personnel

_____

_____

_____

_____

18. Port facility security personnel

_____

_____

_____

_____

19. Routine vehicle traffic or services entering port facility by land

_____

_____

_____

_____

20. Routine vessel traffic or services entering port facility by water

_____

_____

_____

21. Existing security measures (fencing, lighting, locks, alarms, monitoring devices, patrols, etc.)

_____

_____

_____

_____

_____

_____

_____

_____

_____

_____

_____

_____

_____

22. Equipment available for protection of passengers, crews, and port facility personnel (description and location)

_____

_____

_____

_____

_____

_____

_____

_____

_____

_____

_____

Part Two: On-Scene Security Survey

1. Description and evaluation of access control to
ships and restricted areas:

    A. Inspection, control, and monitoring of persons
       and carry-on articles

_____

_____

_____

_____

    B. Pre-employment investigation of new personnel

_____

_____

    C. Inspection, control, and monitoring of cargo,
       ship's stores, and baggage

_____

_____

_____

_____

    D. Safeguarding of cargo, ship's stores, and baggage

_____

_____

_____

_____

    E. General comments regarding access control

_____

_____

_____

_____

2. Evaluation of access points (described in part 1, paragraphs 11 and 13)

_____

_____

_____

_____

_____

_____

3. Evaluation of existing security measures

_____

_____

_____

_____

_____

_____

_____

Part Three: Recommendations

_____

_____

_____

_____

_____

_____

_____   _____
    Date   Signature

during their voyages of which a stop at this port was a part. As of November 20, 1985, the date the International Maritime Organization (IMO) adopted Resolution A.584(14), all vessels are encouraged to submit security incident reports of all unlawful acts and the measures taken to prevent their recurrence to the IMO through both the applicable flag and port states. The port authority security officer or traffic manager should therefore maintain a file of all such reports submitted by vessels while at that port, which the security surveyor should review. The recommended format for a security incident report, as approved by the IMO and sanctioned by the U.S. Coast Guard, appears in appendix A and is entitled "Report on an Unlawful Act."

The next paragraph on the port facility security survey report form requires a narrative of recent port facility history. This includes such events as new construction, addition of service companies, new vendors or other companies authorized to transact business within the port, changes in established agencies and service companies, changes in security procedures or services, and of course, security incidents. If the port authority has had a change in its key personnel during this period, that should be noted as well.

Paragraphs 6, 7, and 8 concern previous security surveys and reports. All previous security survey reports should be on file with the port authority. The security surveyor needs to indicate whether they are on file or not. He should also indicate the date of the security survey report he can find, as well as the date the last security survey was conducted, if known.

The next paragraph concerns the current threat intelligence for the locality. Intelligence can come from any number of different sources, and good places to start are the local Coast Guard, police, and FBI offices. The security surveyor, if he is an independent consultant, may well have his own sources also. He can pick up valuable information, at least so far as the general mood of the port is concerned, by talking to dock workers and others in the local night spots. Hopefully, by piecing his information together, he will be able to arrive at a reasonable intelligence picture and that picture should be described here. He should note the sources of his intelligence so that their reliability can be evaluated as needed.

Paragraph 11 of the security survey report form is devoted entirely to the general layout of the port facility. The surveyor should sketch the layout of the port and include in his sketch all significant buildings, piers, warehouses, storage areas, fences, gates, roads, access points, fuel storage tanks, and so on. He might also want to attach a photocopy of a topographical or other map or chart of the area.

Paragraphs 12 and 13 verbally complement the sketch of the port facility's general layout, with descriptions of significant areas and structures that are within the vicinity of the port and the access points to the port facility itself. All fuel depots, bridges, locks, surrounding roadways and arteries, subways, and waterways should be mentioned. All access points, from the main entrance to service roads and pedestrian gates, should be detailed.

The next two paragraphs concern the port facility's essential services, such as electricity, water, and communications. Paragraph 14 refers to external services upon which the port must rely. Paragraph 15 details the internal services, whether emergency or routine, upon which the port can rely. The two should be considered together when analyzing potential security threats. For instance, the port facility probably receives its electricity from the local municipality but may well have, and certainly should have, its own internal emergency generators. If a terrorist threat scenario calls for the disruption of electrical power to the facility, the backup generators can thwart that part of the operation and possibly prevent its success altogether. Likewise, routine VHF marine radio communications could, in a situation where telephone lines have been accidentally or intentionally severed, be employed as emergency communication.

Paragraphs 16, 17, and 18 all refer to port facility personnel. In paragraph 16 the security surveyor should list all nonemergency or security personnel employed by the port authority or in the port facility. The port authority should maintain lists of all authorized employees of the various service companies, such as stevedores and warehousemen, and require all such entities to provide current employee lists to the port authority as appropriate. If it has done so, the security survey's task will be relatively easy. If it has not done so, the surveyor will have to compile his own lists. He should also note the discrepancy and comment upon it later in the report. This paragraph also requires that all casual labor be listed. This may very well present a problem to everyone concerned since controls over casual labor are usually the most lax. It is for this reason that the casual labor outlet provides good opportunities for terrorist access and must be carefully considered by not only the security surveyor but the security planner as well. Paragraph 17 concerns the emergency port facility personnel, such as any in-house fire-fighting or emergency maintenance personnel. In emergency situations security tends to relax because everyone is concerned with fighting the emergency. Terrorists know this, and security procedures cannot be allowed to slacken at such times. If anything, security should become more alert during periods of emergency since it is possible that the emergency was created specifically to divert attention from security. In paragraph 18 all port facility security personnel should be listed. If private guard companies are utilized they should be required to provide current guard rosters of all employees posted to the port facility. Furthermore, all guard supervisors and responsible managers should also be listed along with their emergency telephone numbers.

Paragraphs 19 and 20 refer to routine vehicle and vessel traffic entering the port. Only vendors and other service companies previously cleared and authorized should be allowed to enter. Certainly, at least, appropriate lists should be maintained by the port authority of vehicles and vessels authorized to enter the facility on routine, recurring business. One way to do this is through the issuance of parking or other permits that can be permanently displayed. In that way, an automobile or boat not displaying the appropriate sticker can be quickly spotted and investigated.

The next paragraph, paragraph 21, is perhaps the single most important paragraph on the form. It will also probably be one of the lengthiest. In this paragraph the security surveyor must detail all the existing security measures within the port facility. This includes all fencing, lighting, access controls, electronic alarms and surveillance devices, security patrols, and so on. Each security measure must be carefully described and analyzed. In part 2, paragraph 3, each security measure must be evaluated; the information contained in this paragraph will form the foundation for such evaluation.

In paragraph 22 the security surveyor should list all equipment within the port facility available for the protection of passengers, crews, and port facility personnel. This can include electronic detection equipment, fire-fighting equipment, security barriers, vehicles, or any other type of equipment designed or capable of being used for protection. All equipment should be described and its location and availability discussed.

Part 2 of the port facility security survey report form, entitled "On-Scene Security Survey," concerns an evaluation of the port facility's access control to ships and restricted areas, the access points into the facility, and the existing security procedures. It begins with the inspection, control, and monitoring of persons and carry-on articles with regard to access to ships and restricted areas. The security intent is primarily to prevent unauthorized persons from gaining access to ships within the port facility and introducing weapons or other dangerous devices aboard. However, the security surveyor should remember to evaluate all such access controls with regard to the port facility's restricted areas as well. If the port contains a cruise ship passenger terminal, some sort of inspection of passengers and carry-on articles has probably been implemented. If it does not contain a passenger terminal, probably no control whatever exists, with the possible exception of ships carrying particularly hazardous cargo such as LNG or explosives. It should be noted, however, that the paragraph refers to persons, not passengers, and therefore the security surveyor needs to consider what access controls are in place that affect everyone wishing to gain access to ships or restricted areas, not just passengers. This includes service personnel, crews, and visitors. It also includes any access control procedures whatever—detection devices, security barriers, locks, and so on. One relatively little-known method of controlling access, or helping to control access, to ships and port facility areas in the United States is the use of port security cards. These cards are issued by the U.S. Coast Guard and resemble military identification cards. The cards are strictly controlled and only issued after the proper background investigation has been conducted. When policy is being set, the port authority should decide whether it intends to utilize this security measure. While the use of port security cards is certainly not fail-safe, obtaining a forged or stolen card is definitely more difficult than simply printing bogus business cards.

The next subparagraph concerns pre-employment investigations of new personnel. There are several alternatives available to the port facility. First, it can have no pre-employment investigation of any kind. It can rely upon the individual service companies to investigate their own employees. Or it can employ a private security firm to perform some or all pre-employment investigations. And, finally, it can perform all pre-employment screening itself. In most ports today, particularly in nonpassenger situations, it is likely that no pre-employment investigations are performed by the port authority itself. It may require some sort of certification from its service companies with regard to their employees, but in such cases there are seldom any control procedures implemented to ensure the service companies are really screening their personnel. Even in port facilities with passenger terminals and well-trained security forces the resources may simply not exist for complete pre-employment screening of everyone employed there. The best solution, so far as the port facility is concerned, is to require all its service companies to retain the services of a qualified, competent, and reliable independent security contractor to perform all pre-employment screening. In any event, the fact that pre-employment investigations are either performed or not performed should be indicated on the survey report form.

The next subparagraph on the form concerns the inspection, control, and monitoring of cargo, ship's stores, and baggage. Again, the primary concern is with the possible introduction of weapons or other harmful devices aboard ships in the port. However, the same security procedures that are designed to prevent such activity can also prevent or help prevent pilferage and smuggling, as well as the unauthorized debarking of stowaways. The procedures utilized in safeguarding cargo, ship's stores, and baggage, if any, go hand in hand with their inspection, control, and monitoring. Such procedures should be listed in the following subparagraph.

Finally, the last section concerning access control simply allows the security surveyor to make general comments regarding access control as he has found it within the port facility. Anything not already mentioned in subparagraphs A through D should be discussed here, as well as anything the security surveyor may wish to emphasize that concerns access control.

Paragraph 2 of part 2 allows for an evaluation of the access points into the port facility that were drawn and described in paragraphs 11 and 13. The evaluation should include for each access point an estimate as to its potential for unauthorized access, the reasons for such estimate, and the possible solutions for any problems envisioned.

The final paragraph in part 2 involves the evaluation of existing security measures within the port. The security surveyor must evaluate all security measures he has observed and reported previously. His evaluation should include an estimate of each security measure's effectiveness. It should also discuss alternative methods, and the possible benefits or liabilities presented by the alternatives.

The last portion of the security survey report is part 3: Recommendations. It is in this portion of his report that the security surveyor draws upon his knowledge and experience, particularly if he is an independent security consultant, and recommends courses of action. These recommendations should not be frivolous. They should be carefully considered and explained in detail, and the security surveyor should expect to be required to defend his recommendations either at the time he submits his report or years later if litigation ensues over security practices engaged in by the port facility.

The last thing the surveyor needs to do is date and sign his report. The date of his signature may not be the same as the date of his survey. In fact, it probably should not be. A good security survey should take a fair amount of time to complete, as should the subsequent report, and although an inordinate amount of time should not elapse between the time the security survey is conducted and when the report is written, a reasonable period is needed in order to consider all the ramifications of the survey.

THE OFFSHORE INSTALLATION SECURITY SURVEY

Offshore installations are, in essence, hybrids of vessels and shore facilities. Though stationary, they are emplaced miles at sea away from all shore-based support. Some are attached permanently to the ocean bottom and some are not. The capital investment for each installation can be enormous—the new semisubmersible tension-leg well platforms (TLWPs) are expected to cost $400 million apiece. The net revenues these installations can produce are equally impressive. Furthermore, one installation can handle production from as many as 24 subsea wells, which means vast quantities of crude oil are moved and controlled by one facility. By their very nature, offshore installations provide wonderful targets for terrorism and extortion. They also present security concerns that encompass aspects of both shipboard and port facility security. Consequently, an appropriate offshore installation security survey will encompass aspects of both shipboard and port facility security surveys. An example of an offshore installation security survey report form appears in figure 4.

Fɪɢ. 4.   Offshore installation security survey report form

Installation_____ Date _____

Location (lat./long.)_____

Owners _____

Operators _____

Type and purpose _____

Part One: Preliminary Assessment

1. Company representatives (names, areas of responsibility, telephone numbers)

_____

_____

_____

_____

_____

_____

2. Crisis management team (if established)

_____

_____

_____

3. Nearest emergency external support representatives

_____

_____

_____

_____

_____

_____

_____

4. Recent installation activity history (new construction or modifications, change in ownership or
operators, significant change in routines, security
incidents)

_____

_____

_____

_____

_____

5. Previous security survey reports on file? Yes___ No___

6. Date of last security survey report found _____

7. Date last security survey taken _____

8. Current threat intelligence for locality

_____

_____

_____

_____

_____

_____

_____

_____

9. Threat intelligence source (FBI, local authorities,
company sources, etc.)

_____

_____

_____

_____

_____

10. General layout of installation

11. Average height above water (main working area)_____

12. Average height above water (helipad) _____

13. Areas and structures within vicinity of installation that should be noted (other installations, shipping lanes, fishing grounds, etc.)

_____

_____

_____

_____

_____

_____

_____

14. Sketch of areas and structures within vicinity

15. Access points to installation (describe and also
note in paragraph 10; include access from both water
and air)

_____

_____

_____

_____

_____

16. External lighting (type, location, and wattage of
all fixtures)

_____

_____

_____

_____

_____

17. External lighting sketch

18. External essential services (electricity, water, fuel, communications, etc.)

_____

_____

_____

19. Internal emergency or routine essential services

_____

_____

_____

20. Installation personnel (functions and numbers of personnel, shore rotation schedules, etc.)

_____

_____

_____

21. Emergency installation personnel

_____

_____

_____

_____

22. Security personnel

_____

_____

_____

_____

_____

_____

23. Routine vessel traffic or services

_____

_____

_____

_____

24. Routine helo traffic or services

_____

_____

_____

_____

25. Routine communication procedures

_____

_____

_____

_____

26. Emergency communication procedures

_____

_____

_____

_____

27. Installation manning requirements

_____

_____

_____

_____

_____

28. Installation manning level at time of survey

_____

_____

29. Existing security measures

_____

_____

_____

_____

_____

_____

_____

_____

_____

_____

_____

30. Equipment available for protection of installation
personnel

_____

_____

_____

_____

_____

_____

_____

_____

_____

Part Two: On-Scene Security Survey

1. Description and evaluation of access control:

A. Inspection, control, and monitoring of persons and carry-on articles

_____

_____

_____

_____

B. Pre-employment investigation of new employees

_____

_____

C. Employee monitoring and control

_____

_____

_____

D. Inspection, control, and monitoring of supplies and baggage

_____

_____

_____

_____

_____

E. Safeguarding of supplies

_____

_____

_____

F. Secured areas

_____

_____

_____

_____

G. General comments regarding access control

_____

_____

_____

_____

2. Evaluation of access points (described in paragraphs 10 and 15)

_____

_____

_____

_____

_____

3. Evaluation of existing security measures

_____

_____

_____

_____

_____

Part Three: Recommendations

_____

_____

_____

_____

_____

_____

_____

_____

_____

_____

_____

_____

_____

_____

_____

_____

_____

_____

_____

_____   _____

Date   Signature

The offshore installation security survey report form begins with the name or designation of the installation and the date of survey. The location of the installation, in latitude and longitude, should then be indicated. The name and number of the applicable nautical chart on which the location of the installation can be found is usually helpful and should be included if known. The names of both the owners and the operators should be recorded, along with a description of the type of installation and its purpose. After this initial information, the survey report form is again divided into three parts: the preliminary assessment, the on-scene security survey, and recommendations.

The first 10 paragraphs in part 1 are very similar to those found on the port facility security survey report form already discussed. The names and telephone numbers of company representatives should be determined and noted. If the company has a designated security manager or officer, his name and emergency numbers should be specifically included. The crisis management team, if it exists, should be detailed. The nearest emergency external support representatives must be determined. Since the installation may be in international waters, it is important to know the nationality of the nearest available help and the specific local requirements for obtaining such help. Recent installation activity history is important for a number of reasons. Movable, semisubmersible installations can be shifted from one geographical area to another and be chartered or leased to different operators. If a recent change has occurred in either ownership or management it should be noted. Likewise, if there has been a significant change in operating routines or personnel the change and its nature should be recorded.

Paragraphs 11 and 12 require the surveyor to determine the average heights above the water of the main working area and the helipad on the installation. This information is important for threat analysis. Also, paragraphs 13 and 14 concern areas and structures within the vicinity of the installation that may bear on the threat analysis, such as other installations, shipping lanes, fishing grounds, and so forth. A sketch of the area should be made and, if helpful, a photocopy of the applicable portion of a nautical chart should be attached.

Paragraph 15 concerns the access points to the installation, which should be described as well as noted on the sketch of the installation's general layout. Most installations have some sort of docking area for crew and supply boats, and this area should be carefully described.

The same is true for the helipad. Once this has been accomplished there may be a tendency to consider that all the installation's accesses have been covered. This would be a mistake. All of the accesses into the interior of the installation need to be identified. Furthermore, if access can be gained to the installation by any other foreseeable means those means should be discussed.

The security lighting considerations are the same for an offshore installation as for vessels or port facilities. All security lighting should be described and a sketch made. Obviously, the sketch should be made at night and all areas of shadow identified.

Paragraphs 18 and 19 concern the installation's essential services. Most offshore installations make their own electricity and water, as do ships. The type, number, and location of generators and desalinators should be described, as well as any security measures that may protect them from sabotage. The installation's communication abilities are also important essential services. These usually take the form of VHF marine or single-sideband radios. Some installations may have satellite communication capabilities as well. All communication equipment should be described, with an indication as to which systems function as primary and secondary systems.

Paragraphs 20 through 22 concern installation personnel, and the considerations are not much different from those involving port facilities. The security surveyor needs to understand the size and nature of the work force on the installation, how often personnel rotations are made, what (if any) emergency personnel are available, and if a security force is maintained.

Routine vessel and helicopter traffic, paragraphs 23 and 24, is important to know. Are schedules maintained and, if so, how readily available is the information off the platform or outside the company? What types of services are provided by vessel or helicopter and what, if any, access controls are employed in conjunction with such services?

Routine and emergency communication procedures should be noted during the security survey. Management personnel need to know not only how to get in touch with those on the platform in times of emergency, but also how to determine if an emergency exists. Codes can, and should, be devised in order to pass vital information ashore if the installation is seized, and the procedures in effect for establishing such codes should be noted.

The installation's manning requirements and manning level at the time of the security survey should be recorded. The surveyor should also try to ascertain whether the manning level, if different from the established requirement, is only temporarily different or chronically incongruous. If the situation is not temporary he should attempt to learn the reason or reasons.

Paragraph 29 details the existing security measures in effect on the platform and within the company. All aspects of security should be discussed, from the physical security procedures found on the installation, such as lighting, access controls, firearms, and barriers, to security policies and programs, such as pre-employment procedures, traffic scheduling, and communication policies. The information contained in this paragraph will form the foundation for the surveyor's analysis of security measures found in part 2 of the report.

The final item in part 1 concerns the equipment available for protecting installation personnel. Firearms can certainly be considered as protective equipment. So can fire hoses. Most platforms are equipped with saltwater pumps and hoses; few if any have firearms. As unfortunate as this may someday be, the security surveyor's task at this juncture is simply to record the availability of whatever equipment he finds. It will be the job of the company's security planner and policy decision makers to determine what, if anything, they wish to do about it.

Part 2 of the offshore installation survey is very similar to the same section in the port facility survey. It is concerned primarily with a description and evaluation of access control and an evaluation of the access points and existing security measures found on the installation. In all instances the concern is one of preventing unauthorized access to the installation or the introduction of weapons or other harmful devices onto the platform. The comments made previously with regard to part 2 of both the port facility and the ship survey forms are applicable and need not be repeated. The same is true for part 3 of the report form, which is the security surveyor's recommendations.

The security survey and the subsequent report, with its threat analysis and recommendations, forms the foundation upon which the security plan is built. The next step in the maritime security process is therefore the preparation of the security plan.

CHAPTER THREE

THE SECURITY PLAN

THE security plan can be prepared by a designated security officer or an independent security consultant. If a security consultant is employed he probably will have performed the security survey in preparation for developing the security plan. If a security consultant is not employed, the security officer may or may not have performed the security survey. In any event, the person who prepares the security plan is referred to as the security planner.

The security planner must carefully weigh and analyze a number of criteria in the process of developing his security plan. These criteria were briefly mentioned in the preceding chapter on security goals and principles. They are:

§ Vulnerability to potential hazards.
§ Effect of security measures on business, efficiency, and operations.
§ Practical limitations imposed by the physical characteristics of the vessel, facility, or installation.
§ Availability of funds.
§ Risk.
§ Alternative measures available.
§ Evaluation of the security capabilities of all available external resources.

Since these factors vary from one instance to another, any security plan taking them into account will also vary from one instance to another. The variables rarely remain constant. Policy changes occur, capabilities change, risks fluctuate. A vessel's shipping route, ports of call, cargo, operating funds, and manning levels vary regularly. When she is sold, her new owners will probably not agree with her old owners' security evaluations. The same can be said for port facilities and offshore installations. Port authorities can change management and policies. Offshore installations can change operators. Consequently, even in situations where consecutive security survey reports appear somewhat consistent the security plan can change significantly. It is imperative that owners and operators remain aware of the shifting winds of their security situation, and plan accordingly. Under most conditions an annual security survey and subsequent security plan review or update will be sufficient.

THE SHIP SECURITY PLAN

A ship security plan should be prepared for every ship. A ship's security officer should be appointed on every ship and be tasked specifically with preparing and/or updating the ship security plan. This security plan should consider all shipboard activities in all geographical locations in which the ship may find herself. It should be sufficiently flexible to allow for different levels of security in the various ports of call, and it should establish preventative measures for unauthorized access to the ship at sea as well as in port. The ship's security officer should be responsible for, but not necessarily limited to:

1. Conducting, or arranging for an independent security consultant to conduct, an initial comprehensive security survey.
2. Developing, or arranging for an independent security consultant to develop, a ship security plan.
3. Maintaining and modifying as necessary the ship security plan.
4. Encouraging security awareness and vigilance.
5. Implementing the ship security plan.
6. Ensuring adequate training for security personnel.
7. Preparing all security reports required by law or policy, including all occurrences or suspected occurrences of unlawful acts (see appendix A).

8. Coordinating shipboard security with port facility security
    officers or local authorities in all ports of call.
9. Conducting, or arranging for an independent security consul-
    tant to conduct, regular security inspections.

The ship security officer should have adequate knowledge of the following:

1. The ship security plan.
2. The layout of the ship.
3. The assessment of risk, threat, and vulnerability.
4. Methods of conducting security inspections.
5. Techniques used to circumvent security measures.
6. Search methods for persons, baggage, cargo, and ship's
    stores.
7. Emergency procedures.

The ship security plan is a combination of the ship's security SOPs
and her security bill. The security SOPs and security bill are
developed on the basis of policy decisions influenced by the seven
policy criteria already mentioned, and are designed to protect
against the security threats faced by the vessel. All vessels face, in
varying degrees, the same six security threats. In ascending order
of seriousness these are:

§ Pilferage.
§ Stowaways.
§ Drug smuggling.
§ Sabotage.
§ Piracy.
§ Hijacking.

To some extent a few of these hazards may be affected by the
geographical location of the ship. Certainly the pilferage and stowaway threats are. Piracy, too, is fairly well confined to certain areas of
the world at the present time. On the other hand, sabotage and hijacking, two of the most serious security threats faced by any vessel, can
occur anywhere and may not be significantly affected by the vessel's
location.

Pilferage of cargo and ship's supplies occurs both on and off the vessel. It is probably the most annoying security threat faced by the ship and her owners. It is certainly the most frequent. Pilferage can, however, become a significant financial detriment to the vessel's operation. Virtually anything that can be carried away by one or two people will be pilfered. The practice has become so widespread in some ports that many owners accept the loss as a cost of doing business. Cargo underwriters pay and then subrogate against the ship's protection and indemnity insurers, who also pay and then raise the calls (similar to insurance premiums) that the shipowner then pays. A vessel with a significant loss history becomes more expensive to operate. Consequently, when pilferage escalates from a few boxes of bananas or grapefruit to entire shipping containers of television sets or computer components the cost of doing business increases substantially.

There are two types of pilferers, casual and systematic. A casual pilferer steals because he is unable to resist the temptation unexpectedly placed before him. The act is usually spontaneous, and the pilferer normally commits it alone. His target may be a box of fruit, or a case of steaks or a portable radio. However, even though casual pilferage involves the unsystematic theft of small items, the cumulative effect of numerous casual pilferers can be extremely serious. A systematic pilferer, on the other hand, steals according to plan. He steals anything of value that is available and sells it for whatever price he can get. He may work alone or with accomplices. Large quantities of goods may be lost to persons engaged in elaborately planned and carefully executed systematic pilferage. Thefts of entire shipping containers of goods are not uncommon. There have been instances where goods have been clandestinely removed from one container and placed in another, new bills of lading and customs declarations prepared, and the goods shipped to a destination chosen by their thieves. In such cases the original container was not removed from the "secure" storage area, its customs seal was not broken, and no one was aware of the theft until long after it had occurred.

A stowaway is another security threat faced by vessels which, on the surface, usually appears more annoying than anything else. However, there can be serious implications connected with stowaways. First and foremost, a stowaway can turn into a saboteur or hijacker. If he can get on board unnoticed, he can do so with weapons and explosives. Secondly, many nations hold the ship responsible for illegally importing stowaways. In the United States, the fine levied against a ship for each stowaway allowed to debark is $1,000. In cases where the vessel is on a standard run from a loading port in an underdeveloped nation to the United States and back again, as many as 12 to 15 stowaways may board the vessel on any given voyage. Since they are usually caught by Immigration authorities as they attempt to leave the vessel at her U.S. discharge port, fines of $10,000 to $15,000 can be levied against the ship each trip. Over the course of a year such fines can amount to several hundred thousand dollars. Furthermore, to add insult to injury, many times the ship is required to take the stowaways with her when she departs, thus having to provide free passage home for the culprits. Also, since many of the underdeveloped countries do not consider stowing away a crime many stowaways are repeat offenders with nothing to lose if they keep trying.

Drug smuggling is another security threat that can have serious ramifications for the vessel owner. Ships calling at U.S. ports present wonderful opportunities for smuggling cocaine, heroin, and other drugs, particularly if a prior port of call is in a drug-producing country. The usual procedure calls for one or more crew members to be paid to secret low-volume, high-priced drugs aboard the ship for transport to the United States. Once the vessel arrives in the United States the drugs are delivered to any of a number of convenient receivers and couriers who come aboard, such as prostitutes, longshoremen, ship suppliers, or "relatives." If the drugs are found aboard the ship by U.S. Customs officials before the crew member has been able to deliver them, the ship most probably will be seized and fined. Furthermore, if a particular ship becomes a repeat offender, regardless of fault on the part of the owners, she can be confiscated and forfeited to the U.S. government. This happened in a case involving the M/V *Ea*. Customs officers observed individuals passing packages of cocaine through a porthole to persons on the dock where the ship was berthed in Tampa. It was established that the vessel's master had either consented to, or was aware of, the illegal importation of cocaine because he had actual knowledge of its presence aboard. The fact that the *Ea*'s owners had no knowledge, or claimed to have no knowledge, of the matter was unimportant. The ship was forfeited to the United States. The 1986 Anti-Drug Abuse Act authorizes Customs to fine common carriers $16,000 per pound of confiscated cocaine and heroin and $8,000 per pound of marijuana. Under this law two well-known carriers have recently been fined $103 million and $59 million. Such fines are mind-boggling and, if allowed to stand, can easily put the shipper and his insurer out of business. Furthermore, on April 11, 1988, the United States quietly enacted a new "zero tolerance" maritime drug policy and now allows the U.S. Coast Guard to seize any boat or ship on which even a minute amount of drug contraband is found. A confiscated boat will be returned to its owners only if the allegations of illegal drugs on board are proved to be false. Shortly after the enactment of this policy, a $2.5-million luxury yacht was seized after less than one-tenth of an ounce of marijuana was found on board. The yacht was ultimately returned to her owner, but only after he had paid a substantial fine.

The next three security hazards—sabotage, piracy, and hijacking—are the most serious threats facing any vessel and crew today. The shipboard security measures and procedures discussed in the next chapter are designed specifically to combat these threats and the enormous terrorist potential that can be realized by them. Sabotage consists of any act which maliciously damages or destroys property, and it is included as part of the basic doctrine of most revolutionary groups throughout the world. Of all the activities available to international terrorists, sabotage offers the widest range of targets and the best potential for success. The devastation that can be accomplished by the skillful employment of sabotage in the maritime arena, and the known existence of certain groups willing to engage in such activity, place this hazard high on the list of serious risks confronting the maritime community. In terms of trained manpower, equipment, costs, and exposure, a sabotage operation involves only minimum expenditure by terrorists. The "profit," however, can be enormous, particularly if the target has been carefully selected. Consider the economic and environmental devastation that could be caused by the well-placed sinking of a fully loaded supertanker. There are more than 500 VLCCs and ULCCs plying the world's oceans. These ships are in excess of 1,000 feet long, over 150 feet wide, and carry more than 250,000 tons of petroleum products. The value of such ships and their cargoes alone exceeds $50 million apiece. The damage a 250,000-ton oil spill can cause on the right coast could easily be valued in the billions of dollars. France claimed damages in excess of $2 billion in the *Amoco Cadiz* litigation. Consider the catastrophic damage that could be caused by blowing up an LNG tanker in New York or Boston. The detonation of 125,000 cubic meters of LNG has been estimated to be the equivalent of a nuclear blast larger than the one that destroyed Hiroshima.

The most common sabotage objective in today's terrorist scenarios is extortion. Indiscriminate destruction is certainly a terrorist tactic, which the bombing of crowded airports clearly demonstrates, but it gains the terrorists nothing but notoriety. Sabotaging a $400-million offshore installation, on the other hand, could lead to millions of dollars in extortion payoffs in addition to the notoriety.

Sabotage tactics take maximum advantage of existing weaknesses in the security system. Accessibility due to inadequate protective measures creates vulnerabilities the nature of which the maritime industry has been far too slow to grasp. There are many ways to commit sabotage, and new methods are being invented daily. A major sabotage effort might be undertaken only after extensive planning and rehearsing. On the other hand, a sabotage mission can also be improvised by taking advantage of opportunity and means as they become available. A sabotage device can be either crude or highly sophisticated, and may be incendiary or explosive in nature. In virtually all cases it will have some sort of time delay mechanism so that the saboteur can get safely away.

Piracy is robbery committed on the high seas, and it is a maritime security threat of greater proportions than most vessel owners are willing to admit. Historically the pirate roamed the seas in an armed vessel and preyed upon whatever merchantmen he came across. Today there are still plenty of pirates and there are more merchantmen than ever. In the United States the crime of piracy has been expanded from simple robbery and is now codified in Title 18 of the U.S. Code, Section 1652: "Whoever, being a citizen of the United States, commits any murder or robbery, or any act of hostility against the United States, or against any citizen thereof, on the high seas, under color of any commission from any foreign prince, or state or on pretense of authority from any person is a pirate, and shall be imprisoned for life." Pirates have been around for as long as men have been going to sea. They are as plentiful today in certain areas of the world as they have ever been. In the Caribbean over the last 15 or 20 years there have been literally hundreds of suspected acts of piracy. Vessels and crews have mysteriously disappeared, with the vessels occasionally reappearing, bloodstained and deserted. The west coast of Africa has long been known to contain a serious pirate threat to merchantmen, which are regularly boarded and looted while at anchor, sometimes by as many as 20 or 30 armed pirates at a time. The greatest number of pirates anywhere in the world, however, swarms in the waters of Southeast Asia. They abound near the active shipping lanes around Indonesia, such as the Strait of Malacca and the Phillip Channel near Singapore. They are heavily armed, fearless, and ruthless. Tankers and other merchant vessels are routinely boarded at night while underway; the pirates employ fast boats, grappling hooks, and lines. Crews are held at gunpoint while their ships are ransacked and looted. At least one master, an Australian aboard the containership *Oriental Ambassador,* has been shot and killed. His ship was boarded in the Philippines.

Owners and operators, even after they are aware of the piracy threat facing their vessels and crews, have steadfastly refused to do anything about the security of their ships. They prefer to rely upon insurance to absorb any losses they may incur. The time has come for the industry to consider the liabilities for negligent security in broader terms than previously. Until now, the argument has always been that the risk is minimal so long as the pirates meet with no armed resistance. The loss of a few thousand dollars, even several thousand dollars, from the master's safe can be absorbed easily. Can $1 million be absorbed that easily? Can $10 million? A $10-million or greater wrongful death lawsuit is not inconceivable where a young shipmaster is killed by pirates and it can be shown that his vessel's owners knew of the piracy threat but refused to do anything to prevent it. The liability scenario can easily be expanded in proportion to the number of other officers or crew who are maimed or killed. Furthermore, it seems for some reason not to have occurred to anyone that once a ship has been boarded and ransacked there is nothing to prevent her from being hijacked. Sooner or later it will occur to the pirates to hold their prizes for ransom. If they can do it, and at the moment they can, so can terrorists; then owners' liabilities will soar into the hundreds of millions of dollars as hijacked vessels are used to create political, economic, and environmental havoc.

Vessel hijacking is the ultimate security threat faced by a ship and her crew. Once a vessel is successfully hijacked, all lives onboard can be considered forfeited and the vessel lost. Owners, operators, officers, and crew will have lost the ability for self-determination. A prisoner of war is placed in precisely the same position. Whether he lives or dies is up to his captors. There are two schools of thought concerning the advisability of becoming a POW, and they apply equally well to vessel hijacking. One school contends it is better to fight to the death than be captured because if captured, one's life may be extinguished at whim. One has, therefore, nothing to lose and everything to gain by resisting. The other school maintains that armed resistance when resistance is futile can only lead to capture or death whereas, by surrendering, death might be avoided. Today's owners appear to have accepted the latter school of thought, forgetting that in most cases it will be the pirates and hijackers who will be at a considerable disadvantage, and who will more than likely lose, against a properly secured vessel. The cost of implementing reliable shipboard security is small when compared to the liability exposure faced by owners, operators, and insurers for negligently not implementing it.

Hijackers, like pirates and saboteurs, must get aboard if they are to succeed. For this reason the focus of shipboard security must be to prevent unauthorized access to the vessel. The security measures and procedures designed to do just that are discussed in the next chapter. The security planner, when preparing his ship security plan, must know and understand those procedures in order to decide which ones to utilize. Before he can make those decisions, however, he must consider the seven planning criteria mentioned earlier. The first is to determine his ship's potential vulnerability to the various security threats just discussed (pilferage, stowaways, drug smuggling, sabotage, piracy, and hijacking). His second task is to consider the effect the various security measures will have on shipboard efficiency and operation if implemented.

Probably the most important consideration regarding vessel efficiency is manpower. Wage cost can determine the profitability of the entire venture. The U.S. merchant marine is a wonderful example. It priced itself out of the maritime market 20 years ago by succumbing to the exorbitant wage demands of the various seamen's unions. U.S. coastwise trade is carried on in U.S. flag bottoms today only because it is the law. International trade is conducted on foreign flag common carriers who can charge lower tariffs due to their lower operating costs. The costs of operating most ships of equal size are about the same with regard to fuel consumption, spare parts, port fees, food, and so on. The only real variable is the cost of manpower, and that cost is considerably lower in non-U.S. flag vessels.

The goal of all owners and operators is to man their vessels at a safe and efficient level without paying for excessive manpower. Unfortunately, proper security requires manning levels that in most cases will be higher than otherwise. If a ship is operating with as few watch standers as possible, and as few watch rotations as possible, no one will be available for security watches. Consequently, if the security needs of the ship are going to be met, the security planner must decide what security measures to adopt and how the manpower will be provided to effect them. In this regard he has three choices: he can try to utilize the existing manning level, pay more overtime, and assign extra security duties to all crew members; he can increase the manning level slightly, pay a little more in regular wages but possibly less overtime, and assign extra security duties to only some of the crew; or he can increase the manning level substantially by employing security personnel in addition to regular crew members, pay extra wages but no overtime, and assign no extra security duties to the other crew members. The decision will be based upon not only the security threat faced by the ship, and considerations of efficiency and shipboard operations, but also the other security planning criteria, notably the availability of funds and the security risks involved.

Manpower, however, is just one of the considerations the security planner must keep in mind when deciding what security procedures to employ. All phases of shipboard operations must be analyzed, including communications, sailing schedules, shipping routes, loading and discharge ports, and types of cargo. For instance, if the primary security threat to the vessel is pirate attacks in the Phillip Channel, additional security forces can be placed aboard only for the duration of the channel's transit. Once the ship is safely clear of the threatened area the extra personnel can be removed. Similar security techniques can be employed in the Persian Gulf to combat attacks by Iranian gunboats. Security professionals can be rotated from ship to ship at a very cost-effective rate without the need for arming and training entire crews.

The practical limitations imposed by the physical characteristics of the vessel provide another factor to be weighed by the security planner. The vessel's configuration will determine to a large extent the methods and manpower needed to secure her. Her interior arrangement will need to be considered if a brig is to be built, or an armory added, or additional security personnel placed aboard. The author was once asked to assist the master of a refrigeration vessel whose standard run was from Turbo, Colombia, to Tampa, Florida, carrying bananas. The master's problem concerned stowaways. By the time the vessel arrived in Tampa on each voyage the master usually had a dozen or so stowaways on his hands. As long as he kept them on board he would avoid any fines, but if they escaped, his ship was liable. The ship had no really secure space in which the stowaways could be confined. Locking a stateroom from the outside had proved futile. The solution was to build a brig, complete with bars and guard station. In doing so the physical characteristics of the vessel had to be considered.

The availability of funds is an important consideration when planning any security program. Obviously, the manpower cost is the greatest concern. Other factors include the cost of weapons, ammunition, lights, alarms, communication equipment, electronic surveillance equipment, and modifications to the vessel.

The risk factor comes into play in two ways. First, a realistic assessment of the risk faced by the vessel must be made with regard to the various security threats. The terms "threat" and "risk" are not synonymous. Piracy is a security threat. The degree of exposure to that threat is the risk. For instance, if a vessel's sail plan calls for her to sail directly from Osaka to Seattle the risk of piracy is probably low. On the other hand, if it calls for her to sail from Singapore to Lagos the risk is probably very high. Likewise, the risk of stowaways and drug smuggling is high on a run from Turbo to Tampa, but low from London to New York. The second way risk plays an important role in security planning is the degree to which the vessel or her crew is placed at risk as a result of the security procedures employed. One of the primary objections raised by owners against arming their ships is that the crews will be placed more at risk as a result. A few years ago the author offered a security proposal to the owners and operators of an LNG tanker line. They seemed genuinely concerned with the security of their vessels, as they should, and appeared interested in the proposal until they realized it included placing firearms on board. They rejected the proposal because they considered their crews to be placed at an unacceptable risk if asked to defend their vessels against hijackers and saboteurs. Strangely enough, they did not consider their crews unacceptably at risk if the hijackers or saboteurs were successful.

There are almost always alternative measures or procedures to any course of action, and the security planner should consider all of them. His task is to determine which alternative procedures are desirable, if any, and whether they are more desirable than the primary measures. Thus, fire hoses may be an alternative to fire arms and CCTV systems can be an alternative to manned security watches. Whether they are more desirable is the security planner's decision.

The last criterion to be considered by the security planner in developing his ship security plan is an evaluation of the security capabilities of other available resources. Certainly, the ship should be secure unto herself and be capable of providing for her own security unassisted, but advantage can sometimes be taken of other available resources. A pierside facility may have its own security personnel who can assist in securing the vessel's berth as well as respond to a security emergency. The local police, military, or Coast Guard may be willing to render security assistance. Customs and Immigration officials may provide information useful to the vessel's security. Private guard companies might be available during extended yard periods. Other ships may routinely be in the vicinity or utilize similar shipping routes and schedules, which might be taken into account when considering combating threats such as piracy.

Having obtained a security survey of his vessel, and having carefully considered the various security planning criteria, the security planner is almost ready to begin drafting his ship security plan. Before he can prepare his security SOPs and security bill, however, he must be provided with one last piece of information. He must know what security policy is to be followed. The dictation of policy must be done by the vessel's owners, operators, or insurers. Those responsible for the ship, crew, and cargo must make the decisions as to the security posture that is to be adopted. Some of the security policy questions needing answers are:

1. Is a security effort needed?
2. If a security effort is needed, should it be conducted by the vessel, home office, or both?
3. If security measures are promulgated on board, should they be passive or active?

    4. Is the operating budget to be increased to allow for additional manpower, modification to the vessel, or installation of electronic devices and, if so, to what extent?

    5. Is the vessel to be armed and, if so, to what extent?

Obviously, the threshold question is whether a security effort is needed at all. For years shipowners have been answering that question in the negative. Worse yet, many have not even bothered to ask the question. Times have changed, and those shipowners who persist in refusing to consider maritime security seriously may well live to regret their struthious attitude. Assuming it is determined that some sort of security effort is needed, however, a decision as to the nature of the program must be made. Is the effort to be made by the home office, receiving security intelligence and making routing and scheduling decisions based upon that information? Or is the ship to be allowed to assume some of the security responsibility for herself? If she is allowed to promulgate onboard security measures, will those measures be active or passive? (Security can be either active or passive depending upon the nature of the actions taken. For the purpose of this book, a vessel which does not intend to protect herself in an active manner by use of force is passive. If berthed, she must rely upon the local law enforcement agencies to protect her. She may still employ lights, alarms, locks, electronic surveillance and detection equipment, and security watches to provide warning of an impending threat, but she will have no reactive capabilities with which to meet that threat. If she is underway, her only option will be to maneuver. If she is at anchor, she has no options. The security procedures discussed in the next chapter can all be considered as active.)

    The operating budget is crucial to any business enterprise, and the maritime industry is no exception. Rarely is there ever enough money for everything that is desired or needed. Consequently, budgetary considerations play an important part in the security policy-making process. Even the simplest and least expensive passive security measure, proper lighting, can be financially significant. When the cost of overtime wages, additional personnel, shipboard modifications, electronic gadgets, and weapons are considered, very real budgetary dilemmas can appear. The trick is to achieve adequate security within the mandated budgetary restraints, and to keep the budgetary restraints reasonable in light of the security needed.

One very important policy decision, and a very difficult one for today's shipowners, is whether to arm their vessels and to what extent. Every merchantman should have an arms locker on board, along with personnel trained and prepared to use firearms when necessary. Also, vessels in danger of missile or other surface-to-surface or air-to-surface attack, such as ships plying the Persian Gulf, should be fitted with a temporarily mounted, autonomous air defense system such as the Goalkeeper or SAMOS naval air defense systems. Even mobile battlefield gun systems such as the Breda Twin 40L70 AA Field Mounting system could be effectively employed aboard. All such systems are fully automated and require no crew involvement. Unfortunately, most shipowners at the present time are not willing to take these steps. In any event, once the ship's security planner has been provided with the necessary security policy guidance he may begin drafting his ship security plan. The flow chart illustrated in figure 5 demonstrates the policy understanding the security planner must have before he can prepare his security SOPs.

The security bill is developed as the security SOPs are formulated. The process is simultaneous, and one cannot be prepared without the other. The security SOPs detail the number and functions of security watch standers for any given shipboard evolution. The security bill assigns each crew member to a particular security task during the same evolution. Consequently, in order to prepare the security plan the security planner must thoroughly understand the recommended security procedures for any given shipboard evolution and decide what can and cannot be done with the manpower and equipment available. The recommended security procedures are discussed in chapter 4. The following is an example of the format a ship security plan might take.

SHIP SECURITY PLAN

Vessel: *Date:*

1. Purpose. The purpose of the ship security plan is to prevent:
   A. Unauthorized access to the ship and restricted areas on board.
   B. The introduction of unauthorized weapons or other dangerous devices on board.

FIG. 5.   Security policy SOP planning

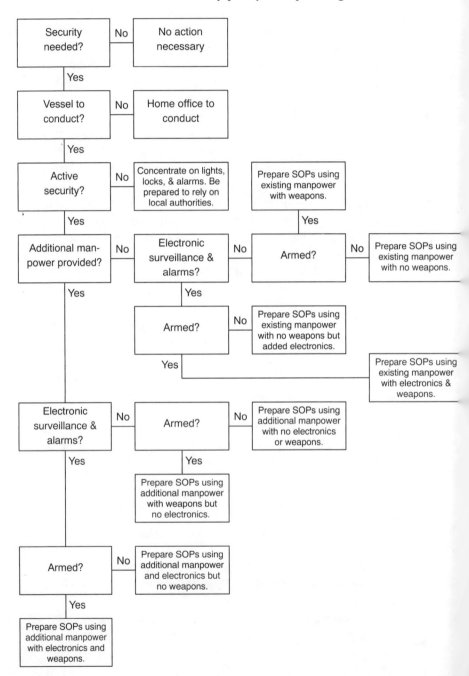

    C. The introduction of illegal drugs or other contraband on board.

    D. Pilferage of cargo while in the care, custody, and control of the ship.

2. Security officer. The ship's security officer shall be the chief officer.

3. Security bill.

    A. All officers and crew shall be assigned security duties and stations to be assumed during any security alert. These assignments shall take the form of the ship's security bill and shall be posted as appropriate.

    B. The security bill is as follows:

Security Bill

Personnel	Duty	Station
Master	In command	Bridge
Ch. ofc.	On-scene OIC	As required
2nd ofc.	OIC sec. team 1	Main deck fwd.
3rd ofc.	OIC sec. team 2	Main deck aft
Ch. engr.	OIC eng. rm.	Engine room
2nd engr.	Assist C/E	Engine room
3rd engr.	Assist C/E	Engine room
R/O	Communicate	Radio room
Bos'n	Assist C/O	As directed
A.B. (Name)	Sec. team 1	Main deck fwd.
A.B. (Name)	Sec. team 1	Main deck fwd.
A.B. (Name)	Sec. team 2	Main deck aft
A.B. (Name)	Sec. team 2	Main deck aft
Oiler (Name)	Runner	Bridge
Oiler (Name)	Runner	Bridge
Oiler (Name)	Throttleman	Engine room
Oiler (Name)	Eng. maint.	Engine room
Cook	Cook	Galley

4. Procedures.

    A. Standing operating procedures (SOPs) shall be maintained and practiced for the following shipboard evolutions:

        1) Moored dockside.

        2) Moored dockside, cargo operations.

3) At anchor.

4) At anchor, cargo operations.

5) Underway.

6) Rendering assistance at sea.

7) Docking/undocking.

8) Receiving/discharging pilots.

9) Receiving ship's stores.

10) Bunkering.

11) Receiving official visitors.

12) Changing crew.

B. The security SOPs are as follows:

(SOPs attached)

5. Security equipment. The following security equipment shall be maintained in good working order and condition at all times:

A. Firearms. The following firearms shall be kept in the ship's arms locker/armory along with 100 rounds per weapon:

(list attached)

B. Security lighting. Exterior security lighting shall be maintained in working order and condition at all times, and shall be turned on in accordance with the security SOPs. Exterior lighting shall be arranged as follows:

(diagram attached)

C. Security alarms and communication systems. All security alarms and communication systems shall be maintained in good working order and condition at all times, and shall be utilized in accordance with the security SOPs.

1) The ship shall maintain the following security alarms:

(diagram and description attached)

2) The ship shall maintain the following security communication systems:

(list attached)

D. Access controls. The following access controls shall be employed aboard at all times:

    1) Crew members shall carry at all times a photo identification document issued by the security officer. All such documents shall be strictly controlled by the security officer, who shall be responsible for maintaining a record of all documents issued and destroyed. Documents of crew members permanently departing the vessel shall be destroyed. Documents of crew members temporarily departing the vessel for periods exceeding two weeks shall be retained on board by the security officer and reissued to the crew member upon his return.

    2) When visitors to the ship are permitted, their embarkation and debarkation shall be strictly controlled. All visitors shall be searched and their carry-on baggage inspected prior to boarding. Visitor passes shall be issued only by the security officer and shall be prominently displayed on the person of the visitor at all times. No visitor shall be allowed to debark until his security pass has been returned to the security officer. All visitors shall be escorted at all times while on board by a member of the crew. All vendors or cargo handlers shall be treated as any other visitor, with the following exceptions:

        a) If visitor is alone at time of embarkation, he shall display an identification document with sufficient information to allow the security officer to verify his identity and employment.

        b) If he is a member of a work gang, the gang leader shall be required to present a list of gang members with sufficient information to verify the identity of each. Only those gang members properly identified shall be issued visitor passes.

6. Restricted areas. The following restricted areas shall be established on board:

A. Bridge

B. Radio room

C. Engine room
D. Armory
E. Ship's office
7. Administration. The administration of the ship security plan
    shall be the responsibility of the ship's security officer under
    the direction of the master. The following shall be conducted:
    A. Security inspections. Security inspections shall be con-
        ducted daily by the security officer in the regular perfor-
        mance of his duties. In addition thereto, inspections shall
        be conducted at any time during periods of potential
        security threat or when directed by the master.
    B. Security training. Security training shall be the respon-
        sibility of the security officer. If a security consultant is
        employed by owners to conduct security training on
        board, the security officer shall coordinate such training
        as necessary.
    C. Security drills. Security drills shall be conducted regular-
        ly, and careful records maintained as to the date, time,
        and nature of the drill. All security SOPs shall be prac-
        ticed.
    D. Inventories. Inventories of all security equipment, includ-
        ing keys, shall be taken at regular intervals. The security
        officer shall maintain a record of all inventories and im-
        mediately report any discrepancies to the master.
    E. Coordination with port facility security officers. Upon
        the ship's berthing at any port facility, the security of-
        ficer shall immediately coordinate with the port facility
        security officer, if there is one, to ensure the security of
        the vessel and her cargo and/or passengers. If no port
        facility security officer is designated then the security of-
        ficer shall coordinate with the port authority's designated
        representative for the vessel's security.

THE PORT FACILITY SECURITY PLAN

As with ships, each port facility should develop and maintain a port
facility security plan. It should provide for measures and equipment
to prevent weapons, munitions, explosives, or other dangerous devices
from being introduced aboard vessels utilizing the port. It should es-

tablish procedures for the prevention of unauthorized access to ships and restricted areas within the port facility, and it should provide for pre-employment evaluations of all security personnel and other personnel who, in the performance of their jobs, will have access to ships and restricted areas.

Like the ship security officer, a port facility security officer should be appointed or designated for every port facility. The port facility security plan should identify the security officer. The responsibilities of the port facility security officer include:

1. Conducting, or arranging for an independent security consultant to conduct, an initial comprehensive security survey in order to prepare a port facility security plan.
2. Developing, or arranging for an independent security consultant to develop, a port facility security plan.
3. Implementing the port facility security plan.
4. Recommending modifications as needed to any existing port facility security plan.
5. Encouraging security awareness and vigilance among the employees of the port facility.
6. Ensuring adequate training for all security personnel.
7. Maintaining all necessary records concerning security of the port facility, including the documenting of all unlawful acts, security training, and intelligence information.
8. Coordinating port security with all vessels using the facility, local and national security services, law enforcement agencies, and fire-fighting agencies.

The port facility security officer should have knowledge of some or all of the following matters:

1. Security administration.
2. Relevant international conventions, codes, and recommendations.
3. Responsibilities and functions of other involved organizations.
4. Relevant government legislation and regulations.
5. Risk, threat, and vulnerability assessments.
6. Security surveys and inspections.

7. Ship security measures.
8. Security training and education.
9. Recognition of characteristics and behavioral patterns of persons who are likely to commit unlawful acts.
10. Inspection, control, and monitoring techniques.
11. Techniques used to circumvent security measures.
12. Dangerous substances and devices and how to recognize them.
13. Ship and local port operations and conditions.
14. Security devices and systems.

The security threats faced by any port facility that must be guarded against are primarily those of pilferage, sabotage, unauthorized access to vessels, and the introduction of unauthorized weapons and other dangerous devices aboard vessels. By far the most serious threats are the latter two, for they allow for any number of terrorist scenarios. In port facilities that administer to cruise ships, and presumably have a passenger terminal within the facility, the task is much more difficult than otherwise. This is due mainly to the large numbers of passengers, visitors, baggage handlers, ticket agents, food caterers, and other service personnel found in and around passenger terminals. The Port of Miami, for example, is the base for 10 cruise ship lines operating 24 cruise ships. The port averages 100,000 visitors and 60,000 vehicles a week.

Recent U.S. legislation and IMO standards have been developed specifically in response to the 1985 *Achille Lauro* cruise ship incident that are designed to increase cruise ship and passenger protection against such terrorist activities. Specific requirements are discussed later in this book in chapter 6. For now it is sufficient to note that counterterrorist concerns, at least for passenger vessels, have increased dramatically. However, few concerns have been voiced regarding cargo vessels, and in most ports throughout the world, including the United States, anyone can walk aboard such ships. The hijacking of a cruise ship and the holding of its hundreds of passengers hostage would certainly have a very great impact on the world community, as the *Achille Lauro* incident did, but so would a 250,000-ton terrorist-orchestrated oil spill. In fact, as maritime passenger terminals become more secure terrorists can be expected to target less troublesome objectives. Consequently, passenger terminal security should be considered as only one item in the grocery list of security items with which the port facility security officer must concern himself. Passenger terminal security, while important, should not be allowed to overshadow all other port security matters.

Preventing unauthorized access to *all* vessels, passenger and cargo alike, should be of primary concern. Because port facilities are generally spread out over a large area and contain numerous piers, warehouses, storage areas, and access points, not to mention pipelines, fuel depots, railways, and anchorages, the problem of physically securing the entire facility is great. It cannot be done simply or cheaply. Even the cost of proper security fencing and lighting, the most basic of security measures, can be enormous. The costs become astronomical when one considers all the possibilities—security personnel, surveillance and communication equipment, vehicles, dogs, electronic or manual access controls, detection machines, and alarm systems. For this reason the port facility security planner must develop his security plan based upon a carefully reasoned and realistic approach to the threats faced and the resources available. To do so he must consider the seven security planning criteria previously mentioned:

§ Vulnerability to potential hazards.
§ Effect of security measures on business, efficiency, and operations.
§ Practical limitations imposed by the physical characteristics of the port facility.
§ Availability of funds.
§ Risk.
§ Available alternative measures.
§ Evaluation of the security capabilities of all available external resources.

Perhaps the most significant of these criteria, as far as the port facility security planner is concerned, is the availability of funds. The second most significant is the practical limitations imposed by the physical characteristics of the port facility. It may well be that the facility cannot be reasonably secured, because of its size and other physical characteristics, without a massive influx of funds that simply aren't available. Realization of this fact, however, should prompt the security planner to rely upon other criteria more than he might otherwise, such as available alternative measures and external resources. One of the external resources available to the port facility security officer might be intelligence data on terrorist activities. Analyzing such data may well allow him to more effectively evaluate the risk of terrorist attack and adjust his security plan accordingly. Just as a ship transiting the Phillip Channel might employ additional security forces for the duration of the transit, so too could a port facility utilize extra security measures only during periods of higher risk.

Next to preventing unauthorized access to vessels and storage areas and the unauthorized introduction of weapons aboard ships, the security problem most often encountered by the port facility is pilferage. In some ports pilferage has reached epidemic proportions, with losses of millions of dollars a year in pilfered goods. There are two primary ways to fight pilferage. The first is to control access to all areas where cargo is handled and stowed. This includes utilizing careful and intelligent pre-employment practices. The second is effective, round-the-clock surveillance of all storage areas, warehouses, and staging depots. This includes the piers during all loading and discharging operations.

Once the port facility security survey has been conducted, and the port facility security planner has carefully considered the various security planning criteria, it is almost time to begin preparing the port facility security plan. Before the security planner can do so, however, he must know what security policies are to be followed. For a port facility, most policy questions will center around funding. The security planner must determine such things as whether contract security services rather than port authority personnel are to be used, and whether individual service companies within the port facility such as stevedores and warehousemen will be required to provide their own security. He will need to know whether the use of dogs is authorized, and if electronic surveillance equipment and alarms can be afforded. He will also need to know what type of response to a security breach is expected. Unlike ships, which in most cases must deal with their security threats alone, the port facility has the resources of local law enforcement agencies at its disposal. Consequently, it may very well be that the goal of the port facility's security program is to provide adequate warning only, and that other agencies will provide the response necessary.

Regardless of the anticipated external support, the port facility security plan should be carefully coordinated with the local law enforcement and fire-fighting agencies. All entities should have designated liaison personnel. In this case, the port facility security officer is the liaison. If a crisis management team has been established, representatives from all applicable local agencies will be members of the team and the necessary liaison will be made through them.

In any event, once he understands the policy considerations applicable to port security, the port facility security officer is ready to prepare his security plan. The following is an example of a simple plan.

PORT FACILITY SECURITY PLAN

Port: *Date:*

1. Purpose. The purpose of the Port Facility Security Plan is to prevent:
   A. Unauthorized access to ships and restricted areas within the port facility.
   B. Unauthorized weapons or other dangerous devices from being introduced aboard ships within the port facility.
   C. Pilferage of cargo while in the care, custody, and control of the port facility.
2. Security officer. The port facility security officer shall be [Name] . He shall be directly responsible to the director of the port authority.
3. Security personnel. All port facility security personnel shall be under the direct supervision and control of the port facility security officer. They shall be employed by the port authority.
4. Security force. The port facility security force shall consist of port facility security personnel. The force shall be divided into four duty sections. Each duty section shall be commanded by a duty section leader who shall be directly responsible to the port facility security officer.

5. Deployment of security force. The deployment of the security force shall be by duty sections. Each duty section shall be deployed in shifts of eight hours. The status of each duty section at any given time shall be one of the following:

> On duty
> On alert
> Stand down

Duty sections shall be rotated through the three eight-hour shifts as directed by the port facility security officer.

6. Security equipment. The following security equipment shall be maintained in good working order and condition at all times:

A. Firearms. All security personnel shall be armed while on duty with a 9mm automatic pistol of their choice which it shall be their duty to provide. Other weapons, such as shotguns and automatic rifles, shall be provided by the port authority as necessary and shall be stored in a secure area designated by the port facility security officer.

B. Security lighting. Exterior security lighting shall be maintained in good working order and condition at all times, and shall be arranged as follows:

> (diagram attached)

C. Security alarms and communication systems. All security alarms and communication systems shall be maintained in good working order and condition.

1) Alarms. The following alarms shall be maintained:

> (diagram and description attached)

2) Communication. The following communication equipment shall be maintained:

> (list attached)

D. Access controls. The following access controls shall be employed:

> (describe by building or location)

7. Restricted areas. The following restricted areas shall be established:

(description or location)

8. Administration. The administration of the port facility security plan shall be the responsibility of the port facility security officer. The following shall be conducted:
   A. Pre-employment screening. Pre-employment screening of all security personnel and other port facility personnel whose jobs require access to vessels or restricted areas shall be conducted.
   B. Security inspections. Security inspections shall be conducted by the port facility security officer on a routine basis.
   C. Security training. Security training shall be the responsibility of the port facility security officer. If security consultants are employed, the port facility security officer shall coordinate such training as necessary. All port security personnel shall maintain a high level of proficiency in the following areas:
      1) Entry control.
      2) Patrols, observation, and communication.
      3) Inspection, identification, and reporting.
      4) Person, vehicle, and building searches.
      5) Apprehension of suspects.
      6) Self-defense.
      7) Recognizing dangerous substances and devices.
      8) Human relations.
      9) First aid.
   D. Security drills. Security drills shall be conducted regularly, and careful records maintained as to the date, time, and nature of the drill.
   E. Inventories. Inventories of all security equipment, including keys, shall be taken at regular intervals.
   F. Coordination with ship security officers and local authorities. The port facility security officer shall coordinate vessel security upon berthing with the designated ship security officer. If no ship security officer has been designated, he shall coordinate security with the vessel's

master. The port facility security officer shall also coordinate port facility security with the local law enforcement and fire-fighting authorities on a regular basis.

THE OFFSHORE INSTALLATION SECURITY PLAN

Each offshore installation should be covered by an offshore installation security plan. The primary purpose for an offshore security plan is to prevent unauthorized access. Consequently, the plan must focus on two distinct security considerations. The first is the physical security of any installation itself. The second is the preventative security measures that can be utilized in controlling routine access to the installation, such as pre-employment evaluations and proper personnel identification procedures.

A security officer need not be appointed for every offshore installation. Since most companies engaged in offshore petroleum production operate many offshore installations, a company offshore security officer can be appointed to oversee the security needs of a number of facilities. In that way a uniform company security policy can be maintained, and company security personnel can be utilized most effectively. The company offshore security officer should be responsible for the following:

1. Conducting, or arranging for an independent security consultant to conduct, an initial comprehensive security survey of all offshore installations owned or operated by his company.
2. Developing, or arranging for an independent security consultant to develop, a company offshore security plan.
3. Implementing the offshore security plan.
4. Recommending modifications, as needed, to any existing offshore security plan.
5. Encouraging security awareness and vigilance.
6. Ensuring adequate training for all security personnel.
7. Maintaining all necessary records concerning offshore security including the documentation of all unlawful acts, security training, and intelligence information.
8. Coordinating offshore security with all affected intra-company departments and local authorities.
9. Developing the company's crisis management team.

The company offshore security officer should have knowledge of the following security-related matters:

1. Security administration.
2. Risk, threat, and vulnerability assessments.
3. Security surveys and inspections.
4. Security training and education.
5. Inspection, control, and monitoring techniques.
6. Techniques used to circumvent security measures.
7. Security devices and systems.
8. Dangerous substances and devices and how to recognize them.

Offshore installations are desirable targets for extortionists and terrorists for a number of reasons, not the least of which are their economic value and their environmental disruption potential. The cost of installing a state-of-the-art rig such as Conoco's tension-leg well platform can be as high as $400 million. The annual net income derived from these installations can easily reach $200 million. Charter rates for deepwater drill ships and semisubmersibles range around $50,000 per day. A $10-million or $20-million extortion demand, even a $50-million demand, would seem cheap in comparison to the loss of the installation. A lot of highly trained professionals can be bought for that kind of money, and it can shelter them from the law for the remainder of their lives. The possibility of massive oil pollution and offshore employee loss of life merely adds to the extorted dollar potential.

Extortion, however, requires control over those extorted. This is usually gained by a threat which is perceived as being potentially capable of materializing. The seizure of an offshore installation and the threat of its destruction would certainly meet that criterion, but in order to seize the installation the extortionists must gain access to it. Access control, therefore, must be the primary concern of the offshore security officer and his offshore security plan.

Would-be extortionists will either walk on board an installation as employees (or disguised as employees) or visitors; or they will board the installation either surreptitiously or by force by boat, helicopter, or swimmer delivery vehicle (two- or four-man minisub). The offshore security plan must be designed to prevent all such eventualities.

The offshore plan, like other security plans, must be based upon security policy. Policy decisions must be made either by the company offshore security officer or communicated to him by his superiors. Not only must the policy that will dictate day-to-day security procedures be established, but also the policy concerning the company's reaction to actual security events must be well delineated. Will the company pay extortion demands? If so, under what conditions will it pay? What limit, if any, will it set on the amount? Are any hostages who may be taken considered expendable? If so, how many are expendable? Should company security policy be published? If so, to what extent should it be published? These and many other questions should occur to the company offshore security officer as he develops his security plan. The following is an example of a simplified offshore installation security plan.

OFFSHORE INSTALLATION SECURITY PLAN

Installation: *Date:*

1. Purpose. The purpose of the offshore installation security plan is to prevent:
   A. Unauthorized access to the installation.
   B. Unauthorized weapons or other dangerous devices from being introduced on board.
2. Security officer. The offshore installation security officer shall be   [Name]   . He shall be directly responsible to the   [Position]   for all security planning involving offshore operations and for the implementation of the company off-shore security plan.
3. Crisis management team. The company crisis management team shall consist of the following:

   (list names and positions)

   The security officer shall be the crisis management team's liaison between the company and all external agency representatives whenever the crisis management team convenes.
4. Security equipment. The following security equipment shall be maintained in good working order and condition at all times:

A. Firearms. The following firearms shall be maintained on board each offshore installation:

(list type and number)

Firearms shall be stowed in a secure space with only the following personnel having access to them:

(list positions)

B. Security lighting. Installation exterior lighting shall be maintained in good working order and condition at all times, and in accordance with the general security lighting plan. The general security lighting plan is as follows:

(diagram)

C. Security alarms. All security alarms shall be maintained in good working order and condition.The following alarms shall be installed on each offshore facility:

(list and diagram)

D. Communication. All installations shall maintain primary and secondary communications. The secondary communication system shall not be located in the same space as the primary system. Both systems shall be in secure locations.

E. Access controls. The following access controls shall be employed on each installation:

(describe)

5. Personnel controls. The following personnel controls shall be implemented to ensure that no unauthorized persons board the installation:
   A. Pre-employment screening.
   B. Security I.D. badges.
   C. Employment rosters.
   D. Vessel and helicopter passenger manifests.
6. Restricted areas. The following restricted areas shall be established on each installation:

(description and location)

7. Administration. The administration of the company offshore
   security plan shall be the responsibility of the offshore
   security officer. The following shall be conducted:
   A. Pre-employment screening.
   B. Security indoctrination of all employees.
   C. Security training of supervisory personnel.
   D. Security inspections and inventories.
   E. Preboarding inspection of all baggage.

The security survey, once conducted, presents a picture of the ship,
port facility, or offshore installation's security posture. The security
plan is designed to ensure viable security. The security measures and
procedures that can be used to ensure this viability are the subject of
the next chapter.

CHAPTER FOUR

SECURITY MEASURES
AND PROCEDURES

THE security threats faced by any vessel, port facility, or offshore installation can be divided into two groups and labelled, for convenience, as category I or category II threats. The most serious are placed in category I and, for vessels, include sabotage, piracy, and hijacking. Category II threats are those that, while constituting hazards to the entity's security, do not reach the magnitude of those in category I. For vessels again, category II threats are pilferage, stowaways, and drug smuggling. The perception and labelling of security threats as category I or II depends a great deal upon the nature and mission of the particular maritime entity under consideration. For instance, whereas pilferage of cargo may be considered by a vessel's security planner to be a category II threat, it may well be considered category I by a port facility security planner (preceded in importance perhaps only by sabotage), and not considered a threat at all by an offshore installation security planner. Consequently, the labelling of threats as category I or II should be made merely for the convenience of the security planner to assist himself in developing his priorities. Category II threats can usually best be defeated by diligent observation, routine inspection, thorough employee security indoctrination, and good pre-employment practices. Category I threats, however, must generally be combatted with more active security measures. Such measures can entail a plethora of alternatives, not the least of which can include armed response and the use of deadly force. A security planner's primary objective should be to meet the category I threats faced by his particular maritime entity. If his security plan manages to do this the category II threats, in all likelihood, will also be guarded against.

Regardless of the nature of the particular maritime entity under consideration, there are certain general comments that can be made concerning multiple levels of defense, security zones, perimeter barriers, protective lighting, guards, dogs, alarms, electronic surveillance, communications, access controls, and so on. The first portion of this chapter will present those comments. Following that discussion, specific security procedures will be presented that are recommended for use aboard vessels, within port facilities, and on offshore installations. It should be borne in mind, however, that such recommendations are just that: recommendations. In any tactical situation the proper solution is the one that succeeds. Textbook solutions are to be studied more for analysis of the tactical situation than for rote resolution of the problem. Consequently, while the author recommends certain security procedures, it is up to the individual security planner to decide whether he wishes to accept those recommendations or develop his own responses.

GENERAL SECURITY MEASURES

In chapter 1 the security axiom of defense in depth was discussed in relation to the maritime security goals of adequate warning and timely reaction. In-depth security is the pivotal concept around which all security measures must revolve. It is the central consideration of any security plan, and it should be the immediate focus of any security surveyor, planner, or inspector. It will certainly be the first thing a prospective saboteur or terrorist looks for when he cases his objective. In short, defense in depth is the single most important security concept applicable to the field of maritime security, and it is for this reason that in-depth security is referred to as axiomatic.

When security experts contemplate in-depth security scenarios they usually think in terms of three layers of protection. These three layers, or zones as they are commonly called, are separated by perimeter barriers through which the attacker must penetrate. The terms "outer perimeter," "secondary perimeter," and "inner perimeter" are used frequently but not exclusively. The terms are not necessarily important, but the concept is. Likewise, the number of security zones will not always be three. There may be as few as two, or as many as four or more. Three is merely considered the optimum in security dogma. The physical characteristics of the entity being secured will ultimately dictate the number of security zones, and hence perimeters, that are established. Whatever their number, perimeters are defined by their barriers, which exist for three security purposes: to detect intruders, to delay their progress, and to destroy their ability to continue. These are known as the "three Ds": detect, delay, destroy.

On land the first layer of defense usually consists of an outer perimeter security barrier of some sort, such as a wall or fence, surrounding the property on which the facility or installation is situated. In medieval Europe this often took the form of a moat or spiked trench. The most phenomenal outer perimeter barrier of all time is probably the Great Wall of China. In any event, the security goal is always the same: to cause the intruders to be detected and to delay their progress sufficiently to allow them to be either turned back, apprehended, or destroyed. The three Ds. There is a fourth D which is also applicable, but which is only present in situations involving less than professional adversaries. That is the D of "discourage." A well-lighted and surveilled or alarmed outer perimeter barrier may well discourage intruders from the outset, but only nonprofessional ones.

At sea the outer perimeter can take several forms, depending upon the security concept developed by the security planner. In traditional naval warfare, a battle group, formed around one or more aircraft carriers or battleships, establishes security "picket lines" of smaller, faster vessels sometimes hundreds of miles away from the main group. Submarines and carrier-based aircraft can extend even this perimeter by yet more hundreds of miles. Radar, sonar, electronic countermeasures (ECM), and a host of other technological advances allow for the establishment of unseen perimeters at just about any desired location or distance from the maritime entity being secured. Of course, commercial vessels and offshore installations do not have surface fleets, submarines, and surveillance satellites at their disposal. They do have, however, the same security concepts utilized by the naval forces of the world and, depending upon budgetary restraints, can employ a number of similar measures. For instance, virtually all oceangoing vessels are equipped with one or more radars. Offshore installations can easily be similarly equipped, although few are at the present time. Consequently, a radar outer perimeter barrier can be established if the security planner desires to do so. Where the security threat is considered serious enough to warrant it, helicopters or other observational aircraft can be employed to provide air cover for offshore installations or vessels transiting dangerous waters. Hydrophones can be utilized by both anchored vessels and offshore installations for security purposes. Protective lighting can create an outer perimeter barrier many yards beyond the physical extremities of a ship or offshore rig, and machine-gun fire makes an extremely effective barrier well beyond that. Consequently, nonmilitary maritime entities can establish outer perimeter barriers that reach beyond their physical extremities, if their security planners so desire. On the other hand, if a security planner prefers not to create an outer perimeter beyond the physical confines of his ship or installation, then his outer perimeter will necessarily be the hull and bulwarks of his vessel or installation. In that case, those portions can be lighted and surveilled just like the outer perimeter barriers of any land-based facility.

After the outer perimeter, the next layer of defense is the secondary perimeter. It is at this perimeter that all intruders who have managed to breach the outer perimeter barrier are expected to be stopped. Whereas the outer perimeter barrier may have been nothing more than a lighted fence, the secondary perimeter barrier is always the main security structure of the installation or facility. If a backyard fence is a homeowner's outer perimeter barrier, the exterior walls of his house constitute his secondary perimeter barrier. Access through this barrier is usually gained not by breaching the barrier itself, such as by blowing a hole in it, but rather by forcing entry through existing openings such as doors and windows. In a security area like a port facility where there may be numerous buildings spread out over a large geographical area the exterior walls of each building become secondary perimeters. Thus, there may be any number of secondary perimeters within such a complex. On the other hand, if a complex contains a single group of buildings clustered fairly closely together the secondary perimeter might be considered to extend around the entire group of exterior walls. The gaps between buildings could be secured by fences, walls, guard posts, or other barriers.

In the case of vessels and offshore installations the secondary perimeter will normally be where access can be gained into the interior accommodations. On vessels this is most often the superstructure; however, care must be taken to consider all other possible ways that access to the accommodations might be gained, such as cargo hatches, scuttles, and so forth. On offshore rigs the secondary perimeter will depend upon the design and layout of the installation. In any case, the

FIG. 6. Perimeters are determined by the physical
layout of the port facility.

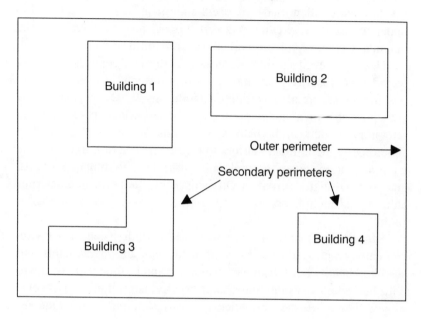

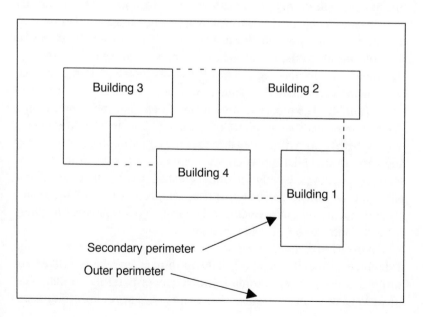

perimeter should be designated and established with the intent of making it absolutely secure. It is this perimeter barrier which must hold if the vessel, facility, or installation is to remain inviolate. All accesses must be identified, analyzed, and made as secure as possible under the existing circumstances. If this perimeter is breached, the defenders' chances for survival are severely diminished.

However, even the best defenses can be overcome, and consequently the security plan must provide for such an eventuality by designating secure areas within the facility itself. These secure areas constitute the final, inner perimeters behind which personnel can retreat and which can be held for a reasonable period of time. They should deny the intruders access to the crucial interior areas such as communication centers, control rooms, armories, lift-support systems, and mission-related activities. On a ship, for instance, the inner perimeters would include accesses to the bridge, engine room, and radio room.

Security barriers can take many forms, including concertina wire, chain link fencing, brick walls, reinforced concrete embankments, and steel bulkheads. The location of the barrier and its intended use, along with budgetary considerations, will usually determine the type employed. Except for port facilities, the barriers found in maritime environments will normally be made of steel. In ships they will consist of the vessel's hull and bulwarks which must be scaled, or her interior or exterior bulkheads which must be breached. The same applies to offshore installations, except that there may be areas on a particular rig where security fencing can be effectively installed. Port facilities, because they are situated on land, have a wide variety of security barriers available. The most common form of outer perimeter barrier utilized by port facilities is chain link fencing. This is primarily due to one specific factor with which port facilities must contend and vessels and offshore installations need not: geographical size. Some sort of security fencing is usually the only economically viable choice for a port facility's outer perimeter barrier simply because of the many miles of barrier required. Even good security fencing can be financially burdensome to install and maintain.

There are effective and less effective types of security fencing, but it should be remembered that, whatever form of fencing is utilized, its purpose is not to keep intruders out. It cannot possibly do that. The Great Wall of China, as impressive as it is, was never able to do that.

An example of inadequate security fencing

Security fencing is designed to discourage amateurs and slow down professionals. Concertina wire on the battlefield is used to delay and channel attackers so that they can be destroyed by the defenders' interlocking fields of fire. The same concept applies to security fencing. By itself it is no more effective than a "No Trespassing" sign, but if it is lighted, patrolled, and alarmed it should delay intruders long enough for them to be apprehended or destroyed.

Security fencing usually takes the form of one of three types, or a combination of the three. These are chain link, barbed wire or tape, and concertina. The choice of type usually depends upon the time available to construct the barrier, the degree of permanence desired, and the availability of materials. Chain link fencing is the most durable and should be used for protection of permanent security areas. It also takes the longest to install. Concertina, on the other hand, takes very little time to install but is not very durable. It is also easily breached. It is a good field expedient, however, when some sort of augmentation fencing is required in a hurry and can be replaced later.

Port facility security fencing should be of the chain link variety. It should be made of at least 9-gauge wire and have a mesh no larger than two square inches. Because it is used in a marine environment, it should be either plastic or aluminum coated to prevent failures due to rusting. The wire should be attached securely to similarly protected rigid metal posts that have been embedded in concrete and braced appropriately. The fence should be laid straight to permit unhampered observation, and its total height should be no less than 9.5 feet. If it is topped with barbed wire, it should be topped with at least three strands. If the fence is placed over concrete, asphalt, or firm ground the wire mesh should extend to within two inches of the surface. If not, it should extend at least six inches below ground level. A good alternative that can be prepared at the same time the fence posts are placed in concrete is to install a concrete channel in the shape of a shallow trough along the entire fence line. This will prevent erosion of the soil along the fence line, provide for water runoff, and, where the fence is properly placed in the center of the trough, effectively prevent someone from quickly scooping out enough soil to allow him to wriggle under the fence. A top guard can be added to the fence if desired. A top guard is an overhang of three or more strands of barbed wire supported on arms extending from the tops of the fence posts at a 45-degree angle. The overhang must angle away from the facility, unless a double top guard is used, which will have the effect of hindering fence-scaling from either side of the barrier. Any opening in the fence larger than 96 square inches will allow human access and should be secured appropriately.

There are certainly many other types of materials and barriers which can be utilized as outer perimeter barriers in a port facility. If a port authority employs an independent security consultant he may recommend several alternatives based upon the variables present. However, for all-around dependability and cost-effectiveness the chain link fence just described is difficult to better.

Of course, a fence is of little use by itself. Its value increases proportionately as it is combined with other security measures. For instance, if the purpose of any security fence is to delay an intruder long enough for him to be detected and hopefully stopped, an unlighted and unguarded fence will fail completely. Any delay is immaterial because he won't be detected. On the other hand, the same fence that is well lighted and patrolled will cause the intruder the same delay, but will now substantially increase his chances of being detected and stopped.

Adequate outer perimeter security requires, at a minimum, three basic security measures. First, there must be an appropriate perimeter barrier. For port facilities this usually means proper security fencing. For vessels and offshore installations the barrier can either be the physical boundaries of the entity itself or some sort of electronically or otherwise projected barrier. Second, that barrier must be lighted. Third, it must be patrolled or in some way regularly surveilled.

The task of providing security lighting (or protective lighting as it is sometimes called) must be accomplished, like fencing, in a particular manner to be effective. The guidelines discussed below are applicable to vessels, offshore installations, or port facilities. The objectives are the same: to discourage intruders, aid in detecting intruders, and assist in repelling or destroying intruders.

Security lighting provides a means during periods of darkness of continuing the protection afforded in daylight, and that is all. Like the unguarded fence, security lighting serves little purpose if no one is around to observe what is lighted. It is generally inexpensive to maintain, and can under some circumstances reduce the need for larger numbers of security personnel. Properly employed, it should allow security personnel to observe activities around or inside an installation without disclosing their presence.

Specific security lighting requirements will depend upon the situation and areas to be protected. Each situation requires careful analysis to determine the best method of obtaining the necessary lighting. Proper security lighting is achieved by providing adequate, uniform light along perimeter barriers, glaring light beyond those barriers and into the eyes of intruders, and relatively little light along patrol routes or security outposts.

In planning to provide security lighting, high brightness contrast between intruder and background should be the first consideration. Even though protective lighting requires less intensity than working light, higher levels of brightness increase the ability of security personnel to spot surreptitious movement and indistinct silhouettes.

There are three lighting coverages that can be employed. First, the outer perimeter barrier and the external approaches to it can be lighted. Second, the outer perimeter barrier and the security zone it surrounds can be lighted. Third, the outer perimeter barrier, the external approaches to it, and the security zone it surrounds can all be lighted. There are advantages to each method. There are also very real tactical advantages to being able to employ any one of the three lighting methods on command in particular intruder situations. The lighting method or methods selected by the security planner should reflect the many variables he must consider when developing his security plan.

Besides selecting the lighting coverage, i.e., what will be lighted, the security planner must also select the lighting system he wants to employ, i.e., how it will be lighted. There are four basic security lighting systems: continuous lighting, standby lighting, movable lighting, and emergency lighting. The type of lighting system will depend upon the overall security requirements of the vessel, port facility, or offshore installation.

The most often used security lighting system is continuous lighting. This system is designed to flood a given area with light continuously during the hours of darkness. The individual cones of light emitted from the various light sources are overlapped so that no area remains unlighted and all areas are lighted to the same degree of intensity.

Standby lighting is very similar to the continuous lighting system just described. It is still designed to flood a given area with overlapping cones of light. The difference is that standby lighting does not remain on continuously. It is designed to be turned on only when suspicious activity is detected or suspected.

Movable lighting is just what the name indicates: movable. The system consists of searchlights, which may be either permanently affixed or portable, whose cones of light can be aimed at targets or areas of suspected activity. The cones of light are movable. This system is normally used in conjunction with either a continuous or standby lighting system and augments it when necessary.

Emergency lighting is any type of lighting system which is used only in times of power failure or other emergencies when the normal security lighting system is rendered inoperable. It can duplicate the normal lighting system or merely provide the minimum amount of lighting required to maintain proper security. In either case, it must depend totally on an independent, alternative power source which, preferably, is autonomous and secure unto itself.

The four security lighting systems just described can all be utilized with any of the three security lighting coverages mentioned earlier. There are also two lighting techniques, which is the way the light is actually projected, that can be applied in any lighting situation. These are glare projection lighting and controlled lighting.

Glare projection lighting is a technique of projecting the glare of lights across a particular area creating, in essence, a barrier of light through which a potential intruder finds it difficult to see and behind which security personnel can operate in comparative darkness. When lighting an outer perimeter barrier and the approaches to it, glare projection lighting is the technique that should be used. Floodlights— to provide a band of light whose horizontal angular dispersal is great, and to direct the glare at a possible intruder while restricting the downward beam—are the preferred lighting for this technique.

Controlled lighting, on the other hand, is that lighting technique whereby the beams of light are generally projected downward in such a manner as to light a particular strip or area. With controlled lighting the width of the lighted strip can be controlled and adjusted to fit the particular need, such as the illumination of the security zone between the outer and secondary perimeter barriers, the topsides of a vessel, or the helicopter landing platform of an offshore installation.

Consider the security lighting of an anchored vessel or offshore installation with regard to the security lighting coverages, systems, and techniques just discussed. Assuming the outer perimeter barrier has been defined as the exterior hull and bulwarks, a security planner might well design his lighting plan so that he employs a continuous lighting system which utilizes glare projection lighting of the hull and bulwarks and the surrounding waters. In this way security watch standers can remain on deck without being detected while at the same time observing all approaches to the vessel or installation. Any prospective intruders must transit the zone of light in order to reach the hull, thereby exposing themselves, while at the same time enduring the blinding light projected from their objective. The tactical disadvantage for such attackers is enormous, and if the vessel or installation is prepared to meet them with virtually any amount of firepower whatsoever, they will most probably be stopped. If they are not stopped and the defenders must withdraw within their secondary perimeter, standby controlled lighting can be activated which will illuminate every square foot of topside space and silhouette the attackers. This will make them easy targets for either security personnel coming to the defenders' assistance or the defenders themselves if secure firing positions exist from inside their secondary perimeter. It will also have a substantial discouraging effect on the attackers, who will most certainly comprehend the purpose and effect of such lighting. Of course, when the standby lighting is activated the outer perimeter barrier lighting should be extinguished. It no longer serves any useful purpose to the defenders, and might well work a considerable disadvantage to anyone coming to their aid. Interior lighting should also be considered by the security planner, for should the intruders gain access to the interior the ability to control such lighting may give enough of a tactical advantage to the defenders to allow them to win. There is nothing darker than the inside of an unlighted ship. Even the most experienced seamen can become disoriented in a large, unfamiliar vessel if trapped below without light. Anyone less than a truly hardened professional who is thrown into complete darkness while facing armed defenders will more than likely panic.

Security lighting is both an art and a science which has developed substantially over the past several years. The increased security awareness of both the business and general populace, along with technological advances in lights and equipment, has created the need for a security lighting expertise not generally recognized earlier. Professional societies, academic courses, and volumes of technical material have all been spawned to meet that need. A ship's security planner can certainly, using common sense and the little technical information imparted here, develop an adequate lighting plan for his vessel. The same can be said for an offshore installation security planner and, possibly, a port facility security planner. However, the really technical considerations such as the types and wattages of lights to be employed and the angles and distances to be incorporated should probably be left to an expert. The same independent security consultant who may have been hired to conduct a security survey and prepare a security plan should have the technical expertise to design an appropriate protective lighting plan. If a security consultant has not been retained, the security planner can either employ one specifically to prepare a lighting plan or seek additional security lighting information from manufacturers of lighting equipment and organizations such as (in the United States) the Army Corps of Engineers, the Illuminating Engineering Society of North America, or the American Society for Industrial Security.

The primary purpose for any security lighting system is to provide the means to detect and combat intruders. The use of light implies human observation, for there are a number of nonhuman detection systems (some animate and some inanimate) that require no light whatever. Dogs, geese,

FIG. 7.   *Upper*, glare projection lighting;
lower, controlled lighting

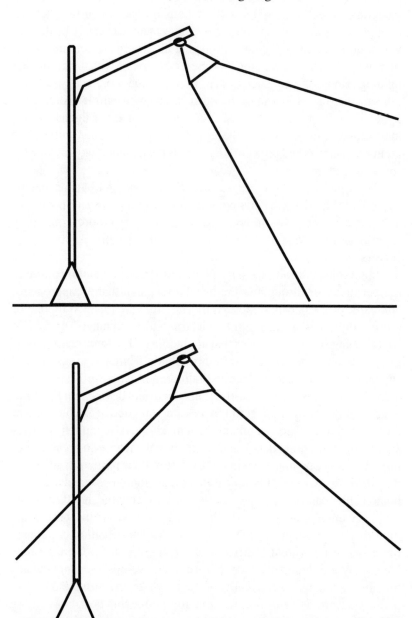

peacocks, and cats have been used as sentries and alarms throughout history. A vast multitude of electronic devices exists today that can either actively or passively detect unwanted visitors. Infrared and ambient light-gathering surveillance systems allow human observation of otherwise nonlighted areas. Consequently, a security system can easily be devised where no protective lighting is needed at all. There are certainly situations where such a system might be preferable to one which incorporates lighting. However, any such system may well be more costly and less fail-safe than one built simply around lights and men. Furthermore, a non-lighted security system relinquishes any deterrent factor a lighted system may provide. In any event, the next topic for discussion concerning perimeter barriers and protective lighting is the methodology involved in surveilling those areas.

There are basically three ways in which perimeter barriers can be surveilled. The first two involve static observation posts or positions, and the third involves moving posts or what are more commonly referred to as patrols. In all three cases security personnel serve as observers.

Static observation posts are placed at strategic locations around the perimeter or throughout the installation such that all approaches and exterior areas can be observed. They may be manned by one or more individuals or they can be electronically "manned" by CCTV cameras and listening devices that are monitored at some central location. There are advantages to both methods. Human beings are not subject to mechanical or electrical failure, nor can a well-trained and alert sentry be disabled as easily as an electronic device. On the other hand, human sentries can certainly become fatigued or frightened and thereby fail to function as reliably as a machine. Also, human sentries usually operate somewhat in an informational vacuum so far as knowing what is happening anywhere else but in their particular sector of responsibility. Good communication among guard posts and the command center can alleviate the problem to some degree, but there is always an unknown factor and time delay that even the best communication cannot prevent. Not knowing the full situation can sometimes cause individual sentries to act inappropriately. On the other hand, they are there at the scene if trouble develops and can take action immediately. In a security system where the surveillance capability is provided by CCTV and the command post consists of television monitors, the duty security personnel may understand the entire situation but immediate action will not be possible. Sentry detection by prospective intruders is another factor to consider. Human sentries are almost always easier to detect than electronic ones, but then an armed, alert human is considerably more formidable than a camera. The deterrent potential of a man versus a camera is therefore another variable in the overall security equation. So far as cost is concerned, neither system can categorically be said to be less expensive than the other; nor is one system necessarily more reliable than the other. The numerous variables present at the time the security plan is formulated, along with the personal preferences of the security planner, will all combine to determine which static observation methods are employed, if any. Of course, there is nothing to prevent the use of *both* human and electronic surveillance systems in combination.

Patrolling is the third and, if properly done, most effective method of surveilling the outer perimeter barrier and preventing intrusion. Patrols are limited only by the ingenuity with which they are employed and, because they are not static like guard posts or camera positions, much harder for intruders to anticipate or render ineffective.

The purpose for either perimeter or area patrols is to provide early detection and warning of any intrusion attempt, and to take immediate action against it. A patrol can consist of any number of security personnel. Depending upon the nature of the area patrolled the patrol can be either motorized or not. Patrols can be conducted by automobiles, trucks, aircraft, boats, or submersibles. They can be either armed or unarmed, and obvious or surreptitious. Patrols can be supported by any number of additional security measures, one of the most common of which is the use of dogs. The only rule that is truly inviolate if patrols are to be effective is that they must not be predictable. They cannot adhere to any externally discernible schedule or route.

Effective patrolling is a highly individualized skill which is usually developed through extensive training and meticulous supervision. It is a skill generally thought to be useful, in an industrial security context, only in large or complex areas like a port facility. However, patrols can also be used to great advantage aboard vessels and offshore installations. Security training that includes patrolling can be conducted on board efficiently and routinely and, where professional security personnel are not regularly employed aboard, should be. Many of the recommended security SOPs for vessels and offshore installations include the use of on-deck patrols.

One way patrol personnel can be augmented or replaced is through the use of dogs. In recent years the use of guard dogs, or sentry dogs as they are known if they are employed in conjunction with a handler, has increased dramatically. Long recognized as assets in the military, guard dogs have now become almost commonplace in nonmilitary applications as well. In fact, many civilian businesses utilize dogs without giving much thought to either their recommended use or the resultant liability exposure. Dogs can certainly enhance a perimeter barrier's effectiveness and either augment or supplant many patrol activities, but a clear understanding of their abilities and/or liabilities should be gained before the decision is made to employ them.

The primary distinction between guard dogs and sentry dogs is the use of a handler. Sentry dogs are accompanied by a handler and remain under his control at all times. Guard dogs, on the other hand, are generally allowed to "patrol" an enclosed area in the absence of any human control from the time they are released into the area until they are retrieved. Both represent the deadliest form of dog known to man. They are not watchdogs, protection dogs, or attack dogs, all of which represent various levels of obedience training in canine pets. Guard dogs are not pets. They are vicious, trained killers capable of maiming or destroying human beings with amazingly little effort. They will usually respond to only one handler whom they have accepted as their master and if he dies, or for some reason can no longer continue as his dog's handler, the dog generally must be destroyed. These dogs are so formidable that some security experts consider the only legitimate use for them to be in time of war against an unconditional enemy.

Of the two, guard dogs and sentry dogs, guard dogs are the least reliable and represent the greatest legal liability to the business using them. This is due to the absence of human control. Because they are generally released into their patrol area at the close of business and left to roam until the next day, there is no one available to pull the dog off an intruder should one be so unwise as to be caught. Furthermore, these dogs do not discriminate. They will attack anyone who enters their area. They are, therefore, similar to but worse than the proverbial "trapgun" with which the homeowner booby-traps his house. A trapgun will only fire once. A guard dog will continue to attack until the intruder is either dead or ceases to move. In the United States trapgun users have invariably been held liable for the death or injury of intruders shot by their booby traps, and guard dog users will be as well, unless legally appropriate warnings are posted. Of course, posting a guard dog warning rather defeats the purpose. Now the prospective intruder knows a dog is on duty and can surmise that probably no one else is around. All he needs to do is incapacitate the dog and he's home free. A guard dog's advantage is his surprise. Once his presence is known he can be defeated.

The sentry dog is a different matter entirely. His job is to detect intruders and alert his handler. When necessary he can pursue, attack, and hold any intruder attempting to escape but, again, this is a legally questionable practice. It is best to leave the detecting and alerting to the dog and the pursuing and apprehending to the humans. The proper use of the sentry dog is as one-half of a dog/handler security team. Because of his keen senses of hearing and smell, the sentry dog is exceptionally well suited for nighttime security work. Furthermore, the added perception of the dog/handler team reduces the need for as much security lighting and allows patrol routes to be lengthened.

There are three basic types of dog patrols. The first is the perimeter patrol. This type of patrol is along either a portion of a perimeter barrier or the entire perimeter barrier; usually the barrier is an outer perimeter barrier such as a fence line. The second type of sentry dog patrol is the area patrol. This patrol is around a group of buildings or within the security zone between the secondary and outer perimeters. The third type of patrol is the specific patrol or post where the team is posted in a particular building or at a particular location.

The sentry dog patrol is especially effective in areas of little activity, such as the isolated perimeters and remote storage areas found in most port facilities. The dog also tends to keep the sentry on duty more alert and gives him added self-confidence. The precise utilization of the sentry dog will depend upon the existing situation and the results desired. In the maritime context, however, sentry dogs are best employed within the port facility and can be extremely useful in curtailing after-hour pilferage.

The sentry dog is an extremely versatile animal. He does have some limitations, however. The odor of petroleum products decreases the effectiveness of his sense of smell, and noise definitely reduces his ability to hear. There are both advantages and disadvantages to incorporating the use of sentry dogs into one's security plan. Some of the advantages are:

1. Dogs provide a strong psychological deterrent.
2. Dogs are beneficial where security personnel have been reduced.
3. A dog's keen senses of smell and hearing enable him to detect the presence of danger and alert his handler.
4. A dog is more effective than a human during inclement weather, and inclement weather usually offers ideal conditions for illegal entry.

Some of the disadvantages are:

1. These dogs are naturally dangerous.
2. Kennels and training areas must be isolated.
3. Care and maintenance of the dogs must be considered in manpower requirements.
4. Public relations must be considered.

Finally, before moving on to other matters, one last use of canine security assistance should be mentioned. This is the use of "sniffer" dogs to detect the presence of drug contraband. With the advent of the U.S. government's "zero tolerance" maritime drug policy, vessel and cargo owners face much greater liability and loss exposure than ever before. Apparently, the United States is no longer interested in an owner's or master's good intentions, and the old seizure safeguard of conducting and logging shipboard drug searches and crew lectures is no longer viable. Consequently, the added time and expense of employing a team of dogs to go through a U.S.-bound vessel prior to her departure but after all crew members are aboard and cargo-handling operations have ceased may now be acceptable. The procedure may in fact be more than merely acceptable, it may be wise and prudent in view of the vessel seizures and massive fines now occurring in the United States.

Moving now from the animate to the inanimate, detection systems, alarms, surveillance equipment, and communications can be discussed together since they are all electronic or mechanical in nature. As discussed previously, the primary purpose for any outer perimeter barrier is to allow for the detection, delay, and destruction (or neutralization) of intruders. The lighting and observation of that barrier increases the likelihood of intruder detection. Alarming the barrier further increases the detection potential. Intrusion detection alarm systems can be installed which are designed to alert security personnel to an intrusion, and the use of these electronic and mechanical warning devices has proven beneficial in many instances.

There is a vast assortment of commercially manufactured alarm devices available that are designed to detect the approach or intrusion of unwanted visitors. New ones are being developed constantly. Of the many electronic security systems, some are suitable only for exterior and others only for interior use. All have inherent weaknesses that must be taken into account when planning for their incorporation into the overall security program. Of course, no alarm system has any value unless it is supported by a security force capable of responding in the event a warning is given.

There are a number of factors the security planner must consider when determining the feasibility or necessity of installing an alarm system. These include:

1. The nature or mission of the entity being secured.
2. The vulnerability of the entity.
3. The accessibility of the entity.
4. The geographical location of the entity.
5. Building or barrier construction.
6. Operational hours.
7. Availability of other forms of protection.
8. Cost (both installation and maintenance).
9. Potential savings in manpower and money.
10. Response time by security personnel.

Every type of intrusion detection system is designed to meet a particular type of security problem. There are, therefore, a number of factors to be considered by the security planner when determining which system to employ. Some of these are:

1. Response time capability of security personnel.
2. Likely intruder time requirements.
3. Operating environment (including climate, noise levels, building and barrier construction, etc.)
4. Radio and electrical interference.
5. Operational hours of entity being secured.
6. Number of equipment operating hours per day.

Frequently, more than one type of system will be required to adequately protect the particular entity. While manufacturers' representatives will usually be more than willing to assist the security planner in his selection of systems, they will understandably be prejudiced in favor of one system or another. The security planner should therefore obtain as much information as possible concerning the various systems under consideration, from as many sources as possible, before making his selection.

Intrusion detection alarm systems should be inherently stable, durable, reliable, and maintainable. They are designed to detect intrusion, not prevent it, and should be integrated into the entire security plan. The essential characteristics of any alarm system include:

1. A sensor unit or detector.
2. Signal transmission lines (if the alarm signal is not radio-transmitted).
3. A central annunciator panel or control board that receives the alarm signal and announces the intrusion both visibly and audibly.
4. System malfunction indicators.
5. Anticircumvention features.

Alarm systems operate on a number of different principles, some of which are:

1. The breaking of an electrical circuit.
2. The interruption of a light beam.
3. The detection of sound.
4. The detection of vibration.
5. The detection of motion.
6. The detection of a capacitance change (resulting from penetration of an electronic field).

No one system is suitable for every location or environment. Often, two or more systems must be utilized to achieve the desired security. Also, in-depth alarm security can be obtained by combining the various systems.

It is important to remember that the primary means of perimeter protection is personal surveillance. It is because such surveillance is frequently limited by the periodicity of patrols that intrusion detection alarm systems are valuable. However, if the vulnerability of the security area does not require constant surveillance, the use of electronic intrusion detection systems may not be warranted. The decision to employ such devices is made by the security planner after careful consideration of the many security factors already discussed.

CCTV is not an alarm system but it can be said to be an electronic intrusion detection system, so long as someone watches the monitors. It is frequently used in conjunction with any or all of the physical security measures discussed so far. A CCTV system consists of one or more television cameras placed in strategic locations (which may or may not be hidden from view), electronic circuitry, and television screen monitors. The monitors are usually emplaced in one central location, generally the security command center. From here security personnel can monitor all areas covered by the cameras simultaneously. The cameras themselves can be installed so that they can be remotely controlled from the command center, thereby giving more flexibility to the system by allowing viewers to zoom in on a particular subject or pan through so many degrees of viewing arc. The greatest problem with TV systems, aside from electrical or electronic malfunctions, is the degree of light needed for the cameras to be effective. Since the use of a CCTV system will either augment or replace on-scene observers, a security lighting plan should already have been developed prior to considering CCTV. It should therefore be a simple matter to determine the light intensities at the prospective camera locations and ensure that the cameras ultimately obtained are designed to function in that amount of light. Like human eyes, television cameras do not function well in inclement weather. However, besides the obvious reduced visibility problem the weather can also create camera malfunctions in instruments not properly weatherproofed. The marine environment is particularly hostile to exposed electronic equipment, although a number of expensive yachts have been fitted with CCTV systems quite successfully. If appropriate precautions are taken there is no reason why CCTV systems cannot be advantageously installed aboard commercial vessels and offshore installations as well as in port facilities or anywhere else. However, the cost of even a moderately complex CCTV system can be quite high, for both initial installation and maintenance. All these factors must be taken into account by the security planner who contemplates using CCTV.

Protective communications systems are also electronic or electrical in nature. Just as there is a vast difference between security lighting and day-to-day lighting, there is the same difference between protective communications and regular workplace communications. Ma Bell's telephones are just not secure, either from unwanted listeners or from sabotage. A protective communication system must provide the ability to communicate both internally and externally under all conditions. Protective communication systems vary in size and type in accordance with importance, vulnerability, location, radio receptivity, terrain, geographical distance, and other variables present at the particular installation. Security forces should certainly have their own communication system with direct lines, auxiliary power supply, and radio external communication ability. Two or more of the following means of communication should be included in any protective communication system:

1. Internal and external telephone service.
2. Internal communications such as intercoms that are not connected to commercial telephones.
3. Radiotelephone capability such as citizens band (CB), marine VHF, or single-sideband (SSB).
4. Satellite communications (satcom).
5. Telegraph and teletype capability.
6. Security command center automatic alarm system.
7. Hand-carried radios.
8. Key-operated electric call box security supervisory system.

Whenever possible, the wiring of protective communication and alarm systems should be in conduits separate from the installation's regular lighting and communication systems. They should also be buried wherever practicable and the knowledge of their location and existence restricted. Tamper-resistant wire and cable, with a sheath of foil that transmits a signal when cut or penetrated, is commercially available and will add to the system's overall security.

The final general security measure that needs to be mentioned before discussing specific security procedures for vessels, port facilities, and offshore installation is access control. In one sense, the term "access control" sums up the entire field of maritime security. No pirate, saboteur, extortionist, pilferer, or stowaway can work his mischief unless he gains access to his objective. Perimeter barriers, security lighting, guard patrols, dogs, alarms, surveillance cameras, and communications equipment all aid in controlling access.

One of the oldest and simplest forms of access control is the lock, which can control access to thousands of square yards of outdoor storage space, hundreds of square feet of building space, or a few square inches of drawer space. A lock can be simple or complex, small or large, manual or electronic. Regardless of its complexity, size, quality, or cost, however, a lock should be considered as a delay device only. There has not been a lock invented that an expert cannot defeat, given enough time and the proper tools. The degree of protection afforded by any properly constructed door, vault, safe, or filing cabinet can be measured in terms of the resistance of the locking mechanism to picking, manipulating, or drilling. Some of the most common locking devices are:

1. Key locks.
2. Conventional combination locks.
3. Manipulation-resistant combination locks.
4. Multiple tumbler (four or more) combination locks.
5. Relocking devices.
6. Interchangeable core system locks.
7. Cipher locks.

Most key locks can be picked by an expert in a matter of seconds or minutes. Keys can also be lost or compromised. Consequently, while key locks are probably the most common form of lock they are also the least secure. Conventional combination locks usually consist of a three-position dial type combination lock. This type of lock can be opened by a skillful manipulator generally in a few minutes and is therefore little more secure than a key lock. Manipulation-resistant combination locks are designed and constructed such that the opening lever does not come into contact with the tumblers until the combination has been set. This mechanism is intended to defeat the skillful manipulator who may be able to determine the settings of the tumblers of conventional combination locks through his senses of hearing and touch. This type of lock is considerably more reliable than the conventional combination lock. Multiple tumbler combination locks merely contain more tumblers than do conventional combination locks. Their degree of security falls somewhere between conventional and manipulation-resistant combination locks. Relocking devices increase the difficulty of opening a combination lock by punching, drilling, or blocking parts of the lock. They are usually found on heavy safes and vaults, and add an appreciable degree of security against forcible entry. Interchangeable core systems utilize a type of key lock with a core that can be replaced by another core requiring a different key. If key locks are to be utilized under circumstances where key compromise is likely, an interchangeable core system provides flexibility in responding to such compromise, and is more economical than replacing locks every time a key disappears. Cipher locks are merely electronic digital combination locks which are usually employed as door-locking devices. Since there are no tumblers to feel or hear, these locks are more secure than conventional combination locks. Of course, being electronic they rely upon circuitry and power sources, all of which can be defeated with the proper high-tech equipment. Finally, there are numerous locking systems presently available that employ neither keys nor combinations, but open by the use of a punched card, or a fingerprint, or voice analysis.

Locks are only the first step in controlling access. Access control necessarily requires an effective lock and key (or combination) control system so that the security of the locks employed can be safeguarded as much as possible. Any such system should include the following:

1. Keys and combinations should be accessible to only those persons whose duties require them.
2. Combinations should be changed at least once in every 12-month period.
3. Combinations should be changed immediately following the possible compromise of the combination, the permanent departure of any person who had access to any combinations, or receipt of any new container with a built-in combination lock.
4. Key padlocks should be rotated every six months.
5. When selecting combination numbers, multiples and simple arithmetic series should be avoided, as should the birth date or other dates easily associated with the keeper of the safe or lock.

6. Records containing combinations and the names of those persons given the combinations should be carefully maintained and secured.
7. The use of keys should be based upon the same general security concepts as combinations.
8. Keys should be stored in a locked, fireproof container when not in use.
9. Keys should not be issued for personal retention or removal from the facility.
10. Access lists for persons authorized to draw keys should be maintained in the key storage container.
11. Control over the key storage container should be maintained by the security officer.
12. Key control records should be maintained by the security officer and should include: the total number of keys in the system, the number of keys issued, the number of keys on hand, and the persons to whom keys have been issued.
13. Key inventories should be conducted at least once in every 12-month period.

Since each vessel, port facility, or offshore installation has its own specific set of circumstances and conditions concerning security requirements, key and lock control systems will vary. Before the security officer (or perhaps the security planner) establishes the system that will be utilized at his facility, he should conduct a lock survey to determine the actual lock requirements and whether those requirements are being met. Thereafter a lock security plan can be prepared and annexed or attached to the ship, port facility, or offshore installation security plan.

Keys and locks are only one form of access control with which the security planner must concern himself. They, along with the other physical security safeguards discussed so far, are designed to prevent unauthorized access by persons who, in most cases, clearly should not have access. However, a large number of persons exist in most instances who should have access in varying degrees, such as employees, visitors, contract workers, vendors, and so on. A positive personnel identification and control system must therefore be established to prevent or control access by persons who appear to belong where they are found.

Access lists, security identification cards and badges, personal recognition, visitor badge assignment procedures, and personnel escorts are all elements of an access control system that contribute to the effectiveness of the system. The best control is achieved when the personnel identification and control system incorporates all of these elements. Simple, understandable, and workable personnel security procedures should be utilized to achieve access control objectives without hampering efficient operations. The well-worn acronym KISS (Keep It Simple, Stupid) applies equally as well here as in many other security situations. Properly organized and administered, a personnel control system not only provides a means of positively identifying those who have a right to gain access, it also allows for detecting unauthorized persons who attempt to enter. The primary access control objectives within a maritime security context are to prevent the introduction of harmful devices aboard ships and offshore installations, or sensitive areas within port facilities; and to prevent the pilferage of cargo and equipment. These access control objectives can best be achieved by incorporating the following procedures:

1. Initially determining who has a valid requirement to be in the area.
2. Limiting access to those persons who have that valid requirement.
3. Establishing procedures for positive identification of those persons allowed access.
4. Issuing special identification cards or badges for those persons allowed access.
5. Instituting proper control procedures for the issuing and use of such cards and badges.
6. Using access lists.
7. Using identification codes.
8. Using duress codes (a word or phrase which, if fitted into normal conversation, alerts security personnel to the fact that the speaker is being forced by an unauthorized person to help him obtain admittance by vouching for him).

Personnel control should begin long before an employee is ever hired. Pre-employment practices are essential in today's maritime environment if vessels, offshore installations, and port facilities are to remain secure. Few maritime operators, however, routinely engage in such practices. There are three basic reasons for such shortcoming. First, there is a general lack of security awareness within the industry. Second, the transient nature of prospective maritime employees and the dearth of truly qualified agencies capable of conducting the necessary background investigations make any realistic pre-employment screening difficult. Third, the cost of conducting background investigations on all prospective crew members, offshore rig workers, or port facility employees is perceived as prohibitive. The key to resolving this impasse lies with explicating owners' and operators' liability for negligent hiring. Once the industry comes to understand its legal exposure in this regard, cost-effective means will present themselves that will help limit that exposure. No pre-employment screening program has to be 100 percent successful. That is impossible. What it must be, however, is reasonable under the circumstances. That means that a limited pre-employment screening system may well be considered legally sufficient today, whereas it may not be five years from now, just as using the hiring practices that were common twenty years ago will not be considered legally justifiable today. The trick, therefore, is to come up with something that can arguably be said to constitute a reasonable effort on the part of the maritime employer to screen prospective job applicants. Such reasonableness will vary under the circumstances, but clearly every employer should utilize pre-employment and security questionnaires at a minimum. Routine polygraph pre-employment examinations are common today, and might be utilized as well, although recent federal legislation may severely limit this practice in the future. It is also, in the United States at least, a relatively simple matter to telephone the local police in order to ascertain whether the job applicant has any record of criminal activity. Availability of such information is controlled by state statute, however, and may be more available in some states than in others. Calls to former employers can also easily be made in order to determine the truth of past employment information as well as any problems the individual may have had. Many maritime nations have established marine index organizations whereby the entire past employment and medical history of prospective maritime employees can be determined for a relatively low subscription fee. These procedures are available to the prudent maritime employer right now. As maritime security awareness increases throughout the industry other means will become more available, such as crewing agencies which offer routine background investigations and psychological profiles for all crew members supplied to their clients.

In any event, once an applicant becomes an employee he should be able to be identified as such. An identification system should be established that identifies not only all employees but visitors as well. Then, assuming the system itself has not been compromised, any person not readily identified as an employee or visitor should be considered an intruder until determined otherwise. One of the simplest identification methods involves the use of cards or badges. Employees should be issued photograph identification cards (although photograph badges can also be issued in place of, or in addition to, the identification cards) and visitors should be issued numbered badges. In high-risk security areas all persons—employees and visitors alike—should wear badges. Any person not prominently displaying a badge is then readily identifiable as a possible security risk. The provisions for identification by card or badge should either be included in the security plan or attached to it, and should include:

1. Designation of the various areas where identification cards and badges are required.
2. Description of the specific identification document or documents to be employed and the limitations placed upon the bearer.
3. The use of such documents and the mechanics of personnel identification upon entering or departing the security area.
4. Procedures to be followed for the control of identification documents, including pre-issue storage, postemployment destruction, and lost or stolen replacement.
5. Procedures to be followed for system-wide re-issue of all identification documents when 5 percent have become lost or unaccounted for.

Identification cards and badges should be of a design and construction which makes them tamperproof as much as possible. Even so, they can be altered, forged, or reproduced by persons having the knowledge, skill, time, and equipment to do so. Consequently, the issuance and accountability of identification documents must be carefully controlled and recorded.

The purpose of a badge or card identification system is to provide a means of positive identification of all persons allowed access to a vessel, installation, or facility. This system assists in the control of all persons arriving or departing, but should not be relied upon exclusively. Just because a person has a badge or card doesn't mean he necessarily belongs there. Personal recognition is the surest method of establishing positive identification. For instance, the gangway security watch posted while a vessel is in port should be familiar with all crew members aboard his ship. Any person attempting to board, even with an employee identification card, whom the gangway watch does not recognize, should be detained until his presence can be verified. Visitor passes or badges should be similarly employed to verify the visitor's right to be there. His name, badge number, and date or dates of his visit should be prelisted. Access lists can also be utilized for employees carrying the proper identification. For instance, the same gangway security watch can be provided a list of all crew members authorized access to the vessel with instructions to admit no one else regardless of identification or personal recognition. This might be necessary where a disgruntled crew member has recently been terminated unbeknownst to everyone onboard. Finally, visitor escorts are an extremely important form of personnel control. Whenever possible *all* visitors should be escorted to their authorized destination. On board ships and offshore installations, safety and security are very viable reasons for an escort, but the possibility always exists that the visitor has gained access by one ruse or another; therefore, an escort is simply a prudent security measure everywhere.

Effective security precautions against sabotage, extortion, hijacking, and pilferage require screening, identification, and control of visitors. Visitors can generally be categorized as follows:

1. Persons with whom every vessel, offshore installation, or port facility must interact in the course of doing business, such as vendors and suppliers, customers, inspectors, contractors, prospective employees, and so on.
2. Individuals or groups who desire to visit for a purpose not essential to, or in furtherance of, the operations of the

vessel, installation, or facility. These may be related to business or educational organizations.

3. Guided tour or other visits in the interest of public relations.

Arrangements for the control of visitors should include positive methods for establishing the reason, validity, and authority for their visit. Limitations concerning access should be identified and, where necessary, addressed. Positive visitor identification is imperative. Visitor registration forms and records should be carefully maintained and should record the identity of the visitor, the date and time of his visit, the object of his visit, and other pertinent information. Visitor identification cards should be issued and, where possible, access lists and escorts should be utilized. Controls for the recovery of visitor identification badges should be emplaced.

Access control does not just involve persons. Package, vehicle, and property control systems must also be instituted if sabotage, hijacking, and pilferage are to be prevented. A positive system should be established to control the movement of packages, vehicles, and property not only aboard (or near) vessels and offshore installations and into port facilities, but also off and out of such entities. Limitations on the types of property and packages that may be brought aboard, or taken off, should be established along with the appropriate methods of ensuring compliance (gate checks, baggage inspections, etc.). Port facilities should institute a motor vehicle registration system whereby all vehicles that make daily or frequent visits to the facility are registered with the port facility security officer. Registered vehicles should be issued a decal or sticker which can be readily observed by security personnel. Wherever possible designated parking areas should be established within the facility as well as restricted areas where no parking will be permitted. The restricted areas should be in the immediate vicinity of vessels or their berths, cargo storage areas, perimeter barriers, or other sensitive locations. A visitor's vehicle should be issued a temporary visitor's parking permit and the process tied into the visitor verification and authorization procedure.

SHIPBOARD SECURITY MEASURES AND PROCEDURES

The security measures and procedures that are ultimately adopted and employed aboard a given ship must necessarily reflect the nature of the security threats faced by that ship during her day-to-day operations. However, an understanding of the security threats facing all vessels engaged in maritime commerce today must be had before a threat analysis can be made with regard to a specific vessel and a decision made as to what security procedures will be adopted. It is for this reason that the initial ship security survey and subsequent report must address the subject of threat analysis. That threat analysis forms the foundation for the development of the ship's security plan.

The concept of category I and category II security threats has already been discussed. For ships, category I threats include sabotage, piracy, and hijacking. Category II threats include pilferage, drug smuggling, and stowaways. Category II threats can best be combatted by diligent observation and frequent inspection by security and management personnel, proper crew indoctrination, and pre-employment screening practices. Category I threats, however, must be met with more active measures along with a mind-set that recognizes the life-and-death ramifications of the dangers being faced.

In chapter 3 the duties and responsibilities of the ship's security planner were discussed, as were the nature and content of the ship's security plan. There are only a limited number of shipboard evolutions that have security significance and with which the ship's security planner should concern himself, but these evolutions must be carefully prepared for by the development of the ship security SOPs. There are twelve evolutions, all of which occur while the vessel is on one of three modes. She is either moored alongside a pier or wharf, at anchor, or underway. These twelve evolutions are:

1. Moored dockside.
2. Moored dockside, engaged in cargo operations.
3. At anchor.
4. At anchor, engaged in cargo operations.
5. Underway.
6. Rendering assistance at sea.
7. Docking or undocking.
8. Receiving or discharging pilots.
9. Receiving ship's stores.
10. Bunkering.
11. Receiving official visitors.
12. Changing crew.

A ship is in most danger during periods of nonmovement, i.e., while she is either moored, lying at anchor, or lying to. Obviously, boarding by unwanted visitors is considerably easier during such periods than when the ship is moving. Of the three, perhaps the most serious threat exists while she is lying at anchor. At such times the vessel's security is completely dependent upon her master and crew (and while she is lying to as well; however, this condition is generally much more temporary and usually farther from shore). There is no available port facility with its lights, security personnel, telephones, and local police and fire departments to assist in her security. Of further significance is the natural tendency to assume that the ship is safer away from shore than at the dock, unless her master has had the dubious pleasure of being boarded by 30 or more Lagos pirates while lying at anchor. On the other hand, the ship is relatively secure underway, assuming no unauthorized persons surreptitiously boarded her at her last port. In order to board a vessel underway the boarders must either employ high-speed craft and grappling hooks, as do the pirates around Singapore, or cause her to slow down or heave to through one ruse or another. The most common is the "vessel in distress" tactic. On February 5, 1978, in the strait of Makassar, the *LNG Aries* received an SOS signal from the Panamanian motor vessel *King Dragon I*. Only two hours after she received the signal, the *LNG Aries* sighted the *King Dragon I* as she sank and rescued all 21 of her crew. The rescue was widely acclaimed and even used to advertise a particular shipboard satellite communications system, but the rescue also provided a wonderful scenario for decoying and boarding a potential target. Of course, underway vessels do not necessarily have to be boarded to be attacked. Persian Gulf shipping has been attacked by Iranian patrol craft, surface-to-surface missiles, and air-to-surface missiles (not to mention mines) for years, and there is no guarantee that this will stop merely because Iran and Iraq have implemented a tenuous cease-fire.

A ship's response to any security threat must be twofold. She must be able to sound an adequate warning and she must be able to respond in a timely manner. The security SOPs must be prepared with these two objectives in mind. They are paramount to the vessel's security. The security measures needed to ensure adequate warning and timely response are the same whether the ship employs additional manpower, electronics, or weapons. Only the methodology differs. Proper perimeter barriers, security zones, protective lighting, barrier surveillance, and access controls must be established, and a security response capability maintained, regardless of the methods employed to do so. For instance, if a ship is not provided additional manpower to maintain security watches and a reactive force, those duties must be performed by the existing crew if she is to remain secure. On the other hand, if specific security personnel are placed on board they will obviously perform those tasks. The security duties, however, remain the same.

Adequate warning is provided by a properly surveilled outer perimeter barrier. Timely response is provided by a well-trained designated reaction force. How and where perimeter barriers are established, how they are lighted and surveilled, what communications are utilized, and what type of reaction force or security response the ship musters must all be detailed in the ship's security plan. The ship's security plan includes her security SOPs, which specify the security tasks to be performed during specific shipboard evolutions, and her security bill, which assigns particular security duties to shipboard personnel. When viewed in its totality, the ship's security plan should allow for all foreseeable contingencies where the ship's security may be threatened.

The ship's first line of defense is her outer perimeter barrier combined with a properly manned security watch. In most cases the outer perimeter will consist of the hull and bulwarks of the ship. However, under some circumstances, electronic outer perimeters may be established. Assuming the exterior configuration of the vessel is defined as the outer security perimeter, the first consideration for the ship's security planner will be the proper surveillance of that perimeter, and protective lighting is the best place to begin.

The security lighting principles discussed earlier in this chapter apply equally well to ships as anywhere else. The security planner must decide what method of lighting he intends to utilize and the types and wattages of lights he wishes to employ. These decisions will be influenced by the configuration of the vessel, her power-generating capabilities, her security operating budget (if she has one), the installation cost of the lighting system chosen, maintenance requirements, reliability, and so on. Also, if temporary lighting is considered either as augmentation or emergency backup, ease of handling and stowage may be important. For instance, high-powered strobe lights can be effectively employed against nighttime underway boarders such as Malaysian pirates, but are relatively ineffective in other situations.

Consequently, the ship's security planner may wish to maintain a strobe light capability for the periods of time his vessel is exposed to such pirate threat but does not desire to affix the lights permanently to his ship. Whether they can be stowed, broken out, and installed in an acceptable manner may determine whether they are utilized at all. It is important to realize that the security planner's lighting decisions should not be made without input from the shiphandlers themselves. Even if he knows the power-generating capabilities of the ship under all conditions, he should certainly confer with the ship's chief engineer before a final decision is made. It is also important to realize that no two ships' security lighting plans are likely to be the same. A vessel's own special configuration, security management policies, operations, and security planner all combine to arrive at a lighting plan unique to her. However, there are two rules of shipboard security lighting which remain in effect no matter what.

The first concerns outer perimeter lighting at anchor or alongside. The outer perimeter barrier, that is, the sides and rails of the ship, and the approaches to it must all be sufficiently lighted. At anchor this means a 360-degree zone of glare-projected light completely surrounding the vessel and extending beyond her hull for a distance of at least 200 feet. Alongside, the same requirement must be met but with the added necessity that the dock, wharf, or pier at which the vessel is berthed must also be lighted for a minimum distance of 200 feet. Usually this lighting can be provided by the port facility with proper liaison by the ship's security officer, but if it can't the ship must provide it for herself.

The second shipboard security lighting rule involves on-deck controlled lighting, or that area of protective light between the outer and secondary perimeters. When the tactical situation requires the lighting of all decks and topsides there can be no shadow anywhere on deck or above. All lighting should be able to be operated from both the bridge and the engine room, independently, and the controlled on-deck lighting should be on a separate circuit from the glare-projected outer perimeter lighting.

Once the vessel's security lighting plan is established, at least so far as the outer perimeter is concerned, the next problem for the security planner involves the surveillance methodology of that perimeter. The most effective is a properly manned topside security watch. The number of watch standers, their duties, and their posts are all dictated by the particular evolution in which the ship is engaged. For instance, when the ship is underway no additional security watches usually need to be posted. Exceptions would be if the vessel responds to an emergency call, picks up or drops off a pilot, or traverses known pirate waters such as the Phillip Channel. On the other hand, when she is anchored or moored alongside, specific security measures must be taken.

In any event, watch standers, when they are posted, must be thoroughly trained in the performance of their duties. An ineffective security watch is as bad as no watch at all. The safety and security of his ship rests on the security watch stander's shoulders, and he had better realize that. Diligence in the performance of his duties is essential. He must remain alert to all possibilities of intrusion even when the possibility seems remote, and even when he is cold, sleepy, or exhausted.

Whether a particular security watch is posted at a fixed location on board or is designed as a roving patrol depends upon the nature of the watch and ship activity at the time. As a general rule, underway security watches should be stationary watches while at-anchor or berthed security watches should be roving. In either case, the same principles apply to shipboard watch standers as to shoreside guards so far as procedures are concerned.

One of the most important security procedural considerations is that of communication, both between the on-deck security watch standers themselves and between the watch standers and whomever has the conn or deck. Hand-held radios (walkie-talkies) are best suited for such communication. Furthermore, if the ship is berthed, communication should have been established between her and port facility security personnel when the ship's security officer made his liaison upon arrival. Communication between ship and shore facility can either be by radio or telephone. If by telephone, the telephone line should be brought aboard and the telephone placed in a secure location. Emergency radio communication should also be established in case the line is intentionally or accidentally severed. All shipboard personnel should be well versed in the use of communication equipment and procedures, and security drills, when conducted, should emphasize communication.

A vessel's ability to post a properly trained security watch is of no value unless she also has the capability to react to any warning sounded by that security watch. In most cases this means a trained reaction force that is prepared to deal with any security threat that may arise. The reaction force should be designated by the master, and can consist of any number of men so long as they are capable of performing the duties required. If additional security personnel are not carried aboard, the security bill should assign all crew members security duties. These duties are to be assumed during any security alert or periods of increased exposure to one or more security threats. This procedure is similar to that employed aboard naval combatants under battle conditions when all hands are called to general quarters. When a warship is at general quarters everyone has a pre-assigned job to perform. It should be the same aboard noncombatants during periods of heightened security. The security bill needs to make a distinction, however, between at-sea and in-port duties. At sea there may well need to be only one designated reaction force per watch, of perhaps only two men, which responds to any security situation. This duty can even be assigned as an additional responsibility with the specification that either the offgoing or oncoming watch respond to the security warning. In either situation, little disruption of normal shipboard routine is likely to occur and additional watches are kept at a minimum. At anchor or in port, however, the security requirements change drastically. Full in-port security watch sections are required to ensure that proper security watches are maintained around the clock and that a reaction force is prepared to respond at any time.

The security procedures employed aboard any given vessel must necessarily be tailored to that vessel. However, there are certain generalized recommendations that can be made regarding shipboard security measures, regardless of the particular vessel or her activity. These can best be made by discussing some of the shipboard evolutions mentioned previously.

A vessel spends, hopefully, more time underway than anything else. She is safer underway than anywhere. Yet even underway she is vulnerable to piracy, hijacking, and sabotage. In the Persian Gulf she is also vulnerable to the traditional naval warfare type of hazards: mines, surface-to-surface and air-to-surface missile attack, high-speed patrol boat hit-and-run tactics, subsurface warfare, and full-scale surface engagements. The particular maritime security aspects of the Persian Gulf situation as far as commercial shipping is concerned will be discussed later. For the moment, however, this discussion shall focus on the category I threats. So far as these threats are concerned, the danger to a vessel lies in her ability to be boarded. Her security rests with her ability to prevent such boarding, and that ability is dependent upon her preparedness. There are three ways in which a vessel may be boarded underway: she can be approached by high-speed watercraft or helicopters and forcibly boarded; she can be duped into picking up "survivors" of distressed or sunken vessels; and she can mistakenly accept boarders disguised as pilots or government officials. Consequently, in order to prevent such boardings, her officers and crew must be alert to the possibilities and have a security plan that covers such contingencies.

There is only one way for a noncombatant vessel to repel armed intruders attempting to board from high-speed watercraft or helicopters, and that is through the effective use of firearms. If firearms are not carried on board, or if the crew is not prepared to use them, the ship might as well heave to and surrender. On the other hand, if she is prepared to fight she stands a good chance of thwarting the boarding attempt. The ship provides a much more stable firing platform, and better cover, than is afforded the would-be boarders. Well-placed automatic rifle fire will cause the attack to be broken off, to be most likely resumed later against a more luckless, unarmed, and less prepared vessel. The key to an otherwise prepared ship's successful repulsion of boarders is her ability to sound an adequate warning. High-speed watercraft and helicopters must operate close to shore, and in order to achieve surprise they must approach from astern or at least abaft the beam. Consequently, a stern security watch posted whenever the vessel is within reasonably close vicinity of land should provide the necessary warning if an attack is attempted. The vessel's radar can also occasionally detect approaching watercraft, but under no circumstances should it be relied upon exclusively. Furthermore, since commercial maritime radars are not combat radars, they will not detect helicopters or other aircraft at all.

As sad a requiem as it may be on the demise of a seafaring tradition of thousands of years, a vessel rendering assistance at sea today exposes herself to a serious security risk. She has no way of ascertaining whether the "survivors" have staged the emergency solely for her benefit. If they have, and if it is properly planned and executed, the operation could place the rescuer in need of rescue. However, a few simple precautions taken at the proper moment can prevent such a ruse from being successful, and a properly prepared ship need never refuse to render assistance at sea for fear of her own safety. Survivors should be taken aboard at only one place on deck, and only one at a time. The ship's at-sea reaction force (of no less than two men) should lay to the place where the survivors will be taken aboard before they are picked up, and carefully search each survivor as he comes aboard. If firearms are carried on board the entire operation should be covered from an appropriate vantage point by at least one rifleman. Once the survivors are on board and determined to be unarmed the security threat has probably subsided, with two exceptions. First, it should be borne in mind that the "survivors" could be acting as decoys to allow the ship to be boarded from a different quarter while the rescue operation is underway. This is only likely, however, if the rescue operation takes place in close proximity to land. If it does, continued all-around security vigilance is imperative during the entire time the ship is lying to. Second, the possibility exists that weapons or explosives could have been cached on board at a previous port for use by the "survivors" or that the ship's own weapons might be intended to be commandeered. In either case, restricting the survivors to certain areas of the ship and following proper weapons security procedures should thwart such actions.

The hijacking of a vessel by someone pretending to be a pilot is a very real possibility. The *Nellie M.* previously mentioned was boarded by hijackers who commandeered a pilot boat. It only takes one man on the bridge with a grenade or pistol to control a ship, at least a ship which is as unprepared for such eventualities as are virtually all commercial vessels today. Commercial vessels routinely take on pilots in most of their ports of call. In most ports in the United States they are required to do so. It is a simple matter to determine sailing schedules and pilot requests. On an inbound ship the pilot usually boards via a pilot boat with the assistance of a pilot ladder. The same precautions that have been discussed concerning rendering assistance at sea should be taken in this instance as well. The ship's reaction force should stand by as the pilot boards. He should be searched and his credentials and identity verified. The pilot will probably not be too pleased with this procedure, but the ship will remain secure. As far as an outbound piloted vessel is concerned, the pilot boarding at the dock should be treated with the same security procedures as all other ship's visitors. When the pilot departs the outbound vessel the security team should stand by until the pilot boat is well away. This precaution is taken against the possibility that the pilot boat might have been commandeered prior to its arrival at the ship with the intention of boarding the ship at the time of the pilot's intended departure.

At anchor, a ship is more vulnerable than she may appear to those on board. Being surrounded by water gives one a false sense of security, as many medieval castle owners discovered. Moats have never been too effective, and in today's world a complacent ship at anchor is easy prey. It is therefore imperative that a ship be protectively lighted and maintain an adequate security watch while lying at anchor. As discussed previously, anchor security lighting should consist of a 200-foot-wide band of 360-degree, glare-projected light around the vessel. This will light the approaches to the vessel and at the same time allow the topside security watch to move about in relative obscurity. The topside security watch should consist of, at a minimum, two roving patrols of one man each. Their areas of responsibility may be divided into port and starboard, or fore and aft. They should carry flashlights, walkie-talkies, and whistles. Where the security risk is sufficient, they should also be armed. The roving patrols should stay in constant communication with each other and the mate on watch as well. During the course of their watch they should be constantly moving, randomly, without establishing a pattern or schedule. They should be alert to all activity on deck, along the ship's sides, and in the surrounding waters. The anchor chain must be checked often, since it is the one convenient conduit to the deck. The watch must remain alert for any approaching boats, swimmers, divers, or submersibles and report everything they see, hear, or suspect to the mate on watch. The mate should position himself where he can best observe the activities of his roving patrols as well as the major portions of his ship. This will usually be on the bridge. An at-anchor reaction force must be designated and standing by someplace within the vessel with quick topside access. Whatever weapons they are to be armed with should already be in their possession. They should be capable of immediate communication with the mate, whether by radio or ship's internal communications, and they should also be able to monitor the communications between the mate and his roving patrols. On command they should be prepared to instantly lay to any area of the ship in order to repel boarders.

If a ship is not underway or anchored there is only one other place she can be: at a dock. Now, there are many types of docks around the world but they all have the same purpose. They exist for ships to either load or discharge cargo. A docked ship is extremely vulnerable, and her security will depend upon more variables than her master or owners may wish to consider. Consider them they must, however, if the vessel's security is to remain viable.

At the dock, the minimum security watch should consist of a gangway watch during the day and a gangway watch and a topside roving patrol during the hours of darkness. The gangway watch should position himself so that he can view as much of the dock as possible while still securing the gangway. His primary job is to allow only authorized persons to board the vessel. At night he also has the responsibility of observing the vessel's dockside outer perimeter. The roving patrol should concentrate on all areas of the outer perimeter not visible to the gangway watch. He should keep moving and check in with the gangway watch frequently by radio. Both watch standers should be equipped with flashlights, walkie-talkies, and whistles. The number of additional watch standers that may be required to secure the ship will depend upon the overall security of the port, the nature of the cargo involved, and the current risk analysis for the area. All security watch standers should be in radio contact with the mate on watch who should be able to call out the reaction force immediately upon the sound of a warning. In-port security watches should be posted and relieved at times other than the usual shipboard routine. For instance, instead of posting security watches from 0800–1200 hours, from 1200–1600 hours, and so on, they might be posted from 0600–1000 hours, from 1000–1400 hours, and so forth. Furthermore, if the ship is to remain in port any longer than a few days the security watch schedule should be varied again. This prevents prospective saboteurs, hijackers, or thieves from ascertaining the security watch routine.

Virtually all of a ship's business is conducted while she is docked. She receives stores and supplies, bunkers, and most of her visitors. Changes in crew usually occur while she is docked, and of course she loads and discharges cargo generally while she is docked. The ship's security policy regarding all of these activities must be clearly established before the security planner can prepare his ship's security plan. What visitors, if any, will be searched as they come aboard? What types of identification will be required? How will the number and type of visitors be monitored? The answers to these questions, and others, will determine how secure the ship can be made.

Many of the access controls discussed previously can be usefully employed aboard ship. Certainly, visitor identification, verification, and escorting should be routine procedures. Hand-held magnetometers allow fast and relatively painless searches of visitors, packages, and baggage, and should also be utilized regularly. Heightened security awareness among the crew is invaluable, and should be fostered at every opportunity. Hired "sniffer" dogs can be posted at the gangway to help discourage the introduction of drugs or explosives aboard.

The shipboard security procedures discussed so far relate primarily to the observation of the outer perimeter and control of the security zone between it and the secondary perimeter. In the security scenarios it has been assumed that any intruders would be stopped at the outer perimeter barrier. However, if they are not stopped, for whatever reason, the ship's security forces must withdraw behind their secondary perimeter barrier. Most ships, fortunately, are made of steel and withdrawing inside and securing all accesses is something like buttoning up a tank. Intruders armed merely with small arms will not get very far at all, and they are not likely to have come aboard prepared to breach steel bulkheads. The secondary perimeter defense tactic is basically the same whether the ship is underway, anchored, or moored. All security personnel should be brought inside (everyone else should already be below) and all accesses secured. (If the ship was not built so that all accesses could be secured from inside, she should have been modified accordingly.) Once inside, the security forces should take up defensive firing positions previously worked out in the security plan. These positions should cover the obvious accesses to the control and accommodation areas of the vessel. Accesses into cargo areas should be ignored, unless they offer access into the control and accommodation areas. If the attack continues once the ship is buttoned up it will be clear that the objective of the attackers is the ship herself, and she will be in a fight for her life. All topside controlled lighting should be turned on. All glare-projected perimeter lighting should be extinguished. If the ship is anywhere other than the open ocean, hopefully help will be on the way. Eighty percent of all violence at sea occurs within 12 miles of shore. This lighting scheme will aid the assisting forces and hinder the attackers.

It is hoped that the attack will be stopped at the secondary perimeter. Either the attackers will give up and depart before help arrives, or they will be repelled when it does arrive. However, if they do succeed in gaining access all is still not lost, if the ship has prepared properly. First of all, if the defenders can predict where the breach will occur they may be able to repel the attackers who, at that point, will be at a considerable tactical disadvantage. If not, they will certainly know where the breach has occurred within a short time. All lights should be extinguished within the passageways. Without light the intruders will be virtually unable to proceed, and will stand a good chance of being defeated by the defenders. If the attackers came equipped with their own lights, which is not very likely, their use will only aid the defenders who presumably will be lying in wait for them in the darkness. Furthermore, the darkened interior passageways of a ship are a booby-trapper's paradise. With a little training the crew could be prepared to set booby traps throughout the ship while the attackers are delayed at the secondary perimeter. Booby traps constitute an extremely cost-effective (in terms of ammunition and manpower) means of inflicting casualties on the intruders. They can also work superbly to discourage and demoralize the attackers who are now faced with, first, a pitch-black maze of interior passageways, with which they are unfamiliar and which have been booby-trapped, and, second, armed defenders who are prepared to ambush them at any turn.

If the attack continues beyond the breach in the secondary perimeter, beyond the booby-trapped darkened passageways, and beyond the defenders' capabilities to stem the assault, the defenders or what is left of them must retreat to their last bastion of defense: the inner perimeters. In most cases these will be the bridge and the engine room. Once these are taken the fight is lost. However, at any time until then the fight is not lost, and a fight not lost is one which can be won. The deciding factor in many cases will simply be the degree to which the ship and her crew are willing to continue to resist. The attackers will be limited in their number and the amount of ammunition they can carry. If properly combatted, they will suffer extensive casualties and they will probably not be reinforced. Any commercial vessel that is prepared to do so should win. The question is only whether her owners and operators want her to win. To date, that question has generally been answered in the negative. Once the maritime community realizes the liability exposure it faces because of its noncombative stance, however, attitudes will hopefully change. In the meantime, pirates and terrorists will become bolder, losses will escalate, and lawsuits will be filed more often.

The subject of lawsuits raises the issue of the Persian Gulf. In the past, owners and operators have allowed their vessels to be indiscriminately attacked by an irrational and fanatic regime which believes it can do so with impunity because no one has made any effort to prevent it. As a result, hundreds of seamen's lives have been lost and billions of dollars in cargo and shipping destroyed. The losses sustained and the personal injury claims paid have been considered merely a cost of doing business in a very lucrative field of endeavor. Such incomprehensible callousness cries out to be stopped. Hopefully, as significantly larger damage awards are made by courts that believe such attitudes should not go unpunished, it will be.

Rocket-propelled grenade (RPG) attacks from puny Iranian patrol craft that are little more than modified ski boats can be prevented so easily that, were it not for the loss of life and limb resulting from such attacks, it would be laughable. Yet owners and operators have allowed such attacks to continue unchecked. Heat-seeking or radar-guided surface-to-surface missiles, such as the Chinese-made Silkworm, can be fought off if the ship is equipped to do so. Yet owners and operators have not seen fit to so equip their vessels. The one-sided surface engagements in which Iranian frigates bravely attack unarmed, slow-moving VLCCs need not be so. Yet owners and operators continue to allow them to be. Shipboard security is not merely a physical condition; it is a state of consciousness, a resolve, an intent. Without the will to make commercial shipping secure against attack, ships everywhere will remain at the mercy of the pirates, extortionists, saboteurs, and terrorists of the world. In the Persian Gulf no intent to make commercial shipping secure has been manifested (other than the U.S. protection policy for certain reflagged vessels), and the majority of the commercial vessels in the area remain at the mercy of Iranian terrorists. These bullies could be stopped dead in their tracks if shipowners would only do the prudent thing and arm their vessels. Merchantmen since the dawn of maritime commerce have armed themselves when necessity called for such measures. During both the world wars in this century commercial vessels were fitted with naval armament that afforded some degree of security. The completely automatic and autonomous weapons systems available today require no crew involvement whatsoever, other than perhaps to activate the system. These systems can automatically engage incoming missiles and aircraft. They can decoy radar-guided rockets and missiles. With a little help they can even engage surface vessels. Yet shipowners refuse to utilize them, preferring instead, apparently, to gamble with the lives and limbs of their crews. Even a two-man machine-gun team, heli-lifted from vessel to vessel, can take out the Iranian gunboats respon-sible for all the RPG attacks vessels have suffered. Yet not even this protective measure has been employed, even though the situation in the Gulf has been notorious around the world.

One area of commercial shipping which has also gained a de-gree of notoriety since the *Achille Lauro* hijacking in 1985 is the cruise ship business. The idea that terrorists could successfully hijack a luxury passenger liner with 800 passengers and 300 crew members aboard sent the maritime nations of the world into a tailspin. All of a sudden everyone became supersensitive to the fact that the security at most cruise ship passenger terminals throughout the world was nonexistent. It is still virtually nonexistent in the vast majority of cruise ship ports of call. However, as a result of the *Achille Lauro,* the International Maritime Organization has made recommendations intended to foster a degree of increased maritime security within the cruise ship industry. Many nations, including the United States, have accepted the IMO's recommendations in one form or another. The focus for passenger liner security has been, and must be, the passenger terminals. Cruise ships are not designed with security in mind. They are designed to accommodate as many passengers as possible in as much luxury as possible. They do not lend themselves to perimeter defenses, security zones, protective lighting, security watches, or armed resistance. The key to pas-senger liner security is access control. While cruise ships can provide a limited amount of access control, the primary respon-sibility for such security must rest with the port facility in which the passenger terminal is situated. Many of the security techniques developed by the airline industry over the past twenty years for use at air terminals can be, and are being, effectively employed in cruise ship passenger terminals. However, while cruise ship security may be an important part of a port facility's security responsibility, it is not its only security responsibility. But if adequate security measures are employed on a facility-wide basis, the security re-quirements of the passenger terminal will be met along with all other facility security requirements.

The Holland America Lines' 34,000-ton *Noordam*, underway. With a
capacity of 1,214 passengers and 559 officers and crew, she and similar
cruise ships are targets for terrorist attacks. Security measures
for these vessels must concentrate on access control.
Courtesy: Holland America Lines.

PORT FACILITY SECURITY MEASURES
AND PROCEDURES

Port facilities, because they are situated on land, lend themselves more
to the traditional security measures and procedures than do either ships
or offshore installations. For this reason, most of the comments made
under the section on general security measures apply to port facilities
directly, and need not be repeated here. The reader should now be quite
familiar with the concepts of perimeter barriers, multiple levels of
defense, security zones, protective lighting, perimeter surveillance,
and access control, all of which the port facility security planner must
carefully consider when he develops the port facility's security plan.

In preparing the plan, the security planner needs to understand the
security threats facing his port facility, for it is these threats his security
plan must be designed to prevent. In order to arrive at this understanding he must realize that the only reason for the port facility's

existence is to service commercial shipping. The vessels that call at his port are seeking more than someplace just to load or discharge cargo, however. They need, in the truest sense of the word, a safe haven. The port facility's security responsibilities are therefore first to the ships which call at the port, and second to the cargo which is either discharged from those ships or stored at the facility awaiting loading. The port facility's third area of security responsibility is to itself: its own buildings, equipment, and sensitive materials. Consequently, port facility security is considerably more complex than either shipboard or offshore installation security because it must be conducted on several levels. The threats therefore facing the port facility are:

1. The same threats facing ships while they are berthed at the facility.
2. Pilferage of cargo stored in the facility.
3. Sabotage of the facility itself.

The threats facing berthed vessels in the United States are primarily sabotage and hijacking. Piracy, by definition, occurs on the high seas, and stowaways and drug-smuggling are generally security threats facing U.S.-bound vessels. The primary concern for the port facility security planner regarding berthed vessels in the United States is therefore to prevent hijacking and sabotage. Both are a function of access control. Preventing pilferage of cargo stored at the facility is also a function of access control, only now the access control is focused on access to the cargo and storage areas and not the ships. Finally, the security of the facility itself is a function of all the traditional security measures and procedures discussed so far, including access control.

Access control is therefore the most important consideration for the port facility security planner. With regard to his ships, if his port facility contains a cruise ship passenger terminal he must make a distinction between cargo vessel security and cruise ship security. He may also need to make a distinction between security for vessels carrying hazardous cargo and for those vessels carrying non-hazardous cargo. The U.S. Coast Guard has promulgated regulations for the handling of hazardous cargoes within the United States, which include some security measures. It has also published "recommended preventative security measures which should be utilized by both passenger vessels and the facilities which serve them." (This is Coast Guard Document 87-019 that is included in the appendix, 52 Fed. Reg. 11,587-11,594.)

Passenger terminals present serious security problems for the port facility primarily because of the huge numbers of people who pass through such terminals. Not only must the port facility devise security procedures designed to prevent unauthorized persons from boarding the cruise ships, and to prevent authorized persons intending harm from boarding the cruise ships, it must also implement baggage and package security measures the primary purpose of which is to prevent the introduction of weapons or other dangerous devices on board. As if this were not enough, the port facility must also closely monitor all permanent employees, contract service personnel, and casual workers whose duties require access to the cruise ships or terminals.

Many of the security procedures developed by the airlines can be effectively utilized by the cruise ship industry. Gate magnetometers, X-ray machines, and sonic detection devices can all be employed in cruise ship passenger terminals, and should be. Passenger identification, verification, and control procedures can and should also be utilized. Passenger control techniques, again pioneered by the airline industry, should be employed. Such techniques allow passengers to be moved from one area to another in an appropriate fashion under controlled conditions. The terminal should be considered, for security purposes, as an installation or facility unto itself that must be secured. Perimeter barriers in the form of fences and walls should be erected, with the appropriate check points, protective lighting, security zones, and surveillance procedures emplaced. Security awareness training among all permanent port authority or cruise line employees who have access to either the terminal or the cruise ships is extremely important, and should be conducted regularly. Pre-employment screening of all such employees, as well as continued employee monitoring by supervisors is also imperative. Involuntary, random drug testing should be made a condition of employment. A drug user can be manipulated by saboteurs or terrorists. From the standpoint of maritime security, the issue of drug use has nothing to do with job performance, or the right to privacy, or the right to work. It has to do with the lives and safety of passengers and crews of recognized potential terrorist targets, and if prospective employees are not willing to accept involuntary drug testing as a condition of their employment they should not be hired.

Cruise ship security, however, should not be the all-consuming objective of the port facility security planner. It must be stressed again that numerous types of cargo-carrying vessels make just as good, if not better, terrorist targets. Hijacking a cruise ship with over a thousand lives at stake may have some degree of perverted appeal to the twisted and demented minds that plan such activities, which of course the world news media merely reinforce with their irresponsible hype. But a truly cold-blooded, calculating terrorist will realize immediately that there are much more lucrative maritime targets, most of which are not protected in the least. Consequently, it is imperative that the port facility security planner not lose sight of his overall security objective, which includes *all* the vessels in his port, their cargoes, and the facility itself.

Many of the security measures and procedures already discussed generally apply to port facilities. Others which could also be considered as general security measures apply, in the maritime context, only to port facilities. Truck and van control is one such measure.

A close and thorough inspection of all trucks and vans which either enter or leave the port facility should be made and their contents duly noted. An orderly system should be established that limits and controls the movement of such vehicles, not only into the port facility, but also around sensitive areas such as passenger terminals, piers, fuel depots, and so on. Wherever possible, loading and unloading platforms should be located outside sensitive areas and within constant view of security personnel. If this is not feasible, turnaround areas for loading and unloading should be established as close to the truck gates as possible. In addition, the number of truck gates should be limited to as few as possible. This will help eliminate pilferage by dishonest employees and truck drivers and will also help prevent the smuggling of unauthorized persons or equipment into the facility.

All motor vehicles either entering or departing the port facility should be required to pass through a service gate manned by security personnel. Automobiles should be checked for the appropriate port facility registration and parking permit. Passengers should be examined and their destination and purpose within the facility noted. At truck entrances all truck drivers, helpers, passengers, and vehicle contents must be carefully examined for both incoming and outgoing conveyances, and should include:

Entrance to a port facility that has absolutely no access control

1. The appropriate entries on a truck register that include the truck's registration and owner's name, signatures of the driver and any helpers, intended destination within the facility, description of load, and the date and time of arrival and departure.
2. The identification of all drivers and helpers, including proof of affiliation with the company or owner of the truck.
3. A driver's license check of the driver.
4. An examination of the truck for unauthorized persons or items.

Identification badges should be issued to truck drivers and helpers, and automobile passengers who have been properly identified and registered. The badges should permit access only to the specific area or areas required for the stated and confirmed purposes. Truck or van loading and unloading operations should be either supervised by, observed by, or performed in sight of security personnel.

One area of truck and van control that needs to have particular attention paid to it by the port facility is the delivery of petroleum products by bulk tank trucks. Pilferage or diversion of bulk fuel oils is a major concern of those who purchase or otherwise deal in such products within the maritime industry. Whether delivery is made by ship or truck, the best preventative measure against pilferage is verification at the point of loading of the amount of fuel oil loaded, and verification at the point of discharge of the amount discharged. There are two caveats to this, however. First, the verification procedures and documentation must be secure; that is, the verification documents cannot have been tampered with and the verification process itself must be performed by qualified and trustworthy people. Second, the same verification procedures used at loading must be used at discharge. In essence, one must utilize the same verification yardstick. In a recent legal case involving a shipment of molasses, the cargo was loaded aboard the carrying vessel at two different loading ports and discharged at two separate discharge ports. Draft surveys were performed for the ship upon completion of all four evolutions, which basically verified that the amount discharged was the amount loaded, which was the amount for which the bills of lading were issued. The tanks into which the cargo was delivered, however, were equipped with high-precision measuring devices and they indicated that considerably less cargo had been delivered than what appeared on the bills of lading. The subrogated consignee of the cargo sued for the difference and the appeals court ultimately held that the same method of measurement must be used at both loading and discharging if proof of loss is to be established. In any event, with these two caveats in mind, and since the port facility is responsible for any cargo within its care, custody, and control, ensuring that proper verification and documentation procedures are followed for bulk cargoes received and discharged is important.

Many port facilities contain rail transport facilities. The movement of railroad cars within the facility as well as into and out of the facility should be closely monitored. Cars should be inspected to prevent the entry or removal of unauthorized personnel or material. All railroad entrances should be controlled by locked gates when not in use, and should be under security supervision when either unlocked or open.

Docks, piers, wharfs, and quays should be separated from the rest of the port facility by perimeter barriers just as the passenger terminal.

Security fencing with controlled gates is usually the form of barrier employed, and it should meet the same standards as previously described. Access to the berthed vessels must be strictly controlled, with the same visitor identification and verification procedures being employed that have already been discussed. In the United States, Coast Guard-issued port security cards should be required for access in addition to any other security procedures. At night the perimeter barrier, and the entire area between it and the berthed vessels, should be lighted by controlled protective lighting, and surveilled appropriately.

Storage area security within the port facility is second in importance only to vessel security. Millions of tons of cargo, valued at billions of dollars, move through an average-sized port facility every year. From the time the port facility, or one of its resident stevedoring companies, receives the cargo until it is loaded aboard its carrying vessel, the port facility is responsible for it. Likewise, from the time the cargo is deposited on the dock by the discharging vessel until it is removed from the port facility by the consignee, the port facility is responsible for it. Millions and millions of dollars in cargo losses are litigated every year in the United States, cases in which the stevedoring companies and the storage facilities are named as defendants. The claim is always the same: negligent care, custody, or control of the cargo lost. Cargo pilferage can be reduced substantially by following the proper storage area security procedures.

A cargo storage area may include a warehouse, shed, open area, dock, or any portion of the port facility that is used for cargo storage purposes. The general security procedures previously discussed concerning security perimeters, lighting, surveillance, and access controls apply to storage areas. The specific security measures employed by a port facility to ensure the security of its storage areas must necessarily be dictated by the nature of the cargo stored, the physical characteristics of the storage area, the geography of the area, the economic or political situation, the potential security threats, and the availability of security support. All of these factors, and possibly others, must be considered by the port facility security planner when he prepares the port facility's security plan. The degree of protection required may vary with respect to the cargo and the activities within the port facility. In some situations, entire areas may require only limited protection. In other areas, a host of additional protective measures may be needed, such as segregation, compartmentalization, and multiplication of security measures. The security plan must therefore not only provide for the general security of cargo storage areas, it must also contain contingency planning for specific types of cargo that may require additional protective measures.

There are basically only two types of storage areas: open storage and covered or enclosed storage. Open storage is normally used for cargo not subject to damage by weather, or bulky, nonperishable cargo which is not particularly pilferable. Steel beams, for instance, can generally be stored in open storage. They are not easily pilfered, nor are they very susceptible to weather damage (light, freshwater surface rust does not damage such cargo or affect its marketability), and they are bulky. Enclosed storage is used for any other type of cargo for which open storage is not appropriate.

When cargo is stored in open areas it should be properly stacked away from, and parallel to, perimeter fences so that security personnel will have an unobstructed view of the fence line. It should not be stacked any closer to the fence than 50 feet, and the stacks should be as symmetrical as possible with wide, straight, intervening corridors. The storage area should be lighted, and patrolled regularly.

Port facility covered storage is usually provided in warehouses or other relatively temporary storage facilities. This is because a port facility is not, and should not be considered as, a storage facility. It is first and foremost a cargo-handling facility, and any storage of cargo should be considered as merely incidental to its primary purpose. Sensitive and highly pilferable types of cargo, such as electronics, drugs, and other high-priced, compact items, should be stored apart from less sensitive cargo, either in a separate building or in a room, cage, or crib. The interior of the warehouse should be well-lighted and checked often by security personnel.

Pilferage of stored cargo is prevented or controlled by utilizing the following security measures:

1. Constant observation of loading, unloading, and moving operations. Pilferage occurs most often when cargo is loaded or unloaded. Security personnel should be particularly alert for the deliberate damaging of packages by cargo handlers to gain access to their contents.
2. Frequent surveillance of stored cargo and cargo storage areas.

3. Controlling access to storage areas at all times, including loading and unloading.
4. Periodically conducting unannounced searches of cargo handlers and their automobiles. As with drug testing, permission to do so should be made a condition of employment. Those refusing to agree to such conditions should not be hired, and those refusing to submit to a search after they have been employed should be terminated.
5. Employing the physical security measures previously discussed: perimeter barriers, protective lighting, guards, dogs, surveillance, and so forth.

Detecting evidence of pilferage and conducting on-scene preliminary investigations of cargo losses are duties of the security personnel assigned to monitor cargo storage areas. Once it appears that a crime may have been committed, however, the local authorities should be notified. Any further involvement of port facility security personnel in investigating or apprehending the suspected pilferers should only be at the request of the authorities.

The last area of responsibility which concerns the port facility security planner is the security of the port facility itself. While vessel security and cargo pilferage control may be his primary security objectives, he must not forget the vulnerability of his particular installation. Some port facilities contain massive fuel oil storage capabilities, for instance, which a terrorist group might well target for sabotage. Others may contain strategically important structures, such as bridges, locks, or tunnel outlets. The key to anticipating as many foreseeable security threats as possible is to remember to use the acronym ACTION: Always Consider The Immediate Obvious Nightmare. If the security planner can look at fuel storage tanks in his port facility and think, "Gee, someone might decide to blow those up," he is subconsciously using ACTION. He needs to train himself to consciously do the same thing. Security disasters always appear to be obvious disasters with hindsight. The usual comment is something like, "Why didn't anyone *think* of that?" The answer is, "No one remembered to use ACTION."

Fuel storage areas and pipelines are prime targets for terrorists.

OFFSHORE INSTALLATION SECURITY MEASURES
AND PROCEDURES

Because of the somewhat unique characteristics of offshore installations, being hybrids of vessels and shore facilities, the offshore installation security planner must be familiar with all the security measures and procedures discussed so far. He must understand, and then apply to his offshore installation security planning, the concepts of perimeter barriers, security zones, defense in depth, protective lighting, barrier surveillance, and access control as they relate both to vessels and port facilities. At the same time he must understand the security threats facing his installation, and tailor his security plan to them.

The two security threats faced by offshore installations are sabotage and hijacking. In all likelihood both would occur for the same reason: extortion. A $200 million rig that makes a net profit of over $100 million per year would certainly fetch a sizable ransom. The newer tension-leg well platforms, which cost about $400 million and are expected to net $200 million or more a year, could reasonably be expected to fetch even higher ransoms. What would be a reasonable ransom for such a rig? $20 million? $50 million? $200 million? With this kind of potential, offshore installations are not going to attract only terrorists. They will attract any crook with enough moxie to put together a team of combat-hardened professionals willing to risk their lives for $5 million or $10 million apiece. There are a lot of combat-hardened professionals, and even more who consider themselves such, out there in the world today who would probably leap at a chance to make one-tenth that amount. The fact that it hasn't happened yet doesn't mean it isn't going to, it just means that no one with enough intestinal fortitude has thought of it. The more than 700 offshore oil rigs around the world present more than enough targets of opportunity.

In order either to sabotage a rig or seize it the culprits must get on board. They will accomplish this, initially, through one of two means. They will either be authorized to go aboard, or they will not be authorized. If authorized, they will be either company employees, contract or subcontract laborers, or visitors. If not authorized, they will come aboard by force. It is important to realize, however, that not all the persons involved in the plot need come aboard at the same time. One disgruntled or money-hungry employee could gain control of the installation with a grenade or pistol, and the rest of his comrades could board at their leisure. Furthermore, it is conceivable that *none* of the extortionists could be on board at the time they work their extortion. It is also conceivable that the rig could be sabotaged for some reason other than extortion, such as revenge or simply to wreak mayhem. In any case, the security planner needs to consider his security options with regard to preventing access to those individuals who may wish to sabotage or seize the installation, and the best way to do that is to categorize his options.

Most of the physical security measures discussed so far are aimed primarily at controlling unauthorized access. The security planner should consider how he will organize his in-depth defense, where his perimeter barriers will be, what his protective lighting scheme will be, and so on. To do so, he must consider his installation as basically an anchored vessel and prepare his security plan according to the security measures discussed for anchored vessels. The main difference between his installation and an anchored ship is the far greater distance from shore his installation is than an anchored vessel would be. This distance will be a significant factor when considering what sources of outside assistance may be available to the installation and the time factor involved in obtaining that assistance.

The outer perimeter barrier for the rig should be its physical boundaries. Radar can certainly be installed and used to form an electronic outer perimeter several miles in diameter, and probably should be, but the problem with doing so involves effectively manning the radar. However, it never hurts to have a radar repeater fired up, even if it is only looked at occasionally. It could be placed in the security office or wherever the security watch stander in charge will be. Anyway, so far as the outer perimeter barrier is concerned, the physical configuration of the rig will determine whether additional barriers are needed. A ship's hull, bulwarks, and rails must necessarily form her outer perimeter barrier, and her very nature precludes the installation of security fencing around her main deck. This is not necessarily so for an offshore rig. Depending upon its configuration and whether it is an exploration or production rig, security fencing may very well be effectively installed in various locations. One obvious place would be in the vicinity of the boat dock.

Once the outer perimeter barrier is defined and augmented as appropriate, the next question concerns protective lighting. The same protective lighting used aboard an anchored vessel should be employed, that is, glare-projected lighting that extends a 360-degree zone of light at least 200 feet from the sides of the installation. In addition, however, an offshore rig needs the capability of lighting the water directly below it as well as its legs or other supports, and this lighting should be controlled lighting.

The next thing the offshore installation security planner needs to do is establish the security zone between the secondary perimeter and the outer perimeter. To do this he needs to decide where his secondary perimeter will be. This will depend upon the configuration of the installation, but the same guidelines apply as on vessels. The secondary perimeter should be located where the accesses into the accommodation and control areas of the installation are. Hopefully, these accesses will be part of reasonably sound walls or bulkheads that can be secured. The security zone between these two perimeters should be lighted with controlled lighting. On an offshore rig, this same area is usually the working area and in all probability will already be lighted. The security planner should ensure that the lighting is adequate for security purposes. Many rigs have more than one working level. If this is the case, the security planner must think and plan in three dimensions.

The inner perimeters should be considered next. As with ships, the control and communication centers are the obvious inner areas which need to be secured. Their accesses will form the inner perimeter barriers, and should be made as secure as possible. Modifications to construction may be required in order to do so.

Surveillance of the outer perimeter barrier is the next problem for the security planner. Guard patrols would normally be used ashore, and security watches would be posted afloat. Are either necessarily needed aboard an offshore installation? The answer depends upon a number of factors. Some of these factors include the size of the rig, its location, the current threat analysis, and the work activity being performed on board. Exploration rigs, for instance, usually maintain a high volume of activity around the clock. The place is a veritable hive of men, lights, and machines for months. Security watches in such cases may well be superfluous, particularly if all workers have been properly indoctrinated concerning security awareness. On the other hand, a production platform may have barely a handful of workers aboard at any given moment. An adequate guard force could require more personnel than the rig does. Are there alternatives? Of course there are! The most obvious is the use of electronic surveillance systems like closed circuit television. An offshore rig is ideally suited for CCTV surveillance, so long as proper lighting requirements are met for camera operation and the cameras are weatherproof. Radar repeaters, television monitors, and communications systems could all be installed in one neat control center that would require only one person to monitor. Of course, the CCTV system could be supported by any number of additional security measures, such as a roving patrol, listening devices, and alarms.

A warning of impending danger is useless, as has been pointed out before, if no reactive capability exists to deal with the danger. Consequently, unless the operator of the installation intends for those aboard to take some sort of action against an attack there is no reason to implement the security procedures just discussed. So assuming the rig personnel are not expected to simply surrender, a decision must have been made regarding the defense of the installation before the security planner started planning his perimeter surveillance procedures. That defense must necessarily include persons capable of repelling the attackers. This means that either additional security personnel will be required, or that installation personnel will be expected to perform security duties when the situation dictates. Either way, the means for repelling the attackers must be placed on board. Normally this would simply involve firearms. However, depending upon the design and construction of the rig, a few alternatives might be available to those offshore installation operators who do not wish to place firearms aboard but who do wish to resist attack long enough to receive professional help. Some alternatives might be: the design and installation of electrically charged barriers, emplacement of water cannon, or the use of chemical reagents and gas. None of these is guaranteed to slow down true professionals for very long, but if help is on the way they might delay the attack long enough for military or police assistance to arrive. Of course, this raises the question as to what government, if any, will respond to such an emergency. Singapore, after all, has refused to do much about the pirates teeming off its shores because it claims it has no jurisdiction to do so. Many offshore installations are located beyond the territorial limits of their nearest countries, so unless an agreement exists that help will be provided if needed the installation may be on its own anyway.

The tactical and logistical hurdles are significant for anyone planning to attack and seize an offshore installation, even if it isn't defended by trained professionals. If it is defended by professionals those hurdles are virtually insurmountable. But unless the threat analysis indicates that a seizure attempt is imminent, keeping highly paid combat-ready troops aboard indefinitely is not the most likely course of action an installation operator would take. A prudent operator will have some sort of reaction force on board, however, and whatever its size and composition, it should be able to repel an assault force of four to six men.

In all likelihood, an armed assault on an offshore installation will be the *last* choice of those wishing to seize it. What they would much rather do is sneak one or two men aboard disguised as employees or visitors, seize control at an opportune moment, and then call in their reinforcements who could arrive shortly by helicopter. The trick, therefore, is to prevent the one or two impostors from getting on board in the first place, or at least prevent them from getting aboard with any type of weapons or explosives. This is what access control is all about.

There are only two ways authorized persons can get on board an offshore installation: by boat or helicopter. In both cases these conveyances should be under the direct control of the offshore operator, and it should be a simple and routine matter to search all baggage, packages, and persons before they are allowed onto the boat or aircraft, as well as to verify identities and authorizations. Any operator not doing this is simply asking for trouble. Furthermore, since there is no reason why any legitimate visitor or employee cannot utilize the company-provided transportation, any other boat or helicopter should be denied access to the installation. "Emergencies" should be treated in the same manner as a mayday request at sea. Both could be deadly ruses.

The comments made previously concerning pre-employment screening, employee monitoring, and drug testing apply here as well. Roustabouts and other offshore personnel are much like itinerant seamen, moving from job to job and place to place. The days of hiring either seamen or offshore workers without some sort of background check are over, or at least they should be. The exposure faced by an employer for not doing so is simply too great.

Sabotage is a far more likely security threat than is seizure of the installation. For one thing, it is simpler and safer. For another, it can serve the purposes of the terrorist or extortionist just as well. A bomb is the most likely instrument of sabotage, and its introduction on board an installation can be prevented in most cases by the same procedures just mentioned: boat, aircraft, and personnel searches, inspection of baggage and packages, and employee and visitor verification and identification.

The security measures and procedures just discussed are some of the options available to the security planner for a vessel, port facility, or offshore installation. Preparing a security plan, however, is just the first step toward securing a particular maritime entity. Once the security plan is prepared and approved it must be implemented. Implementing the security plan is the topic of the next chapter.

CHAPTER FIVE

IMPLEMENTING THE
SECURITY PLAN

ONCE a security plan has been prepared and approved it should be implemented. In order for a security plan to be properly implemented a certain amount of supervision and coordination must be provided, usually by the security planner. Theoretically, a security plan can be prepared by the security planner and then implemented at a later date under the supervision of someone else. The best procedure, however, is to implement the security plan as soon as possible and in doing so utilize the person who prepared the plan in the first place. For purposes of discussion it will be assumed that the security planner will be the person tasked with implementation of the security plan.

The security planner needs to conceptualize the plan as entailing two distinct tasks: implementation of the physical security measures, such as installation of perimeter barriers, protective lighting, locks, alarms, and surveillance equipment; and implementation of the human security procedures, such as employment of security personnel, instituting access and movement controls, and training. By far the more complex of the two tasks involves the human element, which will be discussed shortly.

In developing his security plan the security planner presumably clarified his security budgetary parameters, as well as the security policies affecting the design of his plan, and may now proceed with its implementation. The installation of the physical security measures mandated by the security plan can be an expensive, time-consuming matter if extensive construction or modification must be performed. For instance, the erection of security fencing and other barriers, and the construction of new gates and guardhouses throughout a port facility could be a lengthy project. If new underground wiring must also be installed for all protective lighting and communications systems, the project could become even lengthier. On the other hand, if it is a ship's security plan that is being implemented, very little modification to the vessel may be required to satisfy the security plan requirements, and therefore the implementation of the physical security measures for that particular plan may be quite simple. In either case, physical security implementation is basically a matter of purchasing the materials and equipment needed, arranging for their installation, and ensuring that the installation is performed satisfactorily. Implementing the remainder of the security plan is not that simple.

The security procedures dictated by the plan require human involvement, in one form or another. Pre-employment screening, employee monitoring, access control, security indoctrination, and guard force training and supervision all need full-time leadership not only during implementation of the security plan but continuing thereafter. Since the security planner may not be the person ultimately tasked with such continuing supervision, particularly if he is an independent security consultant, someone must be appointed to perform that duty. He may be designated as the security officer, security manager, security director, or vice-president of security operations, depending upon the scope of his authority and the size of his organization. The supervisory tasks, however, remain essentially the same. During implementation of the security plan he should work closely with the security planner in developing the security measures and procedures that have been planned and approved. After the security plan has been implemented, his duties involve the supervision of all aspects of the plan.

Training of the guard force and supervision of day-to-day security operations are the two most important responsibilities of the security officer. Lack of training is one of the most common deficiencies in any security organization, and is the subject of close scrutiny in any negligent security litigation. A maritime operator can be held liable for negligently refusing or failing to implement reasonable security measures, and he can be held liable for negligently conducting the security measures he does implement. The remainder of this chapter will therefore primarily focus on, first, the legal authority and operational parameters of private maritime security personnel and, second, the training and supervision of such personnel.

Private maritime security personnel are viewed, under the law, in no different manner than private security employees generally. Private security employees have the same authority as private citizens to defend themselves or others, carry firearms, arrest wrongdoers, and investigate suspected criminal activity. The scope of this authority is founded primarily in tort law as opposed to criminal law, although a private security guard will be held criminally responsible if he commits a crime, just like any other citizen. Private security personnel can be either proprietary employees of the maritime operator, or they can be employees provided by a contract security company with which the maritime operator arranges for security services. In either case, they are considered employees or agents of the maritime operator and that operator, as their employer, is liable for their negligence or unwarranted acts. In the case of contract security employees, the service contract should contain an indemnity clause in favor of the maritime operator through which the security service company agrees to accept all responsibility for the acts of its employees. While such contractual arrangements may give the maritime operator the right to sue the security contractor, however, they do not protect the maritime operator from suits by third parties who claim damages resulting from the security employees' actions. Consequently, one consideration in providing the security personnel called for in the security plan is whether the maritime operator should employ its own security forces or contract for such services.

Private security companies, by and large, have very poor reputations so far as providing quality personnel. This is because most of their clients are not willing to pay for quality. Consequently, guards, couriers, and other security personnel are employed at the low end of the pay scale and such positions attract only marginally qualified people. This is not to say that *all* contract security service companies employ marginally acceptable people. There are some very exclusive, specialized security companies that are staffed by professionals of the highest calibre. These companies, however, are not easily located, and they are not inexpensive.

There are substantial pros and cons concerning both the hiring of proprietary security employees and the contracting for security services. Some of the more obvious variables that need to be considered involve budgetary requirements, security duties, guard force size, threat analysis, risk, and liability exposure. Generally, for long-term security requirements, such as those generated by a port facility, permanent security personnel should be utilized. In such cases the maritime operator maintains substantially more control over both the training and performance of security personnel, which can be important from a liability standpoint as well as an operational one. On the other hand, in instances where short-term additional security personnel are required, carefully selected contract security services are more appropriate. Vessel owners wishing to combat piracy in the Phillip Channel or terrorism in the Persian Gulf might well elect to secure the services of professionals willing to ride from one geographical location to another for those express purposes.

LEGAL CONSIDERATIONS

Whichever type of security personnel is ultimately employed, they are all susceptible to the laws and regulations of the country or state in which they operate. For permanent or stationary facilities such as port facilities or offshore installations it is a relatively simple matter to ascertain what those laws and regulations are and how they affect security personnel. For ships, however, as well as for maritime operators who operate facilities in several jurisdictions, the matter is not so simple. The laws and regulations for each jurisdiction in which the vessel may find herself, or in which the maritime operator operates, must be determined and the actions of security personnel modified accordingly. It is impossible to discuss all the worldwide legal ramifications of employing security personnel. However, some general comments can be made.

Throughout the nations of the world there exist only two basic types of legal systems: common-law systems and code law systems. A common law system is that type of system whose jurisprudence is based upon prior legal decisions. Such systems are very fluid and flexible; their law remains in a continuing state of development, changing to meet the needs of the society they serve. All statutes, regulations, or laws enacted under a common-law system must be interpreted by the courts in accordance with the common-law principles developed over many centuries. The common-law nations of the world are primarily those with an Anglo-Saxon heritage: the United Kingdom, the United States, Canada, Australia, New Zealand, and so on. Code law systems, on the other hand, are not based on prior legal decisions. They are founded upon legal codes that may or may not have any historic perspective, and that form the basis for all legal decisions. Some of the more famous legal codes throughout history have been the Ten Commandments, the Code of Justinian, and the Code Napoleon. Code law systems are much more static in nature than common-law systems and considerably more inflexible. Most of the nations of the world have code law systems.

International law is that body of law that consists of agreed-upon rules that control the conduct of nations in their relations with each other. It is important to remember that international law only applies to nations and between nations. Treaties and conventions are the means by which nations of the world agree upon the rules that make up the foundation for international law. A private individual is not bound by any treaty. He is bound by the law of the jurisdiction in which he finds himself. That law may or may not comport with a particular treaty. Public international law, as it affects maritime security, is discussed in chapter 6.

Under common law the rights of the individual are balanced against the rights of the society. In the United States certain rights are guaranteed the individual by the U.S. Constitution. For instance, citizens of the United States have a constitutional right against self-incrimination. This right, however, does not apply between two private citizens. If one citizen interrogates another without the appearance of governmental authority to do so, and that person admits to committing a crime, that admission may be used against him. The rights of individuals with regard to other individuals are governed primarily by what is referred to as tort law. A tort is a legal wrong committed by one person against another, and is a common-law concept. Such wrongs are redressed in the civil court system rather than the criminal court system because they are perceived as wrongs against individuals rather than the society. Crimes are wrongs committed against the society. Sometimes a tort may also be a crime. For instance, the tort of battery under common law is an unlawful or unauthorized touching of the person. This can be anything from an unwanted chauvinistic pat on the behind to a bludgeoning with a club. The unwanted pat is not a crime, the bludgeoning is. Consequently, a particular act may have both civil and criminal ramifications.

Private security personnel, because they are private citizens with no police powers, must understand their relationship both to their employer and the society at large. They are employees who protect their employer's property and, as such, exercise as agents their employer's right to protect himself and his property. This is a right all private citizens have under common law. However, one citizen does not have the right to infringe on the rights of another. Such infringement constitutes a tort, for which the employer can be held liable. Torts that private security personnel can commit include battery, assault, false imprisonment, invasion of privacy, defamation of character, and intentional infliction of mental distress. In addition they can be found negligent in failing to protect employees, customers, or visitors from security hazards, as well as rendering improper emergency medical assistance. They can also be found guilty of crimes such as battery, aggravated assault, and manslaughter; and they can be held criminally negligent in the unauthorized or improper use of deadly force.

The use of deadly force is probably the single most important concept all private security personnel must understand, whether or not they are routinely armed with firearms. Deadly force is *any* force which, when used, is calculated or likely to produce death or serious bodily injury: for example, dogs, stone throwing, electric shock, and even one's fist. There are times, under any legal system, when one is entitled to use deadly force. Generally this is in self-defense when one is under the reasonable expectation of death or great bodily injury. In any jurisdiction, a person under unprovoked attack is entitled to defend himself. Most common-law jurisdictions, however, have refined the rules under which deadly force may be used to encompass more than mere self-defense. Generally, one is entitled to use deadly force to repel an attack on the safety or lives of others as well as oneself if the attack poses a risk of death or serious bodily injury. The key to the use of force, deadly or otherwise, is reasonableness. Deadly force can be used to repel deadly force, but it can never be used to repel nondeadly force. Furthermore, the mere threat of an attack is not sufficient to justify the use of deadly force. For instance, if a man with a knife threatens another but is clearly beyond the range where he can do bodily injury, the man threatened is not entitled to shoot the man with the knife. Likewise, one is not entitled to use deadly force against an attacker who has broken off an attack, even if the attacker has already caused great bodily harm. Many common-law jurisdictions require one to retreat as far as is practical before using deadly force. Exceptions to this rule usually involve one's dwelling or place of business where, if an attack ensues, one is generally not required to retreat. Common law also recognizes the right to use force to intervene during the commission of a crime. Such force must be reasonable under the circumstances, and the nature of the crime will usually determine the amount of force permitted. Most jurisdictions allow the use of deadly force to prevent a deadly felony, such as murder, rape, arson, or robbery. Deadly force is never allowed solely in the defense of property; however, if the defenders of the property reasonably believe they are in danger of serious bodily injury or death from the intruder or intruders, deadly force is allowable once the integrity of the property has been breached. Furthermore, deadly force is permitted to prevent a felonious attack on the property itself, such as arson or sabotage.

In today's world the use of deadly force is usually equated with the use of firearms although, as has been noted, such is not necessarily the case. This is because modern man no longer fights with edged weapons or clubs, except when the exigencies of the situation so dictate. The carrying and employment of firearms by private security personnel is therefore a serious matter indeed, and one to which the maritime operator should give careful attention.

Port authorities are the only maritime operators who conduct business in areas that are at all accessible to law enforcement assistance. For the most part, ships and offshore installations are completely outside any sphere of such assistance. Consequently ships and offshore installations particularly, and port facilities to some degree, must rely solely upon their own security resources if they are to prevent acts of terrorism, sabotage, and thievery. This makes the carrying and employment of firearms by maritime private security personnel a virtual necessity if they are going to be at all successful in maintaining the security of their ship, offshore installation, or port facility. Doing so, however, raises the liability exposure of the maritime operator. In order to reduce this exposure as much as possible, security personnel must be properly trained in the use of firearms. Firearms and training are discussed in more detail in chapter 7.

Restraints on the employment and conduct of private security personnel and the use of firearms exist in the form of rules, ordinances, regulations, and laws governing private security activity. In the United States these can be promulgated at both local and state level and, where state law does not apply, possibly at the federal level. Much of this legislation is in the form of licensing requirements, but there may also exist various applicable statutes that are not specifically written with private security activities in mind and thus are not readily apparent to the maritime operator. The best safeguard against running afoul of such statutes is to confer with local law enforcement agencies during both the planning and implementation stages of one's security development. Security consultants and lawyers can also offer useful advice.

Besides the use of deadly force, and the concepts of civil and criminal liability, there are a number of other legal issues with which maritime private security personnel should be familiar. These include arrest, false imprisonment, search, investigations, interrogations, invasion of privacy, and defamation of character. These subjects are generally taught to all student officers in their police academies, and there are a number of good textbooks on the market that are used in junior colleges and universities as well. One excellent text is *Police Administration: Structures, Processes, and Behavior* (see Selected Reading). The scope of the present book precludes a detailed discussion of such topics; there are, however, some general comments that can be made.

Under criminal law, a proper arrest involves the authority to arrest, the assertion of that authority, and the restraint of the person against whom the assertion is made. The arrest occurs when the individual is deprived of his personal freedom. A simple touch can be classified as an arrest, and one may be liable in tort for battery or false imprisonment if there is no privilege by law to do so. Private security personnel have no more authority to arrest than do private citizens under the common-law or statutory concept of a "citizen's arrest." In the past, at common law, a private citizen was permitted to make a felony arrest in order to protect the safety of the public. He could make a misdemeanor arrest if the misdemeanor constituted a breach of the peace and immediate apprehension was necessary to restore public order. Today, a private citizen in most common-law jurisdictions is allowed to make a citizen's arrest only if the felony is in the process of being committed. Likewise, for a misdemeanor citizen's arrest to be valid, the misdemeanor must be in progress *and* must constitute a breach of the peace that requires immediate restoration of the public order. Finally, any citizen's arrest can only be made if the arresting citizen has the intention to, and does, turn the arrested person over to the proper authorities as soon as possible after the arrest. In the United States many states have enacted statutory provisions concerning the authority of private citizens to arrest, and it therefore behooves private security personnel to know and understand the statutes applicable locally. While private security personnel can, theoretically, make citizen's arrests at any time conditions meet lawful requirements, a good caveat to making such arrests would be that apprehensions should only be made on behalf of their employers and in the interest of asset protection or loss prevention.

Detention of the person arrested necessarily goes hand in hand with the concept of arrest. Unlawful deprivation of a person's liberty, however, constitutes false imprisonment. No jail cell, detention area, or interrogation room is required. *Any* unlawful detention is false imprisonment, even if the intent to detain is only verbally communicated to one standing in an open field. If he reasonably believes he has been unlawfully detained as a result of that communication, he has been falsely imprisoned. Of course the key to whether a false imprisonment has occurred is whether the detention was lawful, which is why private security personnel must understand their authority to make citizen's arrests. In the United States, a majority of the states have enacted antishoplifting statutes that allow temporary detention of suspects for the purpose of investigation, interrogation, or recovery of stolen merchandise. Remember, a misdemeanor shoplifting offense is not a breach of the peace and therefore, under common law, a citizen's arrest is not authorized. Depending upon the wording of such statutes, maritime private security personnel might be able to rely upon them for authority to detain and question suspected pilferers.

The authority to search persons and belongings is another very important concept with which private security personnel should be extremely familiar. In the maritime security arena, it is absolutely vital that security personnel conduct searches in order to prevent weapons and other dangerous devices from being introduced aboard ships and offshore installations. In the United States, citizens are constitutionally guaranteed the right of privacy, which includes the freedom from unreasonable searches. On its face, however, the Constitution does not limit the powers of private security personnel to conduct searches, and common-law authority on this issue is unclear. It appears, however, that there are probably four instances where searches by private security personnel are allowable: where consent is given by the person who is to be searched, where consent is given as a condition of employment, where the search is incidental to a valid arrest, and where the search is incidental to a lawful detention. Conditions of employment and union contracts can express or imply consent to search employees and their belongings; but searches of visitors, customers, and other non-employees in nonarrest situations might be troublesome. Since adequate maritime security requires inspection of visitors, vehicles, packages, and baggage at all access points, the simple solution is to make consent to search a condition for access. Those refusing to give their consent are simply denied access. Such consent should be in writing, and can be made a part of the visitor registration process. Additionally, signs proclaiming the possibility of a search of anyone at any time should be prominently displayed. Besides strengthening the facility's consent to search position, the signs should have a discouraging effect on pilferers, saboteurs, or other mischief makers.

In addition to searches, private security personnel frequently conduct internal investigations and interrogations of witnesses and suspects. There are generally no restrictions by law placed upon soliciting voluntary answers from employees, particularly where conditions of employment require cooperation by the employee. Of course, if the employee chooses not to cooperate he should not be placed under duress or coercion. Physical or mental abuse is actionable under tort law, particularly if the uncooperative employee cannot be proven to have committed any offense. Furthermore, questioning a suspect employee in public, if done in an accusatory manner, may give him the right to sue for either defamation of character or intentional infliction of mental distress. It may, however, be possible to terminate him for such lack of cooperation, depending upon his employment or union contract. A nonemployee suspect can probably be handled less carefully, particularly if the interrogation is incidental to a lawful apprehension or detention. However, it is never a good idea to give a suspect ammunition for a lawsuit, particularly when abusive tactics are not likely to produce results in any event. Polygraph examinations and psychological stress evaluations are frequently used by business and industry in both internal and pre-employment investigations. Some employment contracts include as a condition of employment the right to administer such tests. As already mentioned in chapter 4, however, this practice may now be a thing of the past as a result of recent legislation. Consequently, the best approach to take with regard to polygraph and other similar tests, so far as pre-employment investigations are concerned at least, is to consider them just another tool to be used in formulating the entire employee-candidate picture. Then, if a decision is made not to hire a particular candidate and there are corroborating reasons for not doing so besides the results of the polygraph, the decision will probably be viewed as a fair one if it is ever questioned.

All adequate security programs must include promulgation of written procedures, and maritime security programs are no exception. Written procedures usually take the form of an organization's security procedures manual, security plan, or both. The primary difference between a security procedures manual and a security plan is the audience the document is intended to serve. Generally, a security plan is developed as a management tool whereas a procedures manual is prepared for informational and training purposes. Thus, once a plan has been prepared and approved an appropriate security manual can be written that will aid in its implementation. A security procedural manual should address such topics as company or corporate security policy, rules and regulations, security awareness, professionalism, security chain of command, general security duties and responsibilities, emergency procedures, access control, legal constraints, and so on. It should also describe the security SOPs found in the security plan. A fact to be noted is that the security plan/security manual interface can work on several different levels within a particular organization. For example, if a shipping company maintains a fleet of vessels engaged in worldwide maritime commerce and has the foresight to develop an overall company security plan, it should also prepare a company security procedures manual or possibly a shipboard security procedures manual and disseminate it to the fleet. Individual captains and security officers may then rely upon this manual when they prepare their own ship's security plan. Besides answering the security policy questions the ship's security planner may have, the manual will help ensure uniformity of security procedures throughout the fleet. Once a particular vessel establishes her security plan, a ship's security procedures manual can be prepared for use onboard that can contain any pertinent portions of the company's security procedures manual as well as the master's own security policies and desires.

One of the most important purposes served by the promulgation of a security procedures manual is training. The training of shipboard security personnel will necessarily differ from that of port facility or offshore installation security personnel. However, there are some general comments that can be made concerning security personnel training.

GENERAL SECURITY TRAINING PROCEDURES

The three primary targets in security negligence litigation are the hiring, training, and supervision of security personnel. The three primary causes of compromised security are improper hiring, training, or supervision. In both cases - litigation or security compromise - the maritime operator "takes a hit" for the same reasons: improper hiring, training, or supervision. The acronym that helps the security officer remember these three vitally important security components is HITS. If he doesn't want his security organization to take any *hits,* he had better remember his three most vulnerable areas: HIring, Training, and Supervision.

Of the three, training is probably the most important. A well-trained (and motivated) guard force needs less supervision, and proper training will expose unqualified or otherwise unsuited personnel who possibly should not have been hired in the first place. Improper training is also one of the most common causes of any security deficiency, which is truly remarkable, since it is perhaps the one factor that remains at all times wholly within the control of the organization employing security personnel. There is absolutely no excuse for inadequate training. If an organization is willing to commit the time, money, and other resources to develop and implement a security plan, it does so for one or both of only two reasons: either it understands the need for such actions, or it wishes to insulate itself as much as possible from negligence liability. In either case, allowing inadequate training completely defeats both purposes.

Assuming the need for proper training is recognized by the managerial hierarchy instituting the security measures, the first demand should be for detailed record keeping. Detailed records allow accurate analysis of the training being received, and they also provide documentary evidence and proof of the training that was given. Records should be maintained concerning basic, specialized, refresher, and continuing training. The number of hours and type of training received should be fully documented for each trainee. The names and addresses of all instructors, their qualifications, and the courses taught (with dates) should be recorded. Copies of all training syllabi, course outlines, lesson plans, and handouts should be maintained, along with any revisions (with the dates and authors thereof). The results of examinations or other means of determining knowledge transference should be preserved, as well as grading standards, curves, and other useful statistical information. If independent security consultants are periodically requested to review the training program and offer suggestions (and this should be done), copies of their reports and documentation of any resulting changes should be filed. If any recommendations are not followed, the recommendations and the reasons for not following them should also be preserved. A training log should be maintained at the guard force level, and either monthly or quarterly training reports should be forwarded to the next higher authority. Other record-keeping procedures can be devised and implemented. The purpose, as always, should be to analyze the current training with regard to completeness and effectiveness, and to preserve proof of such training for future litigation if it ensues. Of course, such proof can be a double-edged sword if the training has been insufficient. Consequently, unless the organization fully intends to scrutinize the security training as it occurs, and to take reasonable steps to ensure its adequacy, it may well be that *no* training records should be maintained.

The reason for conducting maritime security training is to ensure that the people whose job it is to maintain security are able to do their jobs, both as individuals and as members of teams. Each maritime entity, whether it be a vessel, port facility, or offshore installation, must necessarily have its own unique training requirements. This is because the training requirements are derived from the nature of the entity itself and the tasks it must perform. The training requirements must, however, be determined by someone and that person will usually be the security officer. His initial decisions may or may not be guided by higher authority, but certainly his training program should be reviewed periodically by his superiors. Training must be a continuing process, and one in which the entire organization participates in varying degrees. There are basically three areas of maritime security training: general employee security training, security personnel training, and material maintenance training.

All nonsecurity employees, supervisors, and managers should receive security awareness training on a regular basis. New employees should be indoctrinated concerning the organization's security policies, rules, and regulations, and, most importantly, the reasons for such policies, rules, and regulations. They must be made to understand that their particular installation is in fact at risk, and that the security and safety of those who work there is dependent in part on their security awareness. They must know and understand all emergency security procedures as they pertain to their own particular job requirements, and they must realize the importance of practicing those emergency procedures when organized drills are called. After security indoctrination has been completed, periodic security awareness refresher classes should be given. Routine procedures for keeping employees informed of security threats, employee security breaches and mistakes, and other security matters should be instituted through the use of posters, announcements, and newsletters.

Material maintenance training should be conducted for *all* maritime employees, both security and nonsecurity alike. Material maintenance ensures, or should ensure, that the physical security measures that have been implemented are properly maintained. This means that security fences, protective lighting, CCTV systems, alarms, locks, and communication systems are all kept in good working order and condition. The maintenance personnel should certainly be inculcated with the importance of both their duty and their ability to effect repairs under routine and emergency conditions, but nonmaintenance personnel should also be aware of the importance of physical security measures and be trained to report any material discrepancies they notice.

Security personnel training is by far the most important aspect of an installation's security training program. It is the security personnel, along with the physical security measures, who deter or prevent security breaches. Security personnel constitute the "combat troops" whose job it is to engage, with deadly force if necessary, all intruders. Their job is certainly the most dangerous of any at their installation, and everyone should be made aware of that fact. Those who authorize security training, those who perform such training, and those who undergo such training must all realize that its primary purpose is to train security personnel to fight. Noncombative security procedures are indeed important, and constitute a significant training objective. In the final analysis, however, it is the ability of the security force to stop armed intruders that is paramount to the security of the installation. In the shock of battle people tend to function only to the extent to which they have been trained. The confusion, uncertainty, and paralyzing terror that can ensue in the heat of battle can be surmounted only by those who have been trained to function under combat conditions. This is what training is all about.

For a training program to work, all managers and supervisors must make a commitment to accomplish genuine training on a continuing basis. This means that when security training is scheduled it must be completed. Except in emergencies, personnel who are scheduled for training must be released from their other duties so that they may undergo the training that has been scheduled. Those persons missing the training, for whatever reasons, must undergo makeup training as soon as possible. Of course, security training scheduling must be realistic. The training itself must not be allowed to leave the installation unsecured, such as would be the case if the entire guard force were taken to the pistol range for marksmanship training. Furthermore, unless the operational readiness of the security force is so poor that there is no other alternative, training should never supplant the primary mission of providing security.

One way of ensuring that security training is conducted routinely and effectively is to prepare a security training plan. This plan should identify the training requirements, schedule the training to meet those requirements, and provide a method of handling changes in the schedule if they must occur (such as inclement weather alternatives or changes due to operational contingencies). The training plan should cover a workable period of time and set realistic training objectives for that time period. Usually, semiannual or annual training plans will suffice, although 90-day training plans may be appropriate under certain circumstances. Reports should be prepared subsequent to each training exercise and filed with, or in close proximity to, the training plan. A quick review of the training plan and the reports can then tell the security officer or anyone else who needs to know what the approximate training status of the security organization is at any given time. An example of a semiannual maritime security training plan appears in figure 8.

In this particular example, the security officer has decided on a requirement of four hours' training time per week for his security personnel. Every week, the security officer has designated two of those four hours for pistol and marksmanship training because proficiency with firearms is vital to reducing the organization's liability exposure—private security personnel cause more injuries through improper use of firearms than anything else. The security officer has also listed the other training requirements he feels are important and allowed two hours per month for any miscellaneous or makeup training.

FIG. 8.   Six-month training schedule

TRNG	HR	JAN (weeks)				FEB (weeks)				MAR (weeks)				APR (weeks)				MAY (weeks)				JUN (weeks)				Cum. Tot.
		1	2	3	4	1	2	3	4	1	2	3	4	1	2	3	4	1	2	3	4	1	2	3	4	
Pistol	2	X	X	X	X	X	X	X	X	X	X	X	X	X	X	X	X	X	X	X	X	X	X	X	X	48
SOPs	2	X				X				X				X				X				X				12
I.A.	2		X				X				X				X				X				X			12
Legal	2			X				X				X				X				X				X		12
Misc.	2				X				X				X				X				X				X	12
Weekly Tot.		4	4	4	4	4	4	4	4	4	4	4	4	4	4	4	4	4	4	4	4	4	4	4	4	96
Cum. Tot.		4	8	12	16	20	24	28	32	36	40	44	48	52	56	60	64	68	72	76	80	84	88	92	96	96

One of the most effective forms of training is drilling. Fire drills are routinely practiced aboard ships, for the simple reason that a fire at sea can be the most devastating emergency to befall a vessel. Fire drills should also be practiced aboard offshore installations and, to a lesser degree perhaps, within port facilities for the same reason. Security drills should also be routinely practiced. They are generally aimed at two different groups of employees. The first group consists of nonsecurity employees. These people should know how to react in a security emergency, and whom to contact for help. Unlike the second group, which consists of security personnel, the nonsecurity employees are not trained to fight the security emergency, and the objective of any security drills should be security breach recognition and communication. Such drills can be either announced or unannounced, and should be critiqued afterwards by announcement or publication. Any number of different types of drills can be devised, and are limited only by the imagination of the security officer. Drills conducted for the benefit of security personnel, however, serve a different purpose entirely. Their purpose is to train the security force to react to security breaches in such a manner that intruders are either apprehended or repelled. The training is essentially combat-oriented, and it requires a substantial amount of discipline and supervision.

One of the most effective types of combat drilling consists of what is termed "immediate action" drills. I.A. drills, as they are commonly called, are designed to provide swift and positive reaction to visual or physical intruder contact. They are simple courses of action in which all security personnel are so well trained that minimal commands are required. They can be designed, developed, and utilized by any security force no matter how it is organized, and they can be developed for any foreseeable combat or security situation. It is not feasible to attempt to design immediate action drills for *every* possible situation, however. Instead, immediate action drills are usually developed for a number of specific *types* of situations, and are then utilized under various conditions. The types of immediate action drills that might be developed by a particular security force could include: suspected imminent contact, close contact, counterambush, and counterpenetration drills. Some examples of immediate action drills are discussed below in the sections on shipboard, port facility, and offshore installation security training.

Another area of training that should concern the security officer, so far as the security force is concerned, is night combat. Night combat training includes movement techniques, night vision development, firing considerations, and emotional preparation. With regard to the latter consideration, darkness provides a great deal of protection, and understanding and believing this can help alleviate most of the irrational fears many people retain from childhood. Darkness, in fact, should be preferred by the well-trained and self-confident security guard who understands the effectiveness of protective lighting, perimeter barriers, and an integrated security system. By training to move at night within their areas of responsibility, and learning to negotiate obstacles and utilize the darkness, security personnel enhance their effectiveness and ability to function at night.

Night vision is essential to nighttime security operations, and can be developed by applying three basic principles of night vision. The first principle requires one to allow his eyes to *adapt to darkness.* The human retina is composed of cone cells and rod cells. Cone cells allow us to see color, shape, and sharp contrast. A great deal of light is required to activate them and they do not function under conditions of low illumination. Rod cells, on the other hand, produce a chemical substance called visual purple which makes them active in darkness. They enable us to distinguish general outlines, black, white, and shades of gray. It takes about 30 minutes for the rod cells to produce enough visual purple to activate them once daylight or bright light is diminished. This is because our eyes are "designed" to function in both daylight and darkness and, under natural conditions, the transition period from day to night and vice-versa (known as twilight) is about 30 minutes. In the modern world we go from artificial light to darkness much more rapidly and therefore, if our eyes are to function as they are supposed to, they must be given a chance to adapt to the darkness. The second principle of night vision is the technique of keeping one's attention focused on an object without looking directly at it. Most of our cone cells are concentrated in an area on the retina directly behind the eye's lens. Most of our rod cells are concentrated *around* the area of the cone cells. When one looks directly at an object the image is formed on the cone cell area of the retina, which does not function in reduced light. Consequently, by looking slightly to the left or right of, or above or below, an object the image is formed on the area of the retina which contains the rod cells and which does function in reduced light. The most sensitive area of rod cells varies in individuals but is usually found by looking 6 to 10 degrees away from an object or, in effect, out of the corner of one's eyes. The third principle of night vision is *scanning*. Scanning is the technique of using off-center vision to observe an area or object. When rod cells are used the visual purple they produce is consumed within 4 to 10 seconds, and thus the image detected by them disappears unless it is shifted to other cells. So, as the visual purple in one area of the retina bleaches out one must shift his gaze slightly so that fresh rod cells are used. This is called scanning. To scan a visual target one must move his eyes in short, irregular movements in such a manner so as to concentrate his gaze all over and around his target for short periods of a few seconds at a time.

Visual purple is chemically related to vitamin A, and a serious deficiency of vitamin A will impair one's night vision. Other factors that can impair night vision are a cold, headache, fatigue, narcotics, nicotine, and alcohol. Night vision is also quickly destroyed if bright light is allowed to enter the eye. One technique for preserving night vision when bright light cannot be avoided is to close one eye, thereby preserving the night vision in that eye. Then, after the bright light has been eliminated, the night vision in the one eye will suffice until the other eye re-adapts. Another technique frequently used aboard vessels and aircraft for preserving night vision when light is required to read by is the use of red light. Red light has the shortest wavelength of all visible light, and consequently the least-destructive effect on night vision. If used sparingly for short periods of time, red light will not appreciably impair one's night vision.

As mentioned earlier, negligent misuse of firearms is the single most frequent cause of litigation against private security personnel. When an organization that employs private security personnel is sued as a result of either an accidental or intentional shooting by a security guard, the claim is always the same: the guard was negligent in the handling of his weapon, or the guard was negligently trained in the use of his weapon, or both. Proper firearms training can do much to prevent the former, and proper documentation of such training can provide enough evidence to completely disprove the latter. The key to insulating an organization from negligent liability is an understanding of the term "negligence." Negligence is the doing of something a reasonable person would not do, or the failure to do something a reasonable person would do, under the same or similar circumstances, *where a duty to act or not act exists.* Negligence always boils down to a question of what was reasonable, but there can be no negligence at all if there was no duty on the part of the actor to either act or not act. For instance, a pedestrian coming upon the scene of an automobile accident has no legal duty whatsoever to do anything, regardless of the seriousness of the accident or the extent of injuries sustained by the participants. He can legally turn his back on the people crying in agony for his help and walk away. On the other hand, if he chooses to assist those who have been injured he assumes, by his actions, the duty to act in a reasonable way, and if those whom he assists are injured further because of his failure to act reasonably he can be found negligent and held liable. A maritime operator who employs armed private security personnel has the duty to ensure they are properly trained in the use of deadly force generally, and in the uses of their weapons specifically. The training must be reasonable under the circumstances, and if it can be proven that the training was in fact reasonable, then the negligent training claim will be defeated. Of course, the issue of how well the guard was trained has nothing to do with the claim that the guard was himself negligent. A guard may act unreasonably no matter how well he is trained, but the likelihood of his acting unreasonably diminishes proportionally to the extent of his training. The legal parameters of employing private maritime security personnel have already been discussed, and the security training should reflect those parameters. Specific training areas in the use of firearms shall be discussed in chapter 7. For the present it is sufficient to note that firearms proficiency training is probably the single most important training security personnel can receive next to, perhaps, training in the legal ramifications of the use of those firearms.

Hand-to-hand combat and nonlethal restraint techniques are another important training subject the security officer should consider. The primary objective of all maritime security personnel is to apprehend or repel intruders, but if the intruders are unarmed the use of deadly force is not legally warranted. It is also not warranted if an intruder is armed but does not threaten to use his weapon. How then is an intruder to be legally apprehended, particularly if he refuses to cooperate? The answer is with nonlethal restraint techniques. Security personnel may use that amount of force, short of deadly force, which is reasonably required to apprehend an intruder under those conditions where a citizen's arrest is legally allowed. But if they do not know how to exercise such force they may well fail to make the arrest or, worse yet, they may successfully make the arrest but severely injure the arrestee in the process and thereby expose both themselves and their employer to legal liability. Proper training should reduce the problem substantially. Martial arts, hand-to-hand combat, and nonlethal restraint techniques are all discussed in more depth in chapter 7.

The last topic for discussion before turning to specific shipboard, port facility, or offshore installation security training procedures is the security officer himself. As has already been noted, the security officer must wear a number of different hats in the performance of his responsibilities. In situations where an independent maritime security consultant is not employed, the security officer may be required to conduct a security survey, prepare a security plan, implement the security plan, and then continue to supervise and train all resultant security personnel. This is a tremendous responsibility. It is also a full-time job so far as port facilities are concerned, simply because of the necessary size of the guard forces and the extent of the facilities. On the other hand, a single offshore installation probably need not have a full-time security officer assigned to it, but the offshore operator should have a security officer designated whose responsibilities may include several, if not all, offshore installations in a given geographical area. Ships, however, because of their nature, require a designated security officer as a member of the crew, but again the job need not be a full-time responsibility. The most likely candidate on most commercial vessels is the chief officer.

Once the security plan has been implemented the security officer is primarily responsible for the training of security and nonsecurity personnel, supervision of the security force, and management of the entire security organization. There is no reason, however, why he should not delegate some of his authority to subordinates or independent consultants, and one obvious area where delegation is appropriate is training. Security officers need not be experts in all aspects of security, in fact few if any will ever be that qualified. They should, however, have a working knowledge of all areas so that they can effectively manage the training required. For example, a particular security officer may not be an expert marksman or qualified firearms instructor, although he may well have had substantial experience with handling and firing guns. He could probably conduct the necessary firearms training himself, and do an adequate job, but part of his responsibilities includes ensuring that his security training program is capable of withstanding litigious scrutiny. Consequently, to be reasonably safe, he should arrange for a qualified expert to conduct the firearms training. He remains responsible at all times for such training, he just simply does not conduct it himself.

Good security officers have certain common attributes. First and foremost, they must understand the serious threat faced by the maritime industry and be able to conceptualize that threat as it pertains to their particular organization. They must know, or be willing to learn, the security business to the extent that they can effectively manage their security organization. They must be intimately familiar with the particular maritime enterprise in which their employer is engaged, and know at all times what major evolutions or activities are planned or expected. They should be constantly on the lookout for security-related information from a variety of sources, and must ensure that their superiors are kept abreast of the security situation and the fluctuating capabilities of their security personnel. Finally, they must fully understand the principles of leadership and develop the personal leadership traits that will make them effective leaders of security personnel.

There are eleven leadership principles that have stood the test of time, the rigor of combat, and the challenge of excellence. The application of these leadership principles within the context of maritime security management is not difficult.

1. A leader should be technically and tactically proficient. A security officer should be technically and tactically proficient by being competent in maritime security operations, training, technology, and administration. Simply stated, he should know his job.
2. A leader should know himself and seek self-improvement. A security officer should know himself, by evaluating his strengths and weaknesses. No one can become a successful leader until he knows his own capabilities and limitations. A good security officer will scrutinize his own knowledge and abilities as they relate to his security responsibilities, and do his best to improve any deficiencies he finds.

3. A leader should know his people and look out for their welfare. A security officer should know the security personnel he manages, and look out for their welfare. An unhappy or troubled security employee is a security risk. A security officer must make a concerted effort to know his people on both a personal and professional level. He should take an active interest in their morale, personal problems, and professional development.

4. A leader should keep his people informed. A security officer should keep his people informed, not only as to what is expected of them, but how they are performing. They should also be kept abreast of current developments within the organization as well as all future events that may have a bearing on their jobs or personal lives. Any security intelligence or other information received from local law enforcement or similar agencies should be quickly disseminated.

5. A leader should set the example. A good security officer will set the example by being physically fit and mentally alert at all times. He should exude confidence, enthusiasm, and professionalism. Without such manifestation of strength his people will feel less secure, and if they feel insecure, the security of the maritime entity with which they are entrusted will diminish proportionally.

6. A leader should ensure the task is understood, supervised, and accomplished. A security officer must ensure this by issuing work assignments clearly and concisely; subordinates should be encouraged to clarify anything they do not understand. A security misunderstanding can turn into a deadly mistake, and mistakes have a way of compounding themselves. Once an assignment is made and understood, it should be supervised. Supervision, however, does not mean looking over a subordinate's shoulder until the task is completed. Proper supervision entails the exercise of thought and care.

7. A leader should develop a sense of responsibility in his subordinates. Subordinate security personnel should be encouraged to take responsibility for their work. If they are willing to accept such responsibility, they should be

given the opportunity to do so. The security officer can check on their work without seeming to, or without dampening their enthusiasm, if he gives a little thought to the situation.

8. A leader should train his people as a team. Security personnel especially should be trained as a team. Individual proficiencies are certainly important, and should be fostered, but the guard force will ultimately need to function as a unit if it is to be successful in maintaining an adequate level of security. This is the primary reason drills are conducted—to ascertain the level of unit proficiency: what has been attained and what must be improved.

9. A leader should make sound and timely decisions. A good security officer assists in his unit's proficiency by being able to make sound and timely decisions. In combat, a leader must have the ability to make a rapid estimate of the situation and arrive at a sound decision. He must be able to reason under the most trying conditions, and decide quickly what action is necessary in order to take advantage of tactical opportunities as they occur. The security officer is no different than the combat leader. His security force should be ready for combat every minute it is on duty, and he should be prepared to lead that force in any security emergency.

10. A leader should employ his people in accordance with their capabilities. Besides knowing his own capabilities and limitations, the security officer must know the capabilities and limitations of the entire security organization. He needs to know the operational effectiveness of his guard force if he is to employ it properly and in such a manner as to ensure success.

11. A leader should seek responsibility and accept responsibility for his actions. Any good security officer will take the initiative when the absence of directives allows it. This is what is meant by "seeking responsibility." By seeking responsibility a security officer develops himself professionally and increases his leadership ability. He should also accept responsibility for everything his security organization does or fails to do.

To be an effective leader, the security officer must not only exercise the leadership principles just discussed, he must develop within himself the leadership traits that all great leaders have exhibited in varying degrees throughout history. Subordinates and superiors alike react to other individuals based on their personalities, which are made up of the sum total of their personality traits. Leadership traits are those personal characteristics that help the security officer earn the respect, confidence, willing obedience, and loyal cooperation of his security personnel, all of which he must have if he is to function effectively in the security environment he has been asked to manage. The leadership traits most often recognized by those who study such behavior are:

1. Bearing.	8. Integrity.
2. Courage.	9. Judgment.
3. Decisiveness.	10. Justice.
4. Dependability.	11. Knowledge.
5. Endurance.	12. Loyalty.
6. Enthusiasm.	13. Tact.
7. Initiative.	14. Unselfishness.

Bearing is the impression one creates by his appearance, carriage, and personal conduct. It can be either good or bad but, whichever it is, it will tend to set the professional standard his subordinates will emulate. It will also establish his reputation among his peers and superiors. The security officer should therefore pay particular attention to his bearing at all times, but particularly when he can be observed professionally. He can develop the bearing of a leader by requiring of himself the highest standards in appearance and conduct, avoiding coarse behavior and vulgar language, applying moderation in all personal activities, and habitually maintaining a dignified manner.

In the profession of arms, of which maritime security must be considered a part, courage in leadership is essential. Courage is a mental quality that recognizes fear of danger or criticism but enables one to proceed under those circumstances with calmness and firmness. In most people it is not an inherent quality. Courage must be learned, usually by self-teaching. A security officer can learn courage by studying his reactions to fear, developing calmness through training and self-discipline, maintaining an orderliness in his thought processes, standing for what he believes is right in the face of popular condemnation, and accepting the blame when he is at fault.

Decisiveness is one manifestation of courage. A leader should have the ability to make decisions promptly and be able to announce them in a clear and forceful manner. Like courage, decisiveness is a mental quality one must consciously develop. The security officer can develop this attribute by learning to be positive in his actions, reviewing his past decisions for soundness, and analyzing decisions made by others so that he may profit from their successes or mistakes.

Security, to be effective, must be dependable. Dependability is the certainty of proper performance to an established standard, and is a quality the security officer must develop in both himself and his security organization. His maritime employer must be able to rely upon dependable security if the enterprise is to function smoothly. Dependability can be developed by not making excuses, performing every assigned task to the best of one's ability regardless of personal belief, being exact in details, being punctual, and carrying out the intent as well as the literal meaning of all directives. Sometimes dependability requires a substantial amount of endurance.

Endurance is the mental and physical stamina measured by the ability to withstand pain, fatigue, stress, and hardship. Courage and endurance are similar in that they both require conscious training by the individual. Endurance can be cultivated by physical and mental conditioning. The security officer should engage in physical training, view strenuous physical or mental tasks as personal challenges, and carry out every assignment to the best of his ability.

Enthusiasm is the display of sincere interest and zeal in the performance of one's duties. It has a tendency to be contagious, and every leader should exhibit it at all times, but particularly when distasteful jobs must be accomplished. Enthusiasm can be developed by understanding and believing in one's mission, remaining cheerful and optimistic, explaining to subordinates the reasons for difficult or uninteresting assignments, and by capitalizing on success.

One leadership trait that all security officers should have is initiative. Initiative is the ability to realize what must be done and the willingness to commence a course of action to achieve this goal, even in the absence of specific directives to do so. In most cases the security officer will be considered by his superiors to be the organization's security expert. They will expect him to do whatever is necessary,

within the operational parameters that have been established, to ensure security is maintained. He cannot afford to wait for someone to
tell him what to do. He can help himself maintain initiative by staying mentally and physically alert, training himself to recognize tasks
that need to be done and then doing them, learning to anticipate by
thinking and planning ahead, looking for and accepting responsibilities, and utilizing available resources in the most effective and
efficient manner.

Integrity is indispensable in both a leader and a security officer,
and can best be described as an uprightness of character and moral
principles with the quality of absolute truthfulness. Governmental
security organizations around the world actively engage in attempts
to compromise their opponents' security operatives. Terrorists and
saboteurs will do the same if given the opportunity. A security officer with integrity cannot be compromised. Personal integrity can
be developed by practicing absolute honesty and truthfulness at all
times, standing for what one believes to be right, and placing one's
sense of duty and moral principles above any temptation for compromise.

Judgment is another important quality that any leader or manager
should have because he makes daily decisions that affect the lives and
welfare of those who work for him. Judgment is the quality of being
able to logically weigh the facts of, and possible solutions to, problems
in order to make sound decisions. Judgment can be improved by anticipating situations that require decisions, practicing making es-
timates of situations as they develop, avoiding making rash decisions,
and approaching problems with a commonsense attitude.

The leadership trait of justice is most commonly discussed in connection with military or governmental leaders who must mete out
punishments to subordinates. In most business enterprises punishments, per se, are not awarded by managers or supervisors. However,
work assignments, rewards, and promotions are made on a routine
basis and the effective security manager will ensure that all such activities are made in a just and fair manner. In order to do this he must
be fair, consistent, prompt, and impersonal. He can play no favorites.
He must be honest with himself and avoid the temptation to give in to
emotion.

Knowledge is important in any profession, and the field of security
is no exception. The security officer cannot be professionally and tac-

tically proficient without having obtained the requisite knowledge, and this knowledge can only be gained by concerted effort on his part. One can increase his professional knowledge by maintaining a personal library and a professional file, studying training manuals and other professional books and periodicals, staying abreast of current events, engaging in serious conversations with other professionals, and evaluating one's experiences and the experiences of others in light of professional objectives.

One of the most important attributes any combat leader can display is loyalty, both to his troops and to his superiors. Loyalty works both up and down the chain of command, and in the heat of battle or under adverse conditions everyone needs to know he is supported. It is this feeling of support that allows an individual to continue to function at his optimum capacity. Security personnel, because they often operate alone or detached from the main group, must know they are supported in everything they do. They must know they will not be abandoned or sacrificed, or made a scapegoat for someone else's mistakes. The security officer who fosters this sense of loyalty among his security personnel will be able to rely on their performance when it matters most. He can develop loyalty by defending his subordinates from abuse, never discussing the personal problems of his subordinates with others, standing up for both his subordinates and his superiors when they are unjustly accused, taking the blame for performance shortcomings of his unit, and being discreet in discussing management problems outside his security organization.

Tact is the ability to deal with others without creating offense. In the field of human and business relations, tact is the ability to say and do the proper thing at the right time. Arguably, this is a very subjective pronouncement, for what may appear to one person as the proper thing at the right time may not appear so to another. In any event, tact is usually helpful when attempting to get things done that require cooperation from others over whom one does not have direct authority. Tact can also create more pleasant working conditions for those over whom one does have authority which, in the long run, can improve job performance. The security officer is likely to be placed in situations where tact is helpful because he must deal with numerous outside agencies and his own superiors in the coordination of his security requirements. He should therefore concentrate on being tactful by being courteous and cheerful, exercising consideration of others, cooperating in spirit as well as in fact, maintaining tolerance toward others, and understanding when to be seen both officially and socially.

The last leadership trait is unselfishness. The unselfish leader is one who avoids providing for his own comfort and personal advancement at the expense of others. Subordinates recognize selfishness in a leader immediately, and lose respect for him just as quickly as a result. The security officer should place his own needs last in any tactical situation, and avoid using his position or authority for personal gain, safety, or pleasure in any other situation. He should be considerate of the problems of his subordinates, and assist them wherever appropriate. His people will appreciate his unselfish attitude and, in all likelihood, will do all they can to support him when the situation calls for it.

The situation usually calls for it when the security officer least expects it, that is, during actual combat or security operations. If he has led and trained his people by following the leadership principles just discussed, and if he has developed within himself the leadership traits needed to make an effective leader, he will more than likely have a security organization capable of meeting any security threat when it occurs. The training of security personnel must differ, however, with regard to the specific entity concerned. The previous discussion has involved general concepts of training and leadership. The following discussions address specific security training considerations for vessels, port facilities, and offshore installations respectively.

SHIPBOARD SECURITY TRAINING PROCEDURES

Shipboard security training procedures must focus on two types of shipboard personnel: those assigned security duties and those not assigned security duties. If additional crew members or professional security personnel have been placed aboard for the purposes of performing security duties the training distinction can be easily made. If, however, no additional security personnel have been placed aboard then the entire crew must be trained in shipboard security procedures. Whichever the case, the first shipboard security training task is security awareness indoctrination of *all* crew members concerning the security threats facing their vessel and themselves. An aware crew is a more alert crew. Once crew members realize that their lives are in danger if their ship is pirated, hijacked, or sabotaged, and once they realize the potential for worldwide maritime terrorism, they will be more likely to take an active interest in the security of their ship. Indoctrination, however, must really begin at the top. When vessel owners and operators refuse to seriously consider the security threats facing their ships their crews cannot be expected to pay much attention to the problem. However, since this discussion concerns the implementation of a ship security plan, it can reasonably be assumed that the vessel's owner is one of the enlightened few who recognizes his massive legal liability with regard to negligent maritime security practices and who has decided to do something about it. Consequently, the next step after security awareness indoctrination of the crew is the implementation of a shipboard security training program. Security training can be conducted in a number of ways. The individual crew member can be taught either on or off the ship, in a classroom, or through the chain of command. Crew members must be trained individually in the various security procedures to be used on board. They must learn how to stand a security watch, communicate properly, and use firearms. They must understand access control procedures and shipboard fighting tactics. Once crew members have learned their individual security skills, they must be taught to work as a team and must be trained together on board. Team training is accomplished in the form of drills.

Initial encounters with terrorists and pirates are sudden, short, and often so unexpected that the opportunity to thwart the attack is lost unless immediate and positive offensive action can be taken. If such action is taken, the chances of repelling the attack are extremely good. For this reason it is essential that simple immediate action drills be taught and practiced. The principles of any immediate action drill are simplicity, aggressiveness, and speed. Drills enable the crew to reduce the reaction time required to assume an offensive posture. Once the immediate threat has been met the master or senior mate aboard can take further appropriate action if necessary. Discipline, prior planning, and decisive leadership are the fundamentals required to successfully execute an immediate action drill.

There are a number of foreseeable shipboard situations for which immediate action drills can be developed. They are:

1. A disturbance or suspicious activity on the pier at which the vessel is moored.

2. A disturbance or suspicious activity in the vicinity of the vessel while she lies at anchor.
3. An intruder or intruders attempting to board from the pier.
4. An intruder or intruders attempting to board while the vessel lies at anchor.
5. An intruder or intruders attempting to board while the vessel is underway.
6. An intruder or intruders attempting to board while the vessel renders assistance at sea, or while she receives or discharges pilots underway.
7. An intruder or intruders aboard.

All ship security personnel must thoroughly understand the significance of these situations and train for their eventuality. Just as a football team develops and practices certain plays to be used under various circumstances, a vessel's security forces must know and understand their "plays." Like the football team, they must practice their drills until they are capable of responding to the given situations in an automatic and effective manner. It is the job of the ship's security officer to tailor such drills to the specific configuration of his vessel and her manning level. The drill scenarios offered below are merely examples of the type of immediate action drills that may be devised.

Situation: Disturbance or suspicious activity on the pier. The first person to become aware of a disturbance or suspicious activity on the pier should be the gangway watch. Remember, this is a twenty-four-hour watch that should be posted at all accesses to the vessel whenever she is lying dockside. Accesses should be kept to a minimum while the ship is working, and should be reduced to only one during periods of inactivity.

Immediate action drill: Once the gangway watch has determined that there is cause for concern (when in doubt he should assume there is), he should immediately inform the roving patrol and mate on watch that there is suspicious activity on the pier. This communication will normally be made by hand-held radio. Upon receiving such information the roving patrol does *not* proceed to the pier side of the vessel. Instead, he maintains a vigilant watch on the opposite side of the ship (where he should be roving in any case—see chapter 4) in case the pier activity is a diversionary tactic. If the roving patrol is armed he should immediately draw his pistol and carry it in a ready but safe position. The gangway watch should do the same.

Subsequent action: The gangway watch should continue to observe the suspicious activity until he is confident the ship is in no danger or until such time as he determines the ship *is* in danger. This may take only a few minutes or much longer, depending upon the situation. If he determines that the ship is in danger, and the mate on watch has not yet arrived at the gangway (which he should do within two minutes of receiving the gangway watch's warning) to make the decision, the gangway watch should muster the duty security team at the gangway. Immediately upon his arrival at the gangway, the mate must take charge of the situation and direct the security team as it arrives. The security team members should take no more than three minutes to respond to the call, and should be armed with shotguns. Upon their arrival at the gangway the mate should rapidly brief them on the situation and post one man to the bow and another to the stern. Thus, within a very short time after the gangway watch notices the suspicious activity, the ship should have security personnel on both the bow and the stern armed with shotguns and on either side of the ship armed with pistols. The mate should also be armed with a pistol, making a total security force of a minimum of five. The security team can consist of any number of individuals, but should have no fewer than two. If more than two security team members muster at the gangway the mate should either direct them to other areas of the ship or keep them with him, as the situation requires. In any event, once the security team members have been posted the mate must assess the situation further. If no immediate action is required, he should physically check to ensure each of his men is in position and then issue whatever orders he deems necessary to protect the integrity of the vessel. If the master is on board, the mate's next obvious duty is to report to him both the nature of the suspicious activity and the security status of the vessel. At that point, the master must decide whether the suspicious activity warrants notifying the local authorities, maintaining the vessel in a security alert status, or standing down the security alert. If the master is not aboard then the mate reports to the senior officer on board, who makes the same decision. If the mate is the senior officer aboard, then he makes the decision. Of course, if the situation is such that the security force was required to immediately engage armed intruders then that decision is not necessary, at least not until after the crisis has passed and the intruders have been repelled.

Situation: Disturbance or suspicious activity in the vicinity of the vessel while at anchor. The first person or persons who should become aware of suspicious activity in the vessel's vicinity while she is anchored is the roving patrol. There should be two roving patrols on watch at all times while the ship is anchored.

Immediate action drill: The roving patrol who becomes aware of the suspicious activity should simultaneously notify the other roving patrol and the mate on watch that he has noticed suspicious activity on or in the water, and describe the location and nature of the activity. This should be done via hand-held radio while the roving patrol continues to observe the disturbance. Upon receiving such communication, the mate should immediately lay to the closest point on board where he can observe the suspicious activity in order to determine whether the duty security team should be mustered. In the meantime, both roving patrols should remain alert and within their assigned areas, drawing their weapons and holding them in a safe but ready position.

Subsequent action: If the mate determines the duty security team should be summoned, he does so and musters it at whatever location is appropriate. This could be at the rail where the roving patrol has spotted the disturbance or where the mate happens to be at the time he gives the order to muster. Once the security team arrives at the designated position the mate should point out the suspicious activity, issue whatever orders he deems important, and post the team members wherever the tactical situation requires. As a rule of thumb, or where the tactical situation may not be clear, one security team member should be posted on the bow and the other at the stern. The mate should position himself where he can best observe the disturbance. As before, the security team members should be armed with shotguns and the mate with a pistol. At this point the mate should report to the master or, more likely, the chief mate. The ship's security bill will dictate the actions of the other crew members once a security alert has been sounded, but in all likelihood the master will have proceeded to the bridge and the chief officer to the location where the mate has positioned himself. Assuming this is the case, the mate reports to the chief officer who then assumes tactical control over the immediate situation while keeping the master informed by radio. If the vessel is anchored in a recognized anchorage, the master should have commenced establishing radio contact with the local authorities as soon as he arrived on the bridge. Once radio contact with the authorities is established, the master should keep them informed during the entire security incident, advising them if he must repel boarders and requesting assistance where necessary.

Situation: Intruder or intruders attempting to board from the pier. As with the suspicious activity on the pier scenario, the first person to become aware of actual intruders should normally be the gangway watch, since he should be in a position to observe the entire length of the pier and should have noticed suspicious activity on the pier prior to any attempt by intruders to board. On the other hand, since the roving patrol should be concentrating on areas not readily observable by the gangway watch, it is possible that the roving patrol will be the first person to notice the intruders. This drill should be employed where no suspicious activity has been noticed prior to an attempted boarding.

Immediate action drill: The gangway watch should command the intruders to stop and identify themselves. As he does so, he should be particularly alert to any indication of hostility or unusual behavior on the part of those approaching his vessel. The term "intruder" applies to anyone who attempts to board without prior authorization and may include bona fide visitors, so the security watch needs to ascertain, if he can, the nature of the intrusion. Any number of factors may be relevant, such as the time of day or night, the number of persons approaching the ship, the packages or baggage carried, and so on. In any event, once they have received the order to stop, the intruders will do one of two things: they will either comply or not. If they do not comply, they may well alter their behavior at this point by producing weapons and/or attempting to forcibly board the vessel. For this reason it is important to give the initial command to stop when the suspicious persons are as far away from the vessel as possible.

Subsequent action: If the intruders stop as they have been commanded, the next duty of the security watch is to proceed with the usual gangway security procedures that have been established for visitor identification and registration, unless the situation appears out of the ordinary (such as the time of night). If the situation does appear out of the ordinary, or if the intruders refuse to stop when commanded, the gangway watch should immediately draw his weapon, muster the security team, and either repeat his command to stop or order those stopped to stand fast. If the intruders ignore his commands he should fire a warning shot. If the intruders open fire he should return their fire. At the sound of gunfire, or upon hearing the security alert on his radio, the roving patrol should draw his weapon and prepare to repel intruders from his side of the vessel. He must refrain from giving in to the urge to rush to the gangway, thus leaving the seaward side of the ship unprotected. If he hears gunfire but no security alert from the gangway watch, the roving patrol should sound the alert as well as contact the mate on watch. The mate, however, should have already been alerted if the gangway watch summoned the security team, or should have heard the warning shot himself, and been on his way to the gangway by this time. When the security team arrives at the gangway it reinforces the watch as required. The mate should arrive at about the same time and take charge of the situation. If the intruders have been successfully repelled by the gangway watch by the time the security team arrives, its members should be posted to the bow and stern by the mate. If, however, the gangway watch still requires assistance the mate should direct one team member to remain with the gangway watch while the other proceeds to a position from which the intruders can be caught in a cross fire, if possible. The mate should also assess the situation to determine whether reinforcements will be required. If so, he should muster the reserve security team, or attempt to make contact with port facility security personnel, or both. If the master and the chief officer are on board, the chief officer should take charge of the immediate tactical situation while the master attempts to contact outside help.

In most cases the intruders will not wish to fight a pitched gun battle in order to gain access to the vessel, and will flee the scene either upon receiving the warning shot from the gangway watch or as soon as the security team arrives. Terrorists have no desire to die for their cause, although many of them recognize the possibility. They would much rather abandon their target for another, less-prepared one at a later date. In fact, truly professional terrorists would have determined prior to the attack whether the ship had the capability of resisting and would have selected another target entirely.

Situation: Intruder or intruders attempting to board the vessel while at anchor. As with the previous drill, suspicious activity should have been noticed prior to an attempted boarding and the appropriate immediate action drill commenced, particularly in this case since *any* activity in or on the water surrounding an anchored vessel should be considered suspicious. Assuming, however, that no suspicious activity has been noted by the time the intruders actually attempt to board, the roving patrol should detect their presence either while they are alongside or shortly after they get on deck.

Immediate action drill: There is no legitimate reason to surreptitiously board an anchored vessel, and the roving patrol should therefore immediately draw his pistol while simultaneously taking cover. If the intruders are unarmed, he should command them to stop, and fire an immediate warning shot if they do not. If they are armed he should open fire without warning.

Subsequent action: At the sound of gunfire the other roving patrol sounds a security alert by summoning the duty security team on his radio, draws his weapon, and prepares to repel boarders. The mate on watch, the chief officer, and the security team, all armed, should arrive on deck at about the same time. The security team should be armed with either shotguns or submachine guns, and should reinforce the roving patrol who is under fire. It should be directed by the mate until the chief officer arrives to take charge. The master should immediately proceed to the bridge and attempt to contact the local authorities for assistance. If the reserve security team is required, the master should instruct it after receiving advice by radio from the chief officer.

Situation: Intruder or intruders attempting to board while the vessel is underway. Pirates or hijackers attempting to board a vessel underway must do so by the use of helicopters or fast watercraft, usually from astern. In either case, they must operate relatively close to land and previous similar activity should be known. Consequently, if the ship is transiting waters where such activity is known to have occurred, such as the Phillip Channel or other similarly notorious areas, an after lookout should be posted. Furthermore, the vessel's underway watch should be alert to possible boarding activity. The after lookout's job is to spot oncoming watercraft or aircraft far enough in advance to alert the bridge of their approach. He should be in direct communication with the mate on watch, and should be posted in a location from which proper observation can be made, communication with the bridge can be had, and control of the ship's spotlights can be effected. Since a gangway watch or roving patrol will not be posted while the vessel is underway, the duty underway security team should consist of four members rather than two. Two of the members should be armed with shotguns or submachine guns, and the other two should be armed with rifles. The after lookout need not be armed.

Immediate action drill: As soon as the after lookout spots aircraft or watercraft astern of the vessel he should notify the bridge and indicate he has them under observation. Once he is convinced that they are in fact approaching the ship he should advise the mate, who should then advise the chief officer that the vessel is being approached. The chief officer should immediately alert the security team and then proceed to the after lookout's position to ascertain the situation.

Subsequent action: If the chief officer concurs with the lookout's assessment he should muster the security team and place the vessel on security alert. The security team should be posted in positions best suited to repel boarders and provide cover. Approaching aircraft and watercraft should be considered hostile and should be fired upon by the riflemen long before they are in a position to effect a boarding. However, before the chief officer gives the order to commence firing the master should attempt to communicate with the approaching craft by both radio and loud-hailer, and if possible the attempted communication and any responses should be taped. If it is dark, the ship's spotlights should be trained on the approaching craft during the loud-hailing attempt. (It should be noted that in this and certain other assault situations like Iranian RPG attacks, a ship with a 30- or 50-calibre machine gun could do a much better job of protecting herself. So far as this drill is concerned, however, it shall be assumed that only personal small arms are available to the crew.) If the rifle fire does not cause the approaching craft to break off, and an attempted boarding ensues via rope ladders or grappling hooks and lines, the boarders should be taken under fire by the security team members armed with shotguns or submachine guns. The riflemen should continue to fire at the delivery vehicles. The boarders and their craft should be spotlighted, in order both to assist the security team in selecting targets and to create a psychological deterrent. If the boarders are delivered by boat, the vessel's protective glare-projected lighting should be used. Also, if the ship has been outfitted with high-intensity strobe lights for just such a contingency, they should obviously be employed. During the boarding attempt the master should commence evasive maneuvering. His ship will certainly not be able to outrun the delivery craft, but he can make it more difficult to land boarders. He should also attempt to contact whatever local authorities may be in the vicinity and request coast guard or military assistance.

Situation: Intruder or intruders aboard. This situation can develop in any number of ways. The vessel can be at sea, at anchor, or at dockside. The intruders may have killed or wounded the security watch and come aboard before the alarm could be sounded or the security team could stop the intrusion. They may have managed to sneak aboard without being detected by the security watch. They may have successfully executed a ruse, such as acting as pilots or distressed mariners. They may have simply overpowered the security force. In any event, the intruders are aboard. In all likelihood they will proceed to either the bridge or the engine room. This situation requires more flexibility than any other security scenario, and is also the most dangerous and difficult to combat. Unless the security force has been able to retreat inside the vessel and lock the intruders out, the intruders must be located, surrounded, and isolated. They may have taken members of the crew hostage. More than likely they will be someplace inside the vessel rather than on deck, and therefore the security procedures that should be followed differ substantially from those previously discussed. However, before the security team can react to the intruders being aboard, it must know they are aboard. The first indication of that may be when the intruders burst upon the bridge in an armed frenzy. Any number of scenarios can be envisioned, but for the purposes of this particular immediate action drill it will be assumed no warning has been given prior to the intruders' arrival on the bridge.

Immediate action drill: The duty security team and all reserve security team personnel must be alerted to the fact that intruders are not only aboard but on the bridge. This can only be done if such an eventuality has been previously planned for and the necessary alarms installed so that they may be activated from the bridge with little or no warning. Two or more silent alarm switches should be installed on the bridge; when activated, they sound an alarm wherever the duty security team stands by, as well as in the master's and chief officer's cabins, but not on the bridge. The alarm should be used for only the one eventuality—that the bridge has been seized. The immediate action drill for those on the bridge is therefore to activate one of the alarm switches.

Subsequent action: All security team personnel must be trained and prepared to act without guidance from the ship's officers if the bridge alarm is sounded. This is because there may be no officers left alive or unrestrained who can assume control. Hopefully, though, both the master and the chief officer would not be on the bridge at the same instant the intruders seized it, and therefore one of them should be available to take charge of the situation. If either of them were in his cabin when the bridge alarm was sounded, or were within earshot of the alarm, he should immediately proceed to the duty security team area and take charge of all security personnel. In either case, whether led by an officer or not, all security personnel must react quickly to contain the intruders, who are now assumed to have gained control of the bridge. In order to do so, the security personnel must surround the bridge. The configuration of every ship is different, but it is probable that at least four men would be required to do this: one at each topside bridgewing approach, one stationed aft on the same level protecting their backs, and one stationed internally at the foot of the ladder leading to the bridge from the deck below. The men should take up covered firing positions from which they can shoot anyone attempting to leave the bridge. To get to these positions they should have moved quickly and silently aft from the security team area to an outside location from which they could move to their topside positions. The level above the bridge should be secured before they settle into position. Once the bridge has been surrounded, the security personnel need to know whether any other areas of the ship have been taken. The most likely areas are the engine room and the radio room. If the radio room is on the same level as the bridge they will not be able to secure it, which is the main reason why either the master or the chief officer should have a radio transmitter in his cabin. At the same time the bridge surrounding detail was dispatched topside, at least one man should have proceeded to the radio room, master's cabin, or chief officer's cabin in order to attempt outside communication. Two others should have proceeded to the engine room in order to secure it. Thus, a minimum of at least seven security personnel are needed to react to an intruder takeover of the bridge. Most commercial vessels are not yet carrying additional security personnel, but if and when they do, six (two per watch) should be the minimum number carried. Assuming that either the master or the chief officer was able to get to the security personnel after the bridge was seized, and assuming no security personnel were on the bridge at the time, the requisite seven people should be available.

Of course, there are some very real questions of policy presented in this scenario, the main one being: Should the ship fight back if intruders manage to get aboard and seize control? Only the ship's policymakers can answer that question, but it is certainly one that the ship's security planner needs to have answered when he prepares the ship security plan.

Another security scenario closely related, but slightly different, involves the situation in which intruders are aboard but no one knows exactly where, and control of the ship has not been seized. This situation might occur if a saboteur managed to gain access to the vessel, planning to plant a bomb and depart. If this is the case, and his presence is suspected but his location is not known, a systematic search of the ship must be undertaken. The search technique is the same, whether local law enforcement personnel or the ship's own security forces are employed. Each deck must be cleared from the uppermost level down. Guards must be posted at all external and internal accesses to each level in order to ensure the intruder cannot return to a previously cleared deck. These guards can move with the clearing force, deck by deck, but must always remain one deck above the clearing force. The clearing force should start at the bow and move aft on each deck or level. Once the intruder is located he must be isolated or captured.

When either searching for intruders or moving toward their last known location, the ship's security personnel should employ certain movement techniques. Such techniques should be the subject of extensive training, and can be combined with the training subjects of interior defense and booby traps mentioned in chapter 4. All security personnel must receive training in moving and fighting within the ship.

Ships are primarily fabricated out of steel. Decks, bulkheads, overheads, doors, and ladders are all made of steel. Passageways are narrow, spaces are confining, and entire decks can become pitch-black labyrinths. Death can lurk around every corner, and ricocheting friendly bullets can inflict more casualties than any aimed fire from the intruders. Passageways are extremely dangerous, for intruder and defender alike. They afford unlimited opportunities for ambush, and should be negotiated carefully by no less than two ship security personnel (one security team) any time intruder presence is suspected. Team members should not move down the center of the passageway. All movements should be against the bulkhead, with both team members moving along the same side of the passageway. Where ambushes or booby traps are likely, movement should employ a leapfrogging technique in which one team member covers the movement of the other team member as he moves 10 to 20 feet down the passageway and then stops. Once he stops, the covering team member moves forward, passes him, and moves another 10 to 20 feet down the passageway. Then they repeat the maneuver.

Ladders must also be negotiated with great care. Before negotiating any ladder a visual search of the immediate area must be made, but in such a manner that the searcher is not exposed to the ladder well or the approaches to it. This can be accomplished most easily with the use of a mirror. One common method of employing a mirror is to attach it to the stock of a shotgun; then, by standing to the side of the ladder well and extending the stock of the weapon into the open space, the person holding it may view the ladder to determine whether it is safe to proceed. A bulkhead opening at either the top or bottom of a ladder must be negotiated as carefully as the ladder itself. If the opening is in the direction of movement, and only to one side of the ladder, the two men should stay as close to the bulkhead as possible on that side as they negotiate the ladder. If there is a T where the ladder terminates (an opening on both sides), either bulkhead may be hugged. Passageway junctions should be negotiated in the same manner.

Once the security teams have located and isolated the intruders the next problem facing the master is what to do with them. If the intrusion has occurred while the vessel was moored or anchored, and the master has confidence in the local law enforcement authorities, he can simply sit tight and await their arrival. This is probably the most desirable course of action since it exposes his crew to the least amount of risk. If, however, he feels he must act immediately or that the local law enforcement response will be inadequate, the master must be prepared to act. The confined spaces of a ship lend themselves wonderfully to the use of riot control agents such as tear gas, Mace, and nausea-producing agents. Intruders who have already been contained by the ship's security personnel, and who refuse to surrender, can be incapacitated through the use of such agents. In their absence large amounts of smoke may achieve the desired result. If smoke devices are also not available (riot control agents should be made a part of the ship's armament), and the intruders have been securely isolated, the master can simply wait them out. Hunger and thirst will take their toll eventually, and in the meantime negotiations for the intruders' surrender can begin.

If hostages have been taken, and riot control agents are either unavailable or inadvisable, negotiations should commence immediately. A cornered terrorist may well barter his hostages for his own release if he is convinced that his mission has failed and that no great publicity will be forthcoming. Hostage negotiation, however, is an extremely delicate operation that should be left to trained professionals if they are available or can reasonably be made available. If a hostage is injured or killed as a result of overzealous or unprofessional hostage negotiations by untrained ship's personnel the ship and her owners may be exposed to unnecessary legal liability.

Situation: Intruder or intruders attempting to board while the vessel renders assistance at sea, or while she receives or discharges pilots underway. Both situations should be handled in about the same manner.

Immediate action drill: Whoever is conning the vessel when at-sea assistance is rendered or pilots are received or discharged should muster the duty security team at the appropriate location on deck.

Subsequent action: The chief officer should supervise the evolution and the duty security team should therefore report to him when mustering. Team members should be placed in locations on deck where they can adequately cover the entire operation. All persons should be searched as they come aboard. The use of tact in this situation may be advisable, and some searches may even be made without seeming to do anything other than provide a helping hand. Regardless of the amount of tact exercised, however, it is important that all persons who come aboard be searched. Once they are on board they should be closely monitored until they depart the ship.

The immediate action drill scenarios just discussed are by no means comprehensive. They are examples of the types of drills that can be devised. Every ship's security officer should give careful thought to the contingencies that might befall his vessel, and plan his shipboard security training procedures accordingly.

PORT FACILITY SECURITY TRAINING PROCEDURES

Port facility security training procedures bear a closer resemblance to shoreside security training methods than any other aspect of maritime security. In fact, they are virtually identical. All of the comments made under the general security training procedures section of this chapter apply to port facilities. Furthermore, most standard law enforcement techniques and procedures are applicable to port facility security. The first training distinction the port facility's security officer must make is between security and nonsecurity personnel training requirements. Security personnel must undergo extensive initial and continuing training in all aspects of security, but nonsecurity personnel should also undergo substantial security awareness training. This training should be on a continuing basis as well. The security officer should therefore maintain two separate training schedules, one for his security personnel and one for all other nonsecurity personnel employed by the port authority or in the port facility by resident businesses.

It is the resident businesses' employees, such as longshoremen, food handlers, fuel oil dispensers, ships' agents, and various office workers who will present the most problems for the security officer so far as security awareness training is concerned. Any training of such personnel will almost certainly be viewed by their employers as a great inconvenience and a loss of time and money. After all, they must continue to pay those employees for the time spent in security awareness training. The port authority, in fact, may take the same dim view. It will be up to the security officer to convince his employer, the port authority, that such training is not only necessary but imperative so far as the security of the facility is concerned, and that they should require compliance by the resident businesses. One of the things he should do is review the service agreements and other contractual arrangements between the port authority and resident businesses in order to ascertain what legal obligations the resident businesses have to the port authority so far as security matters are concerned. What he will probably discover is that no obligations exist at all. Consequently, he should work with the port authority's legal counsel in developing appropriate security clauses for subsequent contracts that will define the resident businesses' security maintenance, training, and pre-employment screening obligations.

Employee security awareness training, while important, is clearly not the security officer's most pressing training responsibility. The training of the port facility's security personnel, however, is. Security training must not be considered as a one-time affair for new employees, or even an occasional or periodic matter for seasoned personnel. It must be looked upon as part of the routine, day-to-day security operations of the port facility. The security officer's job can be summed up in three words: administration, training, and supervision, or ATS for short. What balance the security officer strikes among the three will depend upon numerous variables. For instance, an experienced and well-trained guard force may only require 10 percent of the security officer's time for training. If his administrative duties take 40 percent of his time and he allots 10 percent of his time for nonsecurity employee training, then he will have 40 percent of his time remaining for operational supervision. Thus, the security officer can plan on a 40-20-40 ATS time ratio. On the other hand, an inexperienced guard force in a new security program may require substantially more training and supervision, such that the security officer must initially allot an ATS time ratio of perhaps 10-40-50. Of course, delegating some of his duties in all three areas of responsibility can affect the ATS time ratio as well. So, for instance, even though the security force may need to spend 30 percent of its time training, if the security officer employs outside experts to conduct some of the training he may only need to spend 10 percent of his actual time in this area, which would free up more time for supervisory and administrative duties.

The training of security personnel must focus on two separate areas of knowledge and skills: individual and operational. The individual areas include such things as weapons proficiency, legal knowledge, hand-to-hand combat skills, and so on. Operational areas include security procedures, tactical deployment, and communications networking. From an overall security standpoint, operational skills are much more important than individual ones. From a legal liability viewpoint, they are probably equally important. Individual training considerations have already been discussed. Operational training is best done through the use of drills. The security officer should devise security scenarios based upon foreseeable operational situations and train his security force to respond appropriately. These drills can be referred to as immediate action drills, and any number may be invented. The examples provided below illustrate the concept.

Situation: Intruder or intruders attempting to penetrate the outer perimeter barrier. The discovery of intruders attempting to penetrate the outer perimeter barrier can be made in any number of ways. They could be observed via CCTV; they could activate electronic alarms; or they could be discovered by either security patrols or stationary guards. The initial security response obviously depends upon the method of discovery. So far as getting people on the scene, the response to an alarm triggered half a mile away will be different from the response of a single guard who notices a perimeter disturbance 50 yards from his post. The method of dealing with the intruders, however, should be the same. For the purposes of this drill, it will be assumed the intruders were noticed by a security patrol of two.

Immediate action drill: There are three things the security personnel must do upon discovering intruders, and they must be done in the same order every time. Depending upon the situation they may be performed virtually simultaneously, but they must be performed in the proper order. The guards must mentally assess the situation, report it, and then react to it: *assess, report, react.* The reaction to a single, unarmed pilferer will be different than to three or four armed intruders, so the guards must first assess the situation in order to know the safest way to react. Next, they need to report the situation in order to alert the rest of the guard force and ensure backup support if it is required. Finally, they must react in the safest and most effective manner.

How they assess, report, and react may be determined by whether the guards believe themselves to have been seen by the intruders. If it is likely they have not been spotted by the intruders (glare-projected protective lighting should help), the immediate action drill for the guards is to *freeze* and *observe.* They must particularly ascertain the number of intruders and what weapons, if any, they are carrying. A few seconds of observation may save lives, and they will not appreciably assist the intruders once they have been discovered. Since there are two guards in this scenario, reporting and reacting can be done simultaneously. One can report while the other reacts.

Subsequent action: The initial reaction in almost all cases is to command the intruders to halt. This command may be given from a covered position with weapons drawn or from some other less combative stance, depending upon the circumstances. However, it is always better to be prepared for the worst eventuality. If the intruders are armed they should be commanded to place their weapons slowly and carefully on the ground and step away from them. At this point, if there are more intruders than the two guards can safely handle they should be commanded to lie face-down on the ground with their ankles and wrists crossed while the guards await reinforcements. Otherwise, they should be apprehended, searched for weapons, and then interrogated. All intruders should be turned over to local law enforcement personnel as soon as possible.

Situation: Pilferers discovered inside a cargo storage area. This can be an open area, a fenced compound, or a secured building. They can be discovered before, during, or after an act of pilfering. In all instances the immediate action is the same.

Immediate action drill: Again, the security personnel must assess the situation, report it, and then react to it. Pilferers, unlike most terrorists and many saboteurs, will attempt to flee if discovered. Security guards must therefore be prepared to apprehend fleeing suspects once they make their presence known. If there are more pilferers than guards, the best that can be hoped for is that each guard will successfully apprehend one pilferer. For that reason, the guards may wish to position themselves appropriately before executing the immediate action drill, which is to command the pilferers to freeze.

Subsequent action: As many of the pilferers as possible should be apprehended, searched, and interrogated. All evidence of pilferage should be preserved. Pilferers and evidence should be turned over to the local authorities.

Situation: Moored vessel under attack requests assistance. At first blush, a full-blown firefight on the dock does not seem very likely. However, a reasonable scenario can be developed without stretching the imagination too far. Vessels are moored in port facilities every day that are excellent potential terrorist targets because of their nature or the nature of the cargo they carry. These ships remain completely unprotected, even as maritime terrorism continues to grow. If one were targeted by a terrorist group for a dockside seizure, and that group did not expect to meet armed resistance from the ship, a pitched gun battle could easily erupt as a result of the terrorists' surprise and anger at being foiled. On the other hand, the terrorists might well plan for limited resistance and simply meet more than they had anticipated. In either case, a vessel moored in the port facility could come under attack, respond to that attack, and request assistance from the port facility. Even without such a request, port facility security personnel should certainly respond to any disturbance on one of the facility's piers, not to mention gunfire.

Immediate action drill: The duty security supervisor should immediately dispatch the port facility's security reaction team to the ship in distress, or to the location of the disturbance if the precise nature of the problem is not known.

Subsequent action: As soon as the security reaction team has been dispatched the security supervisor should notify all guard posts and patrols of the disturbance and its location. They should *not*, however, be ordered to assist. The reaction team will be assisted, hopefully, by the local law enforcement agencies which the security supervisor should call as soon as he has dispatched his reaction team and notified his security force. If the fight is not over by the time the law enforcement personnel arrive on the scene, complete tactical control should be passed to their commander or officer in charge.

Situation: Bomb threat received by telephone. Bomb warnings can be delivered by mail or taped messages, but the most common form of delivery is by telephone. The port facility security officer should ensure that all facility telephone operators, receptionists, managers, and other key personnel are provided a telephone bomb threat checklist and that the checklists are kept in locations where they can be referred to instantly. A checklist will help stem the natural tendency on the part of the person receiving the call to panic, and will also assist in obtaining valuable information needed to locate the bomb and perhaps the culprit. The checklist should be designed to obtain as much information as possible about the bomb and its location, and should contain simple, fill-in-the-blank questions which can be read directly to the caller. The questions should elicit information regarding the exact location of the bomb, its appearance, the time set for detonation, the explosive material used, and the reason for its emplacement. The questions should be worded so as to express concern for human lives and *not* the facility or material goods. In addition to the checklist, the same people should be provided a "bomb threat follow-up form" which provides step-by-step instructions as to what to do after the bomb threat has been received (including names of agencies and persons to call, and their telephone numbers). It should also contain informational requests that must be filled in while the call and caller are still fresh in the person's memory. These include such items as the date and time of the call, a synopsis of the language used, the sex and approximate age of the caller, the type of speech employed (tone, speed, characteristics, and accents), and any background noises heard during the call.

Immediate action drill: Upon notification of the receipt of a bomb threat the port facility security officer, or duty security supervisor, should immediately advise all local law enforcement and fire-fighting agencies of the threat and provide them with the information obtained.

Subsequent action: After notifying the proper authorities, the security officer must also make his recommendations to his superiors regarding evacuation of the facility or parts of the facility. Finally, he should arrange to have security and maintenance personnel standing by to assist fire fighters and police in any bomb search that might develop.

These drill scenarios, and others, can be developed by the port facility security officer in the process of training his personnel. One way of augmenting his training program, and possibly raising the level of professional competence among his security personnel, is to encourage them to become reserve police officers within the local community. Many police departments maintain reserve officer programs that provide the same standard of law enforcement training to their reserve officers as their regular officers. Any private security force that can boast of reserve police officers among its personnel can benefit greatly from their training and knowledge of current police doctrine, not to mention their contacts within the law enforcement community.

OFFSHORE INSTALLATION SECURITY
TRAINING PROCEDURES

Offshore installation security training procedures should focus primarily on security awareness training for the nonsecurity employee. The offshore security officer, in all likelihood, will be responsible for a number of offshore installations. These installations will not have full-time security employees on board. What they should have aboard, however, are offshore workers who have been fully indoctrinated in security awareness and who are willing to accept some of the responsibility for the installation's security. In all instances except outright assault, the key to the installation's security is access control. Access control must begin onshore with proper pre-employment screening, employee monitoring, and visitor identification procedures. Thorough searches of all baggage, packages, carryons, equipment, and supplies must be made routinely and consistently, not only ashore but at the installation end as well. Regular inspections of all areas of the installation should be made randomly by supervisory personnel.

The primary security threat faced by offshore installations is sabotage, either terrorist-motivated or otherwise, and, through sabotage, extortion. The July 1988 North Sea disaster involving Occidental Petroleum Corporation's *Piper Alpha* oil platform, in which 166 workers lost their lives, has unfortunately illustrated to the entire world the potential devastation a saboteur could create. There has been no publicized indication that the *Piper Alpha* tragedy was caused by anything other than equipment failure (one common opinion is that the natural gas compression apparatus onboard somehow developed a leak which was then ignited by mechanical failure of some sort), but the horrendous potential for loss of life and revenues (over $1.2 billion per year to the British government alone) raises the fine art of extortion to potentially new heights. If metal fatigue, equipment failure, or just plain old age really did cause the disaster, a small incendiary or explosive device could do the same. One of the major areas of security training the offshore security officer should therefore concentrate on besides access control is bomb identification, bomb searches, and reactions to bomb threats or to extortion demands based upon bomb threats.

The first indication platform workers will probably have that a bomb may be aboard their rig will be some sort of communication from their parent organization. That is because the bomb threat and/or extortion demand will be made to people or organizations who can further the intentions of the saboteur. In the *Piper Alpha* case, had there been an extortion demand it would probably have been made to Occidental Petroleum Corporation's head office in Los Angeles, the BBC in London, or an Aberdeen newspaper. The telephone bomb threat procedures previously discussed are therefore of little importance to offshore installation workers. In addition, there are no telephones on most rigs, although theoretically a rig could receive a radio-transmitted bomb threat. Once the bomb threat is received and the offshore installation alerted, the question is what to do next. A port facility could simply call the local authorities and let them handle the problem from then on, with the possible exception of deciding whether to evacuate or not. An offshore installation can't do that. The owners or operators may well decide to evacuate the rig and call in professional bomb disposal personnel, but the workers have no place to go while they await evacuation—the bomb could detonate in the interim. Any reasonable (remember, "reasonable" is the key word in negligence lawsuits) person faced with such a situation would rather look for the bomb than sit and wait for it to detonate underneath him. In order for him to safely look for the bomb, however, he must be trained in what to look for and what to do if he finds it.

Bombs come in all shapes and sizes. They can be manufactured of all sorts of explosives, and be detonated by any number of devices. The days of simply looking for something that ticks are long gone. The best advice to someone searching for an explosive device is to look for anything out of the ordinary, which is why platform supervisors should routinely inspect all areas of their installations. It is also why workers should be trained to notice and report anything unusual. If something doesn't belong where it is found, particularly if no one knows what it is, it should be suspected of being a bomb.

There are a number of things workers should not do if they find a suspected bomb. They should *not:*

1. Submerge the device in water (unless perhaps to drop it over the side).
2. Shock or jar the device unnecessarily.
3. Attempt to open a suspected package.
4. Turn a package over or on its side.
5. Cut into a box or package with a metallic object.
6. Lay a suspected bottle on its side.
7. Accept identification markings on any suspected package as legitimate.
8. Allow radio transmissions within the near vicinity of a suspected device.
9. Smoke in the immediate vicinity of a suspected package.
10. Allow the diminutive size of a strange package to remove it from suspicion.

Besides training nonsecurity personnel in bomb-search techniques, the offshore security officer should consider some sort of firearms training for at least the installation's supervisory personnel, if firearms are to be kept on board. Emergency communication techniques should also be addressed. Drills can be devised to assist in the training for bomb threat contingencies and can be integrated easily into fire drills and other safety programs. Immediate action drills similar to those already discussed for vessels and port facilities can certainly be developed, but would only be useful on offshore installations where it has been determined the workers will resist any armed takeover attempt. In areas where the local authorities cannot be depended upon to provide rapid assistance to an offshore installation under attack, the security officer may consider either placing security professionals on board or maintaining an offshore security reaction team someplace in the vicinity that can respond to such emergencies. The security professionals would most likely be independent contractors employed for the duration of the perceived threat. The offshore security reaction team, however, should be proprietary employees whose training and supervision are the responsibility of the offshore security officer. If the offshore operator maintains a security reaction team (and negligent security litigation considerations dictate that it should), the team must be trained and drilled in combat operations. Immediate reaction drills should be devised to train the team to rapidly respond to any offshore security emergency.

SECURITY INSPECTIONS

The final requirement for the successful implementation of a security plan is a thorough inspection procedure. Two types of inspections should be routinely conducted: security readiness inspections and operational security inspections. Security readiness inspections are those inspections designed to determine a person's or unit's security readiness, that is, the *ability* to perform the necessary security functions. Operational security inspections, on the other hand, are those inspections which determine the actual security *conduct* of those being scrutinized. Security readiness inspections should be regularly announced and scheduled events in which all personnel strive to achieve high marks in both personal and unit performance. Operational security inspections, however, should be surprise or surreptitious inspections. They tell the security officer what is really happening within his security organization, and exactly how secure his ship, port facility, or offshore installation actually is. These inspections are most effective when they are conducted by someone other than the security officer or a person known to the security force. Independent maritime security consultants are extremely useful for this type of inspection, and can be employed specifically to conduct an operational security inspection and render a written report. The report becomes part of the documentary history of the security organization. If such inspections are conducted routinely (semiannually, for instance), and the subsequent reports are carefully reviewed and acted upon by the security officer and his staff, and their actions are documented, the organization stands a much better chance of successfully defending any negligent security claim which might be made against it.

Some enlightening examples of what can be discovered during surreptitious operational security inspections in airports have been reported recently in various U.S. periodicals. At Washington National Airport a locked door leads to the tarmac and to stairs that bypass passenger screening areas. On the door, in bright red, is posted the following statement: DISPLAY OF PROPER IDENTIFICATION IS REQUIRED TO ENTER THIS AREA. Yet, when a Federal Aviation Administration plainclothes special agent asked an exiting employee to hold the door, he did so without hesitation. The employee was an airport security guard! At Chicago's O'Hare International Airport a man with a briefcase walked through an open baggage room security door, out onto the tarmac, up a boarding staircase, and back into the terminal where he boarded a plane without ever passing through a security checkpoint. At Atlanta's Hartsfield International Airport a woman waiting outside locked security doors watched as airport employees punched the security code into the door's locking mechanism. No effort was made to prevent her from seeing the code, and when she tried it herself the door opened. She also found that the *same* code opened all the other doors she tried. The doors led to the tarmac and crew waiting rooms. The woman also discovered that if she waited long enough outside the same locked doors sooner or later an employee would come along who would hold the door open for her.

It is this type of security dysfunction that operational security inspections are designed to catch. A good security officer will take advantage of any opportunity to conduct even informal operational security inspections. For instance, a ship's security officer might ask the port facility security officer, with whom he has just made his arrival security liaison, to perform an informal operational security inspection of his ship sometime during her stay. The port facility security officer will probably be more than happy to do so. Of course, security officers, like ship's masters who almost subconsciously notice the lay of their vessels, should get in the habit of continuously checking the myriad details that affect the security with which they are entrusted. When placed under oath they should be able to testify it is their habit to conduct security inspections on a daily basis.

Implementation of the security plan is a function of training, supervision, and inspection. It requires planning and perseverance, ingenuity and inspiration, flexibility and accountability, and dedication. It also requires support. Without support from his superiors the security officer's implementation program will fail to achieve the full potential a properly prepared security plan deserves. If a security plan is not implemented to its full potential, the security of the entity it is designed to protect will be less than complete, and less than complete security in today's maritime environment is an invitation for disaster. Full support for security implementation, however, generally comes only after a complete understanding of security management has been gained. Security management, therefore, is the subject of the next chapter.

CHAPTER SIX

SECURITY MANAGEMENT

Security management is the art of managing, not *of* security, but *for* security. It is the way in which a manager views his overall organization, the way he achieves his business goals, in connection with his perception of security and its relationship to his particular enterprise. It is a mind-set that weighs the pros and cons of every business decision against the backdrop of its security ramifications. Maritime security management is no different. It is simply the art of managing for security within a maritime context.

This maritime context, however, presents a variety of unique operational considerations. Shipboard security, for example, is the responsibility of the ship's master who, in this day and age, must be more than a master mariner. He must be fluent in two or three languages, well versed in the maritime law of numerous nations, and cognizant of business management techniques. In other words, a ship's master today must be a sailor, linguist, lawyer, and business executive all at the same time. Where the security of his vessel is concerned, he should also be a capable combat commander. Security, like camouflage, must be continuous. In order to effectively manage his vessel and achieve the results required by her owners and operators, a master must consider the security ramifications of every decision he makes. His vessel, her cargo, and her crew are more at risk now than ever before in the history of peacetime commercial shipping. The potential legal liabilities for inadequate maritime security are greater today than they have ever been, simply because the possibility of massive human, economic, and environmental destruction resulting from maritime terrorism is greater today than ever before in the history of the world.

Maritime security management does not, however, begin with the ship's master. He can only be the instrument of policy decreed by the owners, operators, and insurers of his vessel. If they are incapable or unwilling to consider the security of their ships in day-to-day maritime operations, their masters, no matter how security conscious, will have little latitude in combatting either category I or II threats. Until owners and insurers comprehend that proper shipboard security equates to money saved, through loss prevention and liability reduction, their ships and the men who sail them are doomed by unenlightened security practices in an age of maritime terrorism.

The operation of offshore installations and port facilities presents similar considerations. They too are at risk, and in some cases their liability exposure is greater than any given ship's simply because the potential damages from terrorist acts are greater. Maritime operators are in business for one reason: to make money. The amount of money an operator can make depends to a great extent on the cost of his operation. Consequently, security management must be contemplated in relation to those factors that control operational expenses, because a properly secured enterprise that costs too much to operate or an unsecured enterprise that ultimately collapses from the weight of legal judgments both ultimately fail for the same reason: they were unable to make enough money to offset the cost of doing business. Generally, as operating expenses increase, profitability decreases and, conversely, as operating expenses decrease, profitability should increase. Proper maritime security requires a certain increase in operational expenses heretofore not considered necessary by maritime operators, at least within the last fifty years or so, and the problem therefore lies in balancing increased operational expenses and decreased profitability so that an appropriate level of maritime security can be maintained along with an acceptable profit margin. This requires a consideration of the various strategies, objectives, and priorities to be employed at both the policy-making and operational levels of the enterprise.

At the policy-making level the strategies, objectives, and priorities relate generally to the particular maritime enterprise, and specifically to the character of that enterprise. For instance, for a common carrier the strategies, objectives, and priorities will center generally on the shipowner's business of carrying cargo or passengers for hire, but the specific security concerns will relate to the nature of the cargo carried and the shipping routes utilized. Thus, a general cargo-carrying enterprise may develop different priorities than will perhaps a cargo-specific shipper. Shipping routes and ports of call may need to be scrutinized and security arrangements approved on a regular basis for vessels engaged in general trading, whereas a liner service may need only make such determinations once, at the establishment of the service. A Japanese common carrier transporting bulk lumber from Seattle to Osaka need not consider the same security threats as an LNG tanker service that loads cargo in Borneo or Sumatra and transports it to Boston. A VLCC operator has different security concerns in the Persian Gulf than does an offshore platform owner in the North Sea. A port facility on the coast of Florida from which cruise ship lines operate may establish different security procedures than perhaps a phosphate-loading facility on the same coast. In all instances, however, the strategies, objectives, and priorities set at the policy-making level necessarily impact at the operational level. This chapter will explore some of the topics that directly affect, or should affect, maritime security management decisions, beginning with the concept of negligent security litigation.

NEGLIGENT SECURITY LITIGATION

The liability exposure faced by all maritime operators today in the area of security negligence is enormous. The primary objective of this book is to convince those within the marine industry that this exposure really exists, that it is not the figment of an overactive imagination, and that the realities of maritime terrorism are absolutely horrifying to contemplate. Like the proverbial gold miner's mule that had to be struck between the eyes with a sledgehammer to gain its attention, the marine industry clearly needs to be shocked into a state of security consciousness. In 1985 the *Achille Lauro* incident struck the first overdue hammerblow. The more recent attack in July of 1988 on another cruise ship, the *City of Poros,* in which 9 passengers were killed and 47 others injured, may ultimately serve as a second warning to an industry that persists in burying its head in the sand. The danger, however, is that only cruise ship operators may begin to wise up, when in reality the cruise ship industry is not likely to be the primary target of any well-informed, intelligent terrorist. The lives of three or four hundred passengers pale to virtual insignificance when compared to the hundreds of thousands of lives that could be eliminated by detonating a fully loaded LNG tanker. Furthermore, huge ransoms are more likely to be paid for expensive pieces of offshore equipment by private companies that can afford to do so than for passengers by governments that have sworn not to do so. The sledgehammer between the eyes for the marine industry is, however, not the threat of terrorist activity in and of itself, but rather the threat of legal reprisals far beyond the imagination of many of today's maritime operators. It is that hammer this book hopefully wields, but to do so effectively a description of the American legal system is needed.

Many Americans, and certainly most foreigners, are completely baffled by the legal system in the United States. While the legal concepts are not difficult to understand, they do need to be explained in some language approximately resembling plain English. Most lawyers find this difficult to do, not because they can't speak plain English, but because they have been trained to try and say everything at one time. There are exceptions to any rule of law and one of those exceptions may apply to whatever it is the lawyer tries to explain to his client. Oversimplification is therefore something to be avoided at all costs because the client might misunderstand the explanation, erroneously act on that misunderstanding, and eventually sue the lawyer for malpractice. It is far better to explain the matter in "legalese," which the client can't possibly understand, and thereby ensure that no *mis*understanding ensues. Even if it does, the lawyer remains blameless since he explained everything in proper legal fashion. This book, however, is not written by one of those lawyers who believes oversimplification is a bad thing when trying to explain otherwise convoluted concepts. Therefore, at the risk of being accused of oversimplifying an explanation of the American legal system, an oversimplified explanation of the American legal system follows.

The difference between code law and common-law systems has already been discussed. Because the jurisprudence of the United States is founded upon common-law principles, judicial decisions must be based upon applicable, earlier, precedent-setting cases. This concept is known as the principle of *stare decisis,* which is Latin for "to abide by, or adhere to, decided cases." This is not a difficult concept to grasp, and even those who have never known any legal system other than a code law have no problem in understanding it. The problem in the United States is that not all prior cases that appear similar constitute legal precedent for the particular court deciding the current case. Thus, a court in New York might decide a case very differently from a court in California, even though the facts of the two cases are essentially identical, because the two courts are required to consider different precedent. This concept *is* difficult to grasp, and foreign shippers generally have a very hard time doing so, if they manage to at all. How can similar cases be decided so differently in the same country, they ask, and it is a very reasonable question. The answer lies in understanding the court system of the United States.

The first step to understanding the court system in the United States is to realize there are two distinct and, for the most part, separate court organizations in the country. There are federal courts, and there are state courts. Because of the unique concept of "federalism" upon which the United States was founded, and which has not developed anywhere else in the world, each state in the United States has the authority and power to establish its own jurisprudence; that is, make its own laws, create its own courts, and follow its own decisions. So long as those laws do not conflict with the Constitution of the United States (the founding document of the nation) or with federal legislation enacted for the common good of all the states, they can be developed in any manner the state desires and *no* other state's laws or court decisions can have any effect whatsoever on them. Thus, a California state court will only follow California state law and prior California state court decisions. It couldn't care less what any other state courts around the country, including New York's, do or have done. Most law students hear the story sooner or later of the young lawyer whose task it was to argue an issue in state court that had never before been decided in that state. Since there were no state court decisions in his state on the matter, he decided to research the other 49 states' decisions in an effort to find authority for his position that the judge might accept. He worked day and night for weeks, searching diligently through tome after tome, trying to find cases to support the legal argument he intended to make. Once he had discovered the cases he believed to be helpful he spent yet more days and nights writing the brief he would ultimately submit to the judge when he argued his case. After weeks of work the fateful day arrived, and the young lawyer found himself in front of the judge. Before commencing his argument, which he knew to be absolutely brilliant, he proudly handed the judge his written masterpiece of 40 or so pages. Every applicable case from anywhere in the country that had been decided over the past

200 years was carefully noted and analyzed. When the judge looked at him expectantly he cleared his throat, took a deep breath, and began. "Your Honor, there are no decisions in our state on this particular issue. However, compiled in the brief before you are all the decisions which are to be found in other states . . ." He got no further. The judge, looking first at him, and then at the brief, casually dropped it into the wastepaper basket.

The story illustrates the point that courts in the United States need follow *only* those cases that constitute legal precedent. So the question is, "What constitutes legal precedent?" Generally, it is those cases decided earlier by the *same* court, or those cases decided earlier by a higher court whose decisions are legally binding on that court. There is a judiciary "chain of command" that is basically the same in any state or federal court system. It begins at the trial court level, proceeds to the appellate court, and terminates at the court of last resort (usually referred to as the supreme court). There are only three courts in the chain so far as precedence is concerned, and this is important to remember. A state trial court is only bound by the decisions of the appellate court to which it answers or the decisions of its state supreme court. (Although its own decisions are also considered precedent-setting, it need not be bound by them.) The decisions of any other court, state or federal, are not binding on the trial court. That means that even the decisions of another appellate court in a different appellate district within the same state are not binding on the trial court. At the appellate level, only the decisions of the state supreme court are binding on any of the appellate courts.

The federal court system is set up in the same manner, that is, with trial courts, appellate courts, and the U.S. Supreme Court. The chain of command also works the same, from the trial court to the appellate court and finally to the Supreme Court. Only the names of the courts differ. For instance, in the federal court system the trial court is named the U.S. district court (there are numerous federal judicial districts throughout the country, and the district courts are named after the district in which they sit, such as the Middle District of Florida or the Southern District of New York). The appellate courts are named U.S. circuit courts of appeal, and are numbered in accordance with the number of appellate circuits that have been geographically established. Thus there are the Fifth Circuit Court of Appeals, the Ninth Circuit Court of Appeals, and so on. The circuit courts of appeal must follow

FIG. 9.   Court systems in the United States

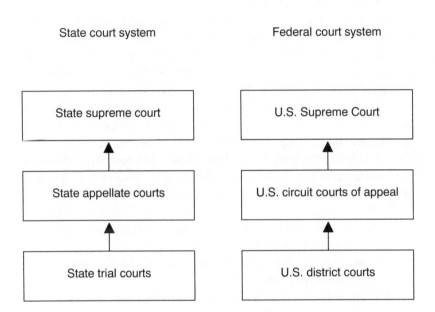

State court system

Federal court system

State supreme court	U.S. Supreme Court
State appellate courts	U.S. circuit courts of appeal
State trial courts	U.S. district courts

only the decisions handed down by the U.S. Supreme Court. A particular circuit court need not agree with or follow the decisions of any other circuit court. The district courts are bound *only* by the decisions of their circuit courts of appeal and the decisions of the U.S. Supreme Court. The diagram in figure 9 illustrates the comparison between the state and federal court systems.

Now, it is important to realize that in neither system, federal or state, is there a right to appeal to the court of last resort. The *only* right of appeal that exists is the right to appeal from the trial court to the appellate court. If an appellant is unhappy with the decision of the appellate court he may *petition* the applicable supreme court to hear his case, but that court has the discretion to hear it or refuse it. Most cases are refused. One of the most common ways to get a case to a supreme court is to argue that different appellate courts have decided similar cases differently and that, in order to unify the law, the supreme court should decide the case. So, unless the Supreme Court of the United States has decided a particular maritime issue, it is quite possible that conflicting appellate decisions can be handed down from different U.S. circuit courts of appeal, which understandably confuses, and angers, foreign maritime interests.

The problem, however, gets worse. The prior discussion has hopefully clarified why different decisions can be rendered on similar cases by different courts. The subject of *which* court one can find oneself in has not been addressed. This is a question of jurisdiction, that power any given court has to hear the case before it. Whether a case can be brought in state court or federal court is a question of jurisdiction that at times can mystify even lawyers and judges. Once the court has determined that it has jurisdiction to hear a case, the next question it must decide is what law, state or federal, should be applied. The rules are sometimes confusing but in maritime negligent security cases there are a number of possibilities. They are as follows:

1. A case might be brought in state court with the court applying that state's law.
2. It might be brought in state court with the court applying some other state's law.
3. It might be brought in state court with the court applying federal maritime law.
4. It might be brought in federal court with the court applying federal maritime law.
5. It might be brought in federal court with the court applying state law.
6. It might be brought in federal court with the court applying federal nonmaritime law.
7. And, finally, it might be brought in federal court with the court applying the law of some other nation.

How, and under what circumstances, cases can be brought in different courts need not be discussed at this time. It should be sufficient to simply note that there are a number of possibilities. Before a case can be brought in any court, however, there must exist what lawyers refer to as a "cause of action." This is the legal right one has to bring suit in the first place. It should not be confused with whether the plaintiff can prove his case. It is simply the determination that he has a legal cause upon which to base his suit. For example, before one can sue for breach of contract (the cause of action) he must allege the existence of a contract. If there is no contract, there is no cause of action for breach of contract. In a negligent security lawsuit the cause of action is negligence, and a simple case would involve one plaintiff and one defendant. More often than not, however, lawsuits involve multiple parties, that is, plaintiffs and defendants. If, for instance, a would-be intruder is shot by a trigger-happy security guard at a port facility and subsequently sues, he will more than likely sue both the guard and the port authority (the guard's employer). If the guard was a contract guard service employee, the plaintiff will sue the guard, the port authority, and the contract guard service. The port authority, however, should have a contract with the guard service that indemnifies the port authority for any negligent or other acts committed by guard service employees, and consequently the port authority might claim against the guard service (it could wait and file a separate suit). Furthermore, since the intruder was clearly not blameless in this entire affair, all defendants will counterclaim against him.

Negligence was discussed in chapter 5. It is the failure to act in a reasonable manner, or the acting in an unreasonable manner, when a duty to act exists. Negligent security, therefore, is the failure to provide reasonable security either through inaction or improper action when a duty to provide that security exists. It can also be the acting in such a manner that, while providing reasonable security, innocent third parties are in one way or another injured. The opportunities for applying this cause of action in the maritime area are boundless. In the Persian Gulf alone, over the past nine years, hundreds of lives and billions of dollars in ships and cargo have been lost, most of which can be attributed to negligent security practices on the part of shipowners. Allowing one's vessels to be pirated over and over again for years on end is not only negligent, it is utter lunacy. A tanker boarded and scuttled, an offshore platform sabotaged and destroyed, a port facility's fuel depot ignited, a cruise ship passenger terminal bombed—if any of these were to be accomplished because of inadequate maritime security, those responsible for providing that security would be liable.

Legal liability, however, is only part of the picture. All lawsuits have two separate and very distinct parts. The first part concerns the question of liability. Was the defendant shipowner, or offshore operator, or port authority, negligent in the manner in which it provided or didn't provide maritime security? The answer to that question rests with the jury hearing the case, and whether its members believe the defendant's actions were reasonable under the circumstances. Reasonability is the key concept. Neither security nor safety can be guaranteed, by anyone. It is the reasonableness of the actions taken, or not taken, that determines negligence. If the jury determines that the defendant's actions were reasonable under the circumstances, the lawsuit, for all intents and purposes, is over. The defendant is not liable, and everyone goes home. On the other hand, if the jury decides the defendant *was* negligent, then the second part of the lawsuit comes into play. That part involves the amount of damages suffered by the plaintiff as a result of the defendant's negligence. This amount, when proven, will be the amount for which the defendant is legally liable. As a result of the *Amoco Cadiz* disaster in 1978 France claimed damages in excess of $2 billion. The litigation took 10 years, and the results are still being appealed. The plaintiffs won on the liability issue, but were not awarded anything close to what they demanded in the way of damages, so *everyone* appealed. The amount of damages to which a successful plaintiff is entitled is a matter of proof. The court cannot replace a lost limb, or restore a life, or reverse environmental damage. All it can do is award money damages as compensation for that which was lost. Consequently, the amount claimed by the plaintiff must be proven as the actual amount lost as a result of the injury suffered. If a thirty-two-year-old chief officer who makes $125,000 a year is killed by pirates aboard a tanker whose owners have repeatedly refused to institute appropriate shipboard security procedures, the damages awarded his widow could easily amount to over $4 million. If it can be proved that he suffered substantially before he died, the award could be significantly higher. If the jury decides that the shipowner was so blatantly callous with regard to the safety concerns of the crew that punitive damages (those damages awarded as punishment) are appropriate, the award could be considerably higher still. When the *Piper Alpha* disaster occurred, in which 166 workers were killed, it was reported that the platform's owner promised an indemnity of some $170,000 to the family of each victim, plus a contribution of $1.7 million to the *Piper Alpha* disaster fund. If the owner is ultimately found negligent in the cause of the catastrophe, those promises will not appear very magnanimous at all. Consider the figures. If the average age of the 166 platform workers was 40, and their average annual income was $75,000, then each worker suffered a loss of income of almost $2 million—over 10 times the indemnity set aside by the owner. The total amount in lost wages alone for which the owner could be liable is some $311 million. The *Piper Alpha* could just as well have been the victim of sabotage as accident, and if that were the case, and negligent security could be established, the liability would be the same: over $300 million. Now consider an LNG tanker explosion in which not hundreds, but thousands, of people lose their lives as a result of terrorist activity. If proper security procedures could have prevented the calamity, the damage award would be one that no company could weather.

There have been literally hundreds of improper security cases decided in the United States over the past 50 years or so. Almost all of these cases, however, were brought by innocent, or sometimes not-so-innocent, third parties who claimed injuries resulting from either negligent or intentional acts of security personnel. The typical cases are those in which a bystander is injured by a stray bullet fired by a security guard at a fleeing suspect, or in which a suspect claims false imprisonment, false arrest, assault, battery, or defamation of character. The potential for such cases can be reduced substantially by training and proper supervision of guard force personnel; and while such concerns are certainly important to those utilizing security forces, the focus of this discussion is on the liabilities faced by maritime operators who fail to provide adequate security rather than the liabilities they may face resulting from particular acts of their security personnel.

The question, therefore, that a jury may be asked to answer in a lawsuit brought after an incident of piracy or maritime terrorism is, "Did the owner or operator act reasonably, under the circumstances, in providing or not providing security?" In order to determine whether or not such action was reasonable, the jury must know what action was taken. This is a matter of evidence, to be offered at trial as proof, as to what the defendant did. There are two types of evidence, physical evidence and testimonial evidence. Physical evidence, quite clearly, is that evidence consisting of physical things such as a gun, a broken lock, a photograph, or a letter. Testimonial evidence is that evidence consisting of testimony given by witnesses or parties. In civil lawsuits, most of the physical evidence offered at trial consists of documentary evidence, such as correspondence, contracts, telephone notes, logbooks, medical records, and so on. Most of the testimonial evidence offered at trial is by either live testimony or deposition testimony. Whatever the type of evidence, physical or testimonial, it constitutes the "ammunition" with which the attorneys fight for their cause. As in any battle, the side with the most ammunition, or the side that can most effectively utilize its ammunition, usually wins. It is therefore the responsibility of any prospective litigant, if he desires to win, to ensure that his attorney receives all the ammunition possible. He can do this by looking ahead and being prepared for the contingency of litigation. This is not difficult to do so long as one understands what happens at a trial.

The first thing to realize is that there are virtually no surprises at trial. The attorneys know who the witnesses are and what they will say if they are called to testify. They know what all the documentary evidence is. They know what other physical evidence exists. They know what experts may be called and what their opinions will be. They know what the law is with regard to the various issues that will be presented. They know the arguments and objections each side will make, and the law relating to those matters. In short, the attorneys know almost everything about the case *except* how the jury will decide the facts.

The second thing to remember is that there are two types of issues in any trial: issues of law and issues of fact. In cases that are tried before a jury, judges only decide the legal issues. They do not decide the factual issues. The facts of the case, that is, what happened, where it happened, how it happened, who did what, why it was done, and whether it was reasonable under the circumstances, are all decided by the jury. In most cases, *the factual findings by the jury are not appealable.* Only the legal rulings or conclusions by the judge may be appealed, such as the admissibility of evidence, the instructions given to the jury, and any particular actions taken by the judge during the pendency of the litigation. The attorneys have no way of knowing before trial who the jurors will be. They have no way of knowing during the trial what the jurors are thinking or what they will decide. It is this unpredictability that causes most attorneys to view a jury trial as little more than a crapshoot. It is also why 9 out of 10 jury trial cases of this type are settled out of court. In any event, knowing the litigation process can help security managers prepare for potential future lawsuits.

There are basically four phases to any lawsuit. The first phase is the pleading phase. This is where the plaintiff files his complaint in the court in which he intends to litigate his claim, and serves on the defendant a copy of that complaint along with the proper court summons or other process that allows the court jurisdiction over the defendant. There can be no case without proper service of process. Once process has been served, the defendant must file his answer or some other responsive pleading (such as a motion to dismiss) to the complaint within a statutory number of days, usually about 20. In his answer, the defendant denies the claim and alleges whatever legal defenses he may have to the claim. At the same time he files his answer, the defendant will usually also file any counterclaim he may have against the plaintiff, and he may also implead (bring in) other third-party defendants whom he believes are either liable to the plaintiff or himself for the claim made. The third-party defendants then have the same statutory period in which to file their answers or other responsive pleadings to the various claims. In complicated cases involving the jurisdiction of state and federal courts, international events, and choice of forum questions, the pleading phase of a lawsuit may take a considerable period of time to complete, sometimes as much as a year or more. Once, however, all questions of jurisdiction, forum selection, and other pleading matters have been decided, and all surviving parties have filed their answers, counterclaims, third-party complaints, and cross claims (claims between defendants), the pleading phase is complete and the case is ready to enter its next phase.

The second phase—and it can be the most important part of the lawsuit—is the discovery phase. It is referred to as such because that is what the parties do, they "discover" everything that might be used at trial. This is why there are seldom any real surprises at trial. By the time this phase is complete, the attorneys have (hopefully) discovered all the evidence there is going to be in the case. Of course there is always the unpredictability of the jury to think about but, generally speaking, everyone knows going into trial roughly what his chances are of prevailing. This is why most lawsuits settle. Consequently, the security manager needs to know how to stack the evidence deck in his favor, not only so far as maintaining the proper records are concerned, but also in responding to the discovery demands of opposing counsel.

The first thing to remember when putting *anything* on paper is that it may wind up in court someday being read to a jury. Correspondence, telephone notes, messages, interoffice memoranda, telexes, file reminders, love letters, poison pen letters, threats, admissions of negligence or wrongdoing, or anything else that can possibly be conveyed in writing may ultimately be enlarged and exhibited in court in letters six inches high. Security managers should form the habit of automatically, almost subconsciously, scrutinizing every word, every sentence, and every paragraph they put in writing for possible legal repercussions or ramifications. They should ask themselves, "Do I really want to put this in writing?" "What will this convey if someone else reads it?" "Do I want this broadcast all over a courtroom?" In a similar manner, a lot of self-serving statements can be placed into an organization's documentary history that may be helpful several years down the line. Security managers should ask themselves questions like, "Is this explanation clear enough for a jury to understand?" "Is this description accurate?" "Are our intentions for doing this good, and are they defined in the best possible manner?" False or questionable information should never be "planted"; this is not the point. The point is that there are always alternative methods of describing events and courses of action, and some may place the operator in a better light than others. Security managers should continually place themselves in the roles of advocate and devil's advocate whenever memorializing anything on paper or, for that matter, on any other recording medium.

It should go without saying that all routine record-keeping ought to be done in a conscientious and detailed manner. *No* records are better than incomplete records, at least when it comes to turning them over to the other side as evidence in a lawsuit. The entire system of record-keeping, report-writing, and log-maintaining should be designed with the possibility of litigation in mind.

Besides simply demanding all records and other documentary evidence the defendant possesses, the plaintiff's attorney will also propound, through counsel, what are called "interrogatories." These are written questions that generally must be answered in writing and sworn to under oath. Many defense attorneys will simply send the questions to their client or his representative and ask that they be appropriately answered and notarized. This is a mistake. Unartfully worded answers to interrogatories can lose a lawsuit. Lay people, and even inexperienced trial attorneys, may not know the best way to word a difficult answer so that its impact can be diminished. The best thing for a security manager to do if he receives interrogatories is to provide his attorney with the most thorough answers he can, but ensure that his attorney realizes these are only rough answers and that all available information is being sent to him so that *he* may prepare the best possible responses to the questions. Once the finalized answers are prepared the security manager should only sign them if he feels comfortable with them, since he can count on having to defend them by testifying under oath in either the courtroom or by deposition, or both.

Testifying is an art that can be acquired only through experience. There are two types of situations where one can be asked to testify: by having one's deposition taken, and by appearing in court at trial. In both instances the actual process of being examined and cross-examined by the attorneys is the same; depositions, however, are usually a little less formal and consequently may not be as stressful. Depositions may be taken for discovery purposes, or for use at trial if the witness lives too far away from where it will be held or will not be available to testify when it occurs. The testimony given is just as important in either case, and a deponent or trial witness should be thoroughly prepared by his attorney beforehand. How he is prepared depends upon the attorney. In some cases practice sessions might be useful in which the prospective witness is taken through the entire process by being examined and cross-examined. In other cases the attorney may simply discuss the case and the expected testimony in either general or specific terms, depending upon the experience and capabilities of the witness.

Once all the documents have been exchanged, the interrogatories answered, rehearsals conducted, and witnesses deposed, the discovery phase of the lawsuit is just about complete. There are other things attorneys may wish to do in particular cases, but by and large most discovery takes the form just discussed. This process, however, can take several years to complete. Once discovery has been completed, the case is ready for trial, the third phase of the lawsuit.

Trials are, in essence, civilized combat. The opposing sides have decided to settle their differences, not by pugilistic or other physical means, but by presentation of their cases to a judge or jury. Lawyers are paid champions who fight for their clients' causes, and that is important to remember. Except for the fact that sometimes their payment hinges upon winning, most lawyers have no personal interest in their cases. They are legally bound to do the best possible job within established ethical parameters and, by and large, they usually do so.

It is also important to remember that not all lawyers are trial attorneys, and the vast majority of lawyers seldom see the inside of a courtroom. So far as trial attorneys are concerned, there are generally two kinds: plaintiff's attorneys and defense attorneys. In the United States the primary difference between the two is the method by which each gets paid, and the United States is unique among all the nations in the world in this respect. Plaintiff's attorneys generally work on what is termed a "contingency fee basis." Their fee is an agreed-upon percentage of any recovery they obtain on behalf of their clients. This percentage usually runs somewhere between 25 percent and 40 percent of the total recovery. If, for instance, an attorney obtains a judgment in favor of his clients of $100,000 and manages to collect that amount (more on collections later), and if he has the case on a 40 percent contingency fee, his fee is $40,000. It comes off the top before any deductions are made for costs or other expenses. The costs of hiring investigators and expert witnesses, and the travel expenses for taking depositions, can easily amount to $10,000 in a relatively simple case. Those costs and expenses, whatever they are, are deducted from the recovery next and the client is left with the remainder, in this example, $50,000. Defense attorneys, on the other hand, are always paid by the hour. Hourly rates vary, depending upon the type of law that is practiced and the location in which it is practiced. The national average for defense attorneys, however, is probably around $125–$150 per hour. On the same $100,000 case in which his brother plaintiff's attorney made $40,000 the defense attorney's fee will probably be around $25,000.

Defense attorneys, however, get paid whether they win or lose, so the higher plaintiff's fee is usually justified, as far as plaintiff's attorneys are concerned, by the higher risk involved in handling the case.

Understanding the economics of litigating is important when it comes to settling cases. The first settlement overture is usually made by the plaintiff's attorney by sending to the defense attorney something called a settlement demand. This is a letter that describes the case from the plaintiff's view based upon the facts that have come out during the discovery process. The letter might discuss such things as what different witnesses have said in their depositions, what the documentary evidence tends to show, what the applicable law is on various issues that might be present in the suit, and what the plaintiff's attorney thinks he can prove in the way of damages He then offers to settle the case by demanding a particular amount—in this instance it might be $85,000.

The defense attorney, upon receiving the settlement demand, usually prepares his own analysis of the case and forwards both to his client along with his recommendations concerning a response. His analysis should contain "worst case" and "best case" scenarios with regard to reasonably foreseeable findings at trial on both liability and damages.

These settlement demands and case analyses cannot be made until most, if not all, discovery has been completed, and this is the reason most cases settle only after the discovery phase and just before trial. If the case can't be settled then, obviously, it must be tried.

Trials consist of several phases themselves. The first phase, in a jury trial, is the selection of the jury. The second trial phase consists of opening statements by both sides. Here the attorneys present to the jury, in as unargumentative fashion as possible, the background of the case and what each side hopes to prove. The next phase of the trial is the most important. It is the proof stage, where all the evidence is presented to the jury in an ordered fashion. The plaintiff's case is delivered first; that is, all the witnesses who will testify on behalf of the plaintiff are called and examined (asked questions) by the plaintiff's attorney. As the plaintiff's attorney finishes his examination of each witness the defense is allowed to cross-examine. Once the plaintiff has called all the witnesses he intends to, his case is concluded and he "rests." The defense then delivers its case in the same manner. Once both sides have rested, the trial enters its next phase: closing arguments. It is here the attorneys "argue," in the fullest sense of the word, their clients' cases. They review the evidence as it pertains to their cases, and attempt to convince the jury to decide in favor of their clients. The trial then enters its final phase as the case is presented to the jury for its deliberation. This simply means that the judge, after instructing the jury on the law that it must apply, turns the case over to the jury which then retires to decide the matter. Once it has decided, the verdict is announced in court and the trial is finished.

There are a number of requests the trial attorneys can make to the judge immediately after the trial has concluded, such as asking that the jury verdict be set aside or that the judge grant a new trial. If the judge denies these requests the case enters its final phase about 30 days afterwards, which is the appeal phase. Very few cases are appealed, but the ones that are usually involve either substantial damage awards or serious injuries for which no liability was found. This is because appealing a case is a fairly expensive undertaking. Many lay litigants don't realize this and assume that their right to appeal somehow shields them from the costs involved. In reality, many cases that probably *should* be appealed never are because of the cost of doing so. A relatively simple appeal can cost $10,000 to $15,000.

Once the judgment in the case becomes final the litigants are left with a piece of paper which decrees the outcome of the litigation. That is all. The court cannot order payment of any judgment that may have been rendered. This sometimes comes as a great surprise to the plaintiffs, particularly foreign ones. Where ships are damaged, for instance, as a result of the negligence of their compulsory U.S. pilots, judgments in favor of the shipowners can be obtained. However, in many cases the pilots do not carry liability insurance and, since they are in a high-risk business, have "judgment-proofed" themselves so that their assets cannot be reached in order to satisfy any judgment rendered against them. Since pilot associations cannot be held liable for the negligence of their members, the unfortunate shipowners are left with an uncollectible judgment. However, so far as negligent security litigation is concerned, the defendants being sued will be shipowners, port facility operators, and offshore installation owners, all of whom will more than likely have some degree of insurance. Of course, this insurance may be completely inadequate when it comes to multimillion- or multibillion-dollar claims. If the claimants prevail in those instances the defendant may simply be put out of business. That is what this book is designed to prevent.

The bottom-line consideration in any negligence litigation, or potential negligence situation, is simply whether the actions that caused the injury were reasonable under the circumstances. Accidents happen. Crimes are committed. The mere fact that an injury is sustained does not give rise to liability. However, if the events that caused the injury were foreseeable and no effort was made to prevent them, or an unreasonable effort was made that failed to prevent them, liability is likely to be found. The shipowner, port facility operator, and offshore installation owner cannot guarantee the safety of their employees or the general populace, but what they must guarantee according to the law is that all reasonable precautions will be taken to prevent injuries form occurring through inadequate security practices. This should be the primary goal of security management.

EXECUTIVE SECURITY AWARENESS

Security management must begin at the top of any organization, and until all top-echelon managers are fully security conscious the organization will remain at risk on a daily basis. No top executive attains his position today without knowing when to call his company's lawyer. Many managers, in fact, have law degrees. The days of managing a business without due consideration for the legal ramifications of any contemplated action are gone forever. In the maritime industry the days of managing a business without due consideration for the security ramifications of any contemplated action should also be gone forever. Unfortunately, many marine enterprises haven't yet realized that security is even a management consideration at all. This book will hopefully change that.

Maritime security awareness training for executive personnel can be easily integrated into other management programs. One-day and half-day seminars can be tailored specifically for the organization by either the in-house security manager or an independent security consultant. If an independent security consultant is employed, however, he should have maritime security experience. He should also have both management and legal experience so that the matters discussed will have a direct correlation to the tasks and responsibilities of the managers for whom the seminar is designed. Security awareness training is *not* security training. Its purpose, as its name implies, is to make those being trained *aware* of the security considerations that are applicable to the particular field of endeavor in which they are engaged. A one-day introductory executive maritime security awareness training program for a shipping organization might look like this:

MARITIME SECURITY MANAGEMENT SEMINAR

Topics	Schedule
Maritime terrorism	0900–1000
Security principles	1000–1100
Shipboard security	1100–1200
Lunch	1200–1330
Legal considerations	1330–1430
Security management	1430–1630
Questions and answers	1630–1700

Multinational corporate executives are at risk all over the world, and the maritime industry is no exception. Security- and liability-conscious organizations might institute an executive protection training program that could provide the following benefits:

1. Increase executive security awareness.
2. Reduce company liability in cases where executives are kidnapped or injured.
3. Increase executive morale.
4. Increase executive physical fitness.

A training program can easily be devised, with a little outside help, and busy executives would find it both enjoyable and relatively painless so far as time requirements are concerned. An example of a ten-week syllabus that utilizes a 2.5-hour class one evening a week and a 3-hour class on Saturday mornings is as follows:

EXECUTIVE PROTECTION TRAINING

Week 1 Evening: Introduction/Terrorism/Fitness scan/ Fitness education
        Saturday: Self-defense indoctrination/ Weapons indoctrination

Week 2 Evening: Security principles/Marksmanship
        Saturday: Pistol range

Week 3 Evening: Personal security
        Saturday: Self-defense (hand-to-hand) training

Week 4 Evening: Terrorist tactics
        Saturday: Shotgun and automatic weapons

Week 5 Evening: Physical security/Defensive driving
        Saturday: Self-defense

Week 6 Evening: Kidnapping/Security in foreign lands
        Saturday: Self-defense

Week 7 Evening: Ambushes/I.A. drills
        Saturday: Self-defense

Week 8 Evening: I.A. drills
        Saturday: I.A. drills (practical)

Week 9 Evening: Miscellaneous
        Saturday: Weapons qualification

Week 10 Evening: Course review
        Saturday: Self-defense qualification

The author once taught a continuing Saturday morning self-defense and rape-prevention class to the women employees of the marine equipment manufacturing company where he was employed as in-house counsel. He was asked to do so by the corporation's president (who knew of his background in security) after one of the women workers started receiving threatening telephone calls both at home and at work. What started out as a short security awareness class turned into a weekly event that the class eagerly awaited. Morale improved, among not only the women employees but the men as well, and there were many requests to expand the training to include male employees. Security awareness increased substantially throughout the plant, even though the training was directed only toward personal protection and was not given to everyone. Security measures that had caused some grumbling among the employees ceased to be a source of irritation, at least outwardly, and there appeared to be a better all-around feeling pervading the workplace. All of this caught upper management by surprise, and it was finally identified as a reaction by the employees to the manifestation of caring on the part of the corporation. There is no reason to suspect any different reaction by company executives who might feel personally threatened as a result of their respon-sibilities. Even if they don't, just the release of doing something that is perhaps "fun" but at the same time personally beneficial, and en-couraged by the company, can improve their outlook on life and their jobs immensely. It can also improve security awareness, which is what all of this is about.

Maritime security awareness among executive personnel is impor-tant for other reasons besides those already mentioned. Probably the most important is how crisis management capabilities within the com-pany can be affected. Crisis management is an organized, strategic response to security crisis situations that employs pre-established emergency procedures and pre-assigned managerial support. The managers assigned to the crisis management team must possess a high degree of security training in order to perform their tasks effectively, but other managers within the organization need to be aware of the crisis management team and its responsibilities. Executive security awareness plays a vital role in this regard.

Crisis management teams will vary in composition from one or-ganization to another, but all should consist of senior managers and security professionals capable of collecting and processing emergency security information as it becomes available and acting on that information to resolve the crisis. Each respective team member should have pre-established contacts with the necessary outside support agencies, and should be prepared to coordinate the resources within his area of responsibility with theirs. He should also have a close working relationship with the other team members and know the responsibilities of each. Ideally, all team members should reside in the same city or area and be capable of gathering at a pre-arranged location within an established short period of time. Consequently, managers who must travel extensively should not be considered as crisis management team candidates due to their likely unavailability at a time of crisis. Alternate crisis management team members should be chosen and trained, however, to allow for the eventuality of a particular team member's unavailability. The areas of responsibility that should be covered by members of the crisis management team are:

1. Top management.
2. Security.
3. Legal.
4. Communications.
5. Financial.
6. Personnel.
7. Public relations.

The crisis management team should be provided with documentation describing organizational security crisis policy and with crisis management team decision-making authority. Individual responsibilities for each team member should be carefully delineated, along with internal team authority or chain of command. Contingency plans should be developed that include checklists for tasks to be performed in various foreseeable security situations such as hijacking, kidnapping, bomb threat, sabotage, and so on. Drills should be performed, and critiques rendered, to ensure crisis management team operational readiness.

Appropriate executive security awareness also helps ensure rapid response up the organizational chain of command to any security incident or crisis. An incident may occur thousands of miles away from company headquarters, and it is important that all field managers know how to respond and whom to contact in such an emergency.

ORGANIZATIONAL SECURITY POLICY

All maritime enterprises should have some sort of security policy. Security policies can vary substantially. From a liability standpoint, the policy itself is not as important (so long as it can be defended as being reasonable under the circumstances) as is the derivation of the policy in the first place. Having *no* security policy can be worse than having a potentially inadequate security policy, because failing to take cognizance of the security threats facing the maritime industry or doing nothing about them is clearly negligent, whereas implementing a security policy that in the long run may prove to be inadequate might still be considered by a jury as reasonable under the circumstances. An organization should therefore be able to show that it carefully evaluated its security posture in a reasonable fashion, and that it subsequently derived a security policy that it believed to be adequate under the circumstances. This process should be well documented, and should include the security evaluation process as well as the reasoning behind the policies ultimately adopted. Independently conducted security surveys are extremely helpful in documenting this evaluation process. As part of the security survey assignment, the organization can ask the surveyor for policy recommendations that can then be evaluated in light of technical, legal, financial, and logistical restraints. Even if the recommendations are ultimately held to be inadequate, the organization's reliance on the recommendations of an apparently qualified security expert should be held to be reasonable under the circumstances. The security survey and its policy recommendations, the analysis of those recommendations, and the policy decisions themselves should be incorporated into the organization's security policy document. This document, or appropriate portions of it, can then be disseminated throughout the managerial organization.

The topics for security policy consideration will necessarily vary with the particular organization. Obviously, a port facility need not ponder whether it is prudent to place firearms or naval weapons systems aboard cargo-carrying vessels; an offshore installation operator need not worry about cruise ship passenger terminal security considerations. However, there are some general categories of security policy topics which can be listed. They are:

1. Organizational security.
2. Executive personnel security.
3. Vessel, facility, or installation security.
4. Security forces.
5. Firearms and other weapons.
6. Contingency planning.
7. Crisis management.

Organizational security is just what the term indicates: security of the organization. So far as policy decisions are concerned, the organization needs to consider whether it, as a whole, is at risk and, if so, what should be done about it. Many multinational corporations are prime targets for international terrorists who equate their names and products with capitalist oppression. Offshore oil platforms and fully loaded VLCCs or ULCCs clearly represent their parent organizations, and they constitute tremendous targets in terms of destruction, extortion, and propaganda potential. However, shoreside support facilities and regional offices also represent their multinational parent organizations, and their security should also be carefully considered.

Executive personnel security is another policy consideration closely related to organizational security. Because top executives represent the multinational corporations that employ them, they too are prime targets for terrorists. Any executive not willing to admit this fact is only deceiving himself. Any organization not willing to admit this fact is not only deceiving itself, it may well be leaving itself wide open for liability when its executives do become victims of terrorist activity. Is an organization responsible for the safety and security of its executives, even when the risks of terrorist activity are open and obvious? Is it responsible for negotiating with, or simply paying ransoms to, kidnappers and extortionists if the lives of its employees are at stake? If so, is it liable no matter what the ransom demand? These are questions that have yet to be answered in the courts. In the United States employers generally have a nondelegable duty to provide a safe place in which to work. Can this concept be extended to include employers of executive personnel who are assigned overseas either with or without their express consent? Are those same employers duty-bound to provide 24-hour-per-day security and security training for such personnel? Again, those questions have yet to be answered in court. The most germane case so far was decided in 1980 in the U.S. District

Court for the Southern District of New York. The name of the case was *Curtis v. Beatrice Foods Company,* and it involved the kidnapping of the manager of a subsidiary industrial company of the defendant's located in the Republic of Colombia. The manager, Gustavo G. Curtis, was kidnapped by terrorists and held for ransom for eight months, during which time Beatrice Foods voluntarily undertook to negotiate for his release and, after protracted negotiations, succeeded in freeing him alive by paying a ransom of 15.5 million pesos. Curtis and his wife sued Beatrice in federal court claiming over $200 million in damages for allegedly not doing enough on his behalf while he was being held prisoner, and for not transferring him from Colombia in the first place after he had requested it. Beatrice Foods denied legal liability and claimed that its conduct was voluntary, reasonable, and in good faith in freeing Curtis from captivity, and that it was not his employer nor was it obligated to provide him with employment elsewhere. The case was tried without a jury, and the plaintiffs lost on all counts. They appealed, and the decision was affirmed. Unfortunately, however, the case did not address the important liability issues, but focused instead on the interpretation of Colombian law, which all parties had stipulated applied, and the lack of proof offered by the plaintiffs. Consequently, the extent of an employer's liability, if any, for the kidnapping of one of its employees is not known. The claim will most certainly be made again, however, and it therefore behooves any prudent organization faced with such potential threats to explore its policy options.

Vessel, facility, and installation security procedures have been discussed at length. Underlying the implementation of those security procedures, however, must be the policy decisions that allow for such implementation. Consequently, the security threats faced by the ships, installations, or facilities of the particular maritime organization must be carefully studied and the subsequent security policy decisions made. All such policy decisions, and their reasons, should be well documented, and the organization's liability exposure should be carefully considered in the process. Underlying all policy decisions should be the question of reasonableness under the circumstances. Is it reasonable to expose a ship and her crew to the danger of RPG attacks when such attacks can be prevented easily and inexpensively? Is it reasonable to expose a ship and her crew to pirate attacks when such attacks can also be prevented easily and inexpensively? Is it reasonable to send ships into areas where they can be attacked by surface-to-surface or air-to-surface missiles without placing on board those ships some means of self-defense? Is it reasonable to expose offshore workers to potential disasters such as the *Piper Alpha*'s, which could just as easily have been an act of sabotage as it was an accident, without providing reasonable security measures to prevent it? These questions, and many like them, must be asked by those making security policy decisions if they wish to limit the liability exposure faced by their organizations.

Two of the toughest security policy decisions faced by any maritime organization involve the employment of security forces and the arming of those forces. If security forces are required, are they needed on a full-time or part-time basis? Should they consist of proprietary or contract personnel? Should they be armed, and if so, with what? The security response must be reasonable under the circumstances to meet the security threat faced, otherwise those providing the response as well as those it is intended to protect are unreasonably placed at risk. Unreasonable, inadequate security is negligent security. A department store guard, whose sole function is to prevent shoplifting, need not be armed with anything more than a nightstick. However, a guard whose duty it is to prevent a terrorist hijacking had better be armed with something more effective, otherwise he might as well not be there at all. If he is not there, and the security threat is known, it is negligence. If he is there, and improperly armed, it is negligence. If he is not there because the threat is not known, but it should reasonably be known, it is negligence (the law does not accept the head-in-the-sand excuse). Once the security threat is recognized or should have been recognized, the maritime operator has a duty under the law to provide reasonable security. There is no way around it. If it fails to provide reasonable security, and people are injured or property damaged as a result, it will be liable. The damages can be astronomic; consider the *Piper Alpha* example of lost wages alone. The policy decision-makers must consider such eventualities.

Contingency planning and crisis management policies go hand in hand. The key to both is foreseeability. Once the security threats are recognized, their eventualities must be planned for throughout the organization. The security policies relating to each potential incident must be well understood by all personnel likely to be involved. What will the onboard response be to pirate attack? How should a sabotage attempt be handled on an offshore installation in the North Sea? How will bomb threats be handled for a cruise ship passenger terminal? What should an LNG carrier's response be to an attempted hijacking? What should the organizational response be to all of these events? If an oil rig is hijacked or sabotaged and a ransom demanded, will the ransom be paid? Will negotiations be attempted? What parameters will be set for payment of a ransom demand? What tasks will be set for the crisis management team, and who will ensure they are complete? These questions and many more must be asked and answered by those responsible for developing the organization's security policies. The answers, or the resulting policies, cannot be arbitrary, however, and the reasons for the positions taken should be carefully explained and documented. They should also be reviewed for reasonableness. One effective contingency planning tool that can be utilized at various organizational levels is the practice of gaming. For over ten years the U.S. military has used gaming for both the strategic and tactical training of its officers. The recent popularity of role-playing gaming among American consumers has spawned a large variety of complex, military-oriented, and tactically accurate games, many of which can have substantial organizational training and planning value if used properly. One particular game even has as its scenario the terrorist hijacking of an Italian luxury cruise ship, which roughly recreates the *Achille Lauro* incident.

RISK MANAGEMENT

Risk management is the term most often used by insurance professionals to describe an organization's management of its liabilities. Although it usually encompasses more than the mere purchase of insurance, self-insurance and commercial insurance considerations are the two conceptual cornerstones of risk management. Through risk management an organization identifies its risks, analyzes and evaluates them in relation to the liabilities they present, and then either reduces, transfers, or accepts those risks depending upon the management policies of the organization. Commercial insurance is the primary method employed in today's business environment to either reduce or transfer financial risks, and it can be obtained to protect an organization against losses sustained as a result of terrorist activity.

The concept of insurance, as it is practiced today, has been around for about 700 years. It is said to have originated in the town of Bruges, one of the leading seaports of the Hanseatic League, and by the fifteenth century insurance practices were well established throughout Europe. By the late sixteenth century rules and regulations had developed requiring, among other things, that contracts of insurance had to be in writing and recorded as public acts before a register. To this day, the insurance contract is the single most important item regarding insurance coverage and the payment of claims. Contracts of insurance are highly technical, complex, and legalistic documents that contain numerous words and phrases of art not readily understood by laypersons. They abound with definitions and exclusions that delineate, or attempt to delineate, the insurer's obligations under the contract to pay for losses sustained by the insured. They also describe preconditions and other requirements that must be met by the insured before coverage can attach.

Insurance companies have been responding to losses sustained from pirate activity for hundreds of years, including the payment of ransoms to release crews held hostage by pirates in the East Indies during the eighteenth century. More recently, they have paid for the loss of aircraft that have been hijacked and destroyed by Palestinian terrorists, as well as millions of dollars in ransoms for numerous executives kidnapped in Third-World countries. Kidnap insurance is available to qualified corporations and individuals at this moment, as is just about any other type of insurance for which there is a willingness to pay. The key word is "pay." Insurance companies are in business to make money. They gamble on not having to pay for the loss that their insured pays them handsomely to protect against. As the risk of the loss occurring increases, so do the insurance premiums, until at some point the cost of the insurance equals the cost of the potential loss. At some time prior to that point most insureds become self-insured; that is, they assume the risk of the loss themselves. Statistically, therefore, insurance companies can't lose, and they seldom do unless they make an error in their calculations. They do realize, however, that they cannot assume liabilities for potential losses that could affect their own solvency, no matter how much they charge for premiums. That is why in times of war certain coverages are suspended: Potential liabilities simply exceed the premium income minus operating expenses (not to mention profit). Consequently, the potentially astronomical damages that could result from the maritime security scenarios previously discussed raise some interesting questions so far as insurance coverage is concerned. The initial fines of $103 million and $59 million levied by the United States against shippers for importation of cocaine, heroin, and marijuana, mentioned earlier, sent shock waves through the maritime underwriting industry and almost assuredly caused those concerned to review the applicable protection and indemnity policies for excuses not to pay. If the *Piper Alpha* was not self-insured by Occidental Petroleum one can bet its underwriters are having a fit over the potential $300 million-plus claim for loss of life, not to mention the lost revenues. If the claimants in the *Amoco Cadiz* oil spill are successful on appeal, who will come up with the sought-after $2 billion? If an LNG tanker were hijacked and ignited in Boston Harbor, how could any underwriting or shipping enterprise possibly pay for the massive destruction that would ensue?

Maritime underwriters have only two choices once they realize the magnitude of their potential exposure arising from terrorist activity. They can either suspend coverage, as they have done in the past, or they can exclude it completely unless certain security requirements are met by their insureds. The only logical course of action is to exclude coverage until maritime operators enact security measures and meet security standards that will greatly reduce the likelihood of successful terrorist action. Any ship, installation, or facility can be adequately protected. The problem lies in forcing the marine industry to take the necessary steps to provide such protection. The underwriters will ultimately wield the hammer that forces the issue, but they won't do so until they are convinced such action is necessary. They may wait too long.

While they are waiting, there are a number of things a security manager should do to solidify his organization's legal position so far as insurance coverage is concerned. First, he should obtain copies of all current insurance policies and study them from the standpoint of having to make a claim on behalf of the organization either for losses it might suffer as a result of terrorist activity, or for coverage from claims that might be made against it as a result of terrorist activity. The best way to do this is to make a list of all the foreseeable events that could occur, and a list of all the foreseeable claims that could be made as a result of those events, and then read each policy to see if those claims are more likely to be covered or excluded. In order to arrive at a conclusion with respect to possible coverage, the security manager must read the policies the same way the insurance companies' lawyers will, and not the way most insureds do. He should also know the basic legal rules of contract interpretation. In the United States these rules can vary somewhat from state to state, and each state may vary from federal law. Consequently, it is important to know what law applies to the construction of the various contracts under consideration. Generally speaking, the following rules apply:

1. Unless stated otherwise in the contract, the law of the country or state in which the contract was executed controls.
2. Federal law applies to all maritime contracts made in the United States. (Contracts for marine insurance are maritime contracts.)
3. If the language of the contract is clear and unambiguous it will be construed according to normal usage.
4. If the contract is ambiguous such that there are two or more reasonable interpretations, it will be construed against the party who drafted the contract.
5. Contracts must be read *in pari materia;* that is, as a whole.

Insurance policies can almost *always* be shown to be ambiguous. That is because underwriters are so concerned with covering themselves for events they don't wish to insure they get tangled up in the contract language. The language used may appear to cover an event in one part of the contract and exclude it in another. If so, the contract is ambiguous and must be construed in favor of the insured. In any event, the trick to reading insurance policies is to determine first what events are covered by studying the definitions section for such terms as "loss," "event," "accident," "insured," and so on. Then, if the event in question appears to fall within the policy coverage, the "exclusions" section of the policy should be read to see if the event is one which is excluded. If the event still appears to be one that is covered, a close reading of the warranties and other preconditions should be made to determine whether the insured may have violated any warranty that would have the effect of voiding the insurance. Throughout this entire process it should be remembered that when faced with a large claim the first thing underwriters do is attempt to find some reason not to pay it. Years ago the more disreputable underwriters would refuse to pay *any* large claim, no matter whether they thought coverage existed or not. This would force the insured to sue, and the case could then be settled for less than the claim amount. Now, however, at least in the United States, if an insured is forced to sue his underwriter and he prevails, the underwriter must pay not only the claim but the insured's attorney's fees as well. Also, if it can be proven that the claim was denied in bad faith the insured may be awarded punitive damages. This has made some underwriters a little more careful in denying claims, but one can rest assured that if the coverage question can be decided either way, and if there is at least a chance of prevailing in court, the insurer will deny the claim. In any event, once the security manager has reviewed the insurance policies in light of all foreseeable claims, he should make lists of those claims for which he suspects no coverage exists and of those he believes the underwriters will deny (the two are not necessarily the same). He may then wish to confirm his analysis with the organization's legal counsel, because the next thing the organization must do is decide how it intends to manage those risks for which there appears to be a coverage question. A number of options are available, some of which include clarifying in writing with the underwriter whether coverage exists for specific claims, obtaining additional insurance, or considering the risks self-insured for the time being and planning to litigate the disputed coverage if necessary.

OTHER LEGAL CONSIDERATIONS

There are a number of other legal considerations with which the security manager should be concerned besides risk management and negligent security litigation. All of them cannot be discussed here. Many, in fact, will only become apparent as a particular organization develops its security policies and implements security procedures. The security manager should, however, remain constantly aware of the possible legal ramifications or requirements of any security options under consideration. In this regard, he may wish to enlist the aid of legal counsel at some time during the policy development stages. Even without the aid of counsel a certain amount of legal inquiry and analysis can be made with a little forethought to the problem.

Maritime activity is regulated, by and large, by national statutes, treaties, and international conventions. Treaties and international conventions only affect individuals so far as they are manifested in the laws of the jurisdiction in which the individual finds himself. Thus, maritime security policies, measures, and procedures will be affected and possibly regulated by the laws of the country in which the security measures are taken. Actions taken on the high seas will be scrutinized according to international law or the law of the flag of the vessel involved. Security planning must therefore take into account such laws and regulations that are applicable to the particular maritime endeavor.

In the United States the laws and regulations affecting ships and shipping are found primarily in the following sources: Title 46—Shipping of the U.S. Code, Title 33—Navigation of the U.S. Code, and the corresponding volumes of the *Code of Federal Regulations* (known as the CFR). Official notices and other governmental announcements are published in the *Federal Register.* In certain circumstances other sections of the U.S. Code may have maritime security applications, such as Title 14—Coast Guard, Title 15—Commerce and Trade, Title 18—Crimes and Criminal Procedure, Title 19—Customs Duties, Title 21—Food and Drugs, and so on. It is not the intent of this book to discuss all the applicable laws and regulations in the United States or elsewhere that may affect maritime security. However, it *is* the intent of this book to raise the security consciousness of the maritime industry; therefore, some of the applicable statutes and regulations as they may relate to maritime security should be discussed.

Title 46 of the U.S. Code is entitled "Shipping," and this is what it pertains to. It is divided into subtitles I and II. Subtitle I has nothing in it, as it has been reserved for future legislative use. Subtitle II is entitled "Vessels and Seamen" and is divided into 10 parts, which are alphabetically designated. They are:

A. General Provisions.
B. Inspection and Regulation of Vessels.
C. Load Lines of Vessels.
D. Marine Casualties.
E. Merchant Seamen Licenses, Certificates, and Documents.
F. Manning of Vessels.
G. Merchant Seamen Protection and Relief.
H. Identification of Vessels.
I. State Boating Safety Programs.
J. Measurement of Vessels.

Each part is divided into a number of chapters, each with numerous sections. The first noteworthy section, so far as maritime security is concerned, is section 2302, "Penalties for negligent operations." It reads:

(a) A person operating a vessel in a negligent manner that endangers the life, limb, or property of a person is liable to the United States Government for a civil penalty of not more than $1,000.

(b) A person operating a vessel in a grossly negligent manner that endangers the life, limb, or property of a person shall be fined not more than $5,000, imprisoned for not more than one year, or both.

(c) An individual who is intoxicated when operating a vessel, as determined under standards prescribed by the Secretary by regulation, shall be
  (1) liable to the United States Government for a civil penalty of not more than $1,000; or
  (2) fined not more than $5,000, imprisoned for not more than one year, or both.

(d) For a penalty imposed under this section, the vessel is also liable in rem unless the vessel is
  (1) owned by a State or a political subdivision of a State;
  (2) operated principally for governmental purposes; and
  (3) identified clearly as a vessel of that State or subdivision.

This section clearly allows the imposition of both civil and criminal penalties for the negligent operation of a vessel, and it raises some interesting questions concerning negligent security. Could operating a vessel without security, or with inadequate security, be said to be operating a vessel in a negligent manner such that it endangers the life, limb, or property of another person? If so, the master (and possibly the owner and operator) can be held liable for a civil penalty of $1,000. Where the security threat is known, such as attacks by pirates in the Phillip Channel, and the vessel is operated without security, could that be said to be operating a vessel in a grossly negligent manner? If so, the master (and possibly the owner and operator) can be fined up to $5,000 and imprisoned for up to one year. Furthermore, in both instances the vessel can be arrested and sold to pay the monetary penalties imposed. If this seems far-fetched, consider what *has* been found to be negligent operation under this section: operation of a vessel at night without navigation lights, leaving a wheelhouse unattended for 5–10 minutes with another vessel in the vicinity, failure to secure exit hatches in heavy weather, and failure to assure cargo containers were stowed securely before leaving the loading dock. Operating a vessel with no security where a threat is known to exist is certainly comparable to leaving a wheelhouse unattended or hatches unsecured. Furthermore, if a seaman injured in a pirate attack sues, is it not likely that he will also file charges under section 2302, if he knows about it?

Another section that can have serious maritime security ramifications is section 2304, "Duty to provide assistance at sea." It reads:

(a) A master or individual in charge of a vessel shall render assistance to any individual found at sea in danger of being lost, so far as the master or individual in charge can do so without serious danger to the master's or individual's vessel or individuals on board.

(b) A master or individual violating this section shall be fined not more that $1,000, imprisoned for not more than 2 years, or both.

Seamen for thousands of years have been quick to go to the aid of other seamen in distress, and this section merely codifies that tradition. Failure to do so, however, can result in a fine of $1,000 and imprisonment for two years. Most maritime nations have similar laws, and consequently ship's masters are generally well aware of their obligation, both morally and legally, to render assistance at sea. Terrorists, however, planning to hijack a vessel, can use such obligations to their advantage. A properly security-conscious and wary master should understand that, at least under this law, he does have a choice. Even though the statute reads that he *shall* render assistance, it also indicates such assistance need only be offered where it can be made without seriously endangering the ship or those on board. Consequently, if a master comes upon an assistance-at-sea situation that to him looks suspicious he may legally refuse assistance. Even if the situation later turns out to have been legitimate, if he can show it looked like a trap and smelled like a trap, he should be exonerated.

Section 8102 is interesting in that it pertains to watchmen aboard passenger vessels. It states in part:

(a) The owner, charterer, or managing director of a vessel carrying passengers during the nighttime shall keep a suitable number of watchmen in the vicinity of the cabins or staterooms and on each deck to guard against and give alarm in case of fire or other danger. An owner, charterer, or managing operator failing to provide watchmen required by this section is liable to the United States Government for a civil penalty of $1,000.

This section is interesting for a number of reasons. First, it applies only to passenger-carrying vessels. Second, it requires security watches to be posted at night in the vicinity of cabins or staterooms *and on each deck,* which presumably includes all weather decks, to guard against fire *or other danger.* It is foreseeable that cruise ships that ply island waters could be boarded by hijackers in the same manner that pirates board tankers and freighters in the South China Sea and similar areas: by high-speed watercraft and grappling hooks. Even though the intent of the statute is to guard against fire and perhaps the theft of passengers' valuables, it clearly has a broader applicability within the context of maritime security.

The next section that bears mentioning is a lengthy one on watches. The portions of section 8104 that are quoted demonstrate an *authority* to do something, rather than a requirement. Section 8104 reads in part:

(b) On an oceangoing or coastwise vessel of not more than 100 gross tons (except a fishing, fish processing, or fish tender vessel), a licensed individual may not be required to work more than 9 of 24 hours when in port, including the date of arrival, or more than 12 of 24 hours at sea, except in an emergency when life or property are endangered . . .

(d) On a merchant vessel of more than 100 gross tons . . . the licensed individuals, sailors, coal passers, firemen, oilers, and water tenders shall be divided, when at sea, into at least 3 watches, and shall be kept on duty successively to perform ordinary work incident to the operation and management of the vessel . . . A licensed individual or seaman in

the deck or engine department may not be required to work
more than 8 hours in one day . . .

(f) Subsections (d) and (e) of this section do not limit the
authority of the master or other officer or the obedience of
the seamen when, in the judgment of the master or other officer, any part of the crew is needed for

(1) maneuvering, shifting the berth of, mooring, or unmoor-
ing, the vessel;

(2) performing work necessary for the safety of the vessel,
or the vessel's passengers, crew, or cargo;

(3) saving life on board another vessel in jeopardy; or

(4) performing fire, lifeboat, or other drills in port or at sea.

Shipboard security watches have been recommended elsewhere in this
work that can be stood by existing members of the ship's crew if
professional security personnel or additional crew members are not
placed on board. This suggestion is not expected to gain much favor
with American seamen's unions, and one objection that might be
raised by such unions is the apparent statutory prohibition for additional watches under section 8104. However, subsections (b) and (f)
both appear to allow the standing of additional security watches. On
vessels of less than 100 gross tons additional security watches may be
ordered in cases of "emergency when life or property are endangered,"
and on vessels of more than 100 gross tons such watches may be ordered when "necessary for the safety of the vessel, or the vessel's passengers, crew, or cargo" or when performing security "drills in port
or at sea."

The final section in Title 46 that will be quoted is section 10902,
"Complaints of unfitness." The section concerns itself mostly with
possible onboard unfitness of food and water and the available
remedies for the crew, which have little to do with maritime security.
The first part of the section, however, does have some rather startling
security significance. It reads in part:

(a)(1) If the chief and second mates or a majority of the crew of
a vessel ready to begin a voyage discover, before the vessel
leaves harbor, that the vessel is unfit as to crew, hull, equipment, tackle, machinery, apparel, furniture, provisions of food
or water, or stores to proceed on the intended voyage and re-

quire the unfitness to be inquired into, the master immediately
shall apply to the district court of the United States . . . for the
appointment of surveyors . . .

The significance of this section lies in the statutory recognition that a
vessel may be unseaworthy as to crew or equipment to proceed on her
intended voyage, and that the vessel's master may refuse or be unable
to do anything about it. It provides a remedy for the vessel's crew so
that they need not go to sea in an unseaworthy vessel. In order to be
seaworthy, a vessel or a piece of equipment must be fit for its intended
use. Federal maritime law has long recognized the fact that a vessel
can be unseaworthy if she is improperly manned. Inadequate or nonexistent security measures can likewise make a vessel unseaworthy to
proceed on her intended voyage, particularly if that voyage will take
her into known jeopardy where such security measures may be needed.
Under this section, a crew can demand that their ship be outfitted with
reasonable protection against missile and RPG attacks before sailing
for the Persian Gulf, or that an antipiracy capability be installed aboard
before sailing for pirate-infested waters. If such a demand were to be
made, and if it caught the shipowner by surprise, the resultant sailing
delay could be extremely costly while the matter was resolved in court.
It could also force the shipowner to install court-ordered security
measures aboard.

Before leaving Title 46, several other sections should be mentioned, all of which appear in the appendix to Title 46. An entire chapter, chapter 37, is devoted to the congressional voicing of concerns
about international maritime and port security, but in reality it says
very little. The chapter, entitled "International Maritime and Port
Security," contains sections 1801 through 1809. None of the sections
requires much action other than the promulgation of a few reports on
the part of some governmental agencies. All nine sections are
reproduced in appendix B to this book. Chapter 38 of Title 46 is entitled "Drug Abuse Prevention On Board Vessels" and it contains section 1901 through 1904. These sections are reproduced in appendix F
to this book, and need not be discussed in much depth. The most important feature of this chapter is the authorization of seizure and forfeiture of any property, including vessels, used to commit or facilitate
a drug-related offense under the Comprehensive Drug Abuse Prevention and Control Act of 1970. The final two sections of Title 46 to be

mentioned have spawned massive amounts of litigation over the years. They are section 688, "The Jones Act," and section 761, *et seq.,* "The Death on the High Seas Act." Both provide statutory causes of action to sue for death or injury resulting from negligence in the operation of a vessel. The two statutes apply in different instances, and neither shall be quoted here. It is sufficient to note that throughout this work when discussions have been had with regard to shipowners' liabilities for injury or death of seamen or passengers resulting from negligent security practices those liabilities stem wholly or in part from these two statutes.

Title 33 of the U.S. Code is entitled "Navigation and Navigable Waters." This is a lengthy title, encompassed in four volumes that contain 35 chapters and over 2,100 sections. As the title suggests, all aspects of navigation and matters concerning the navigable waters of the United States are included. Only a few of these matters will be discussed here since most of them apply to navigational rules or pollution of the navigable waters and do not concern the security of vessels, port facilities, or offshore installations.

One section of Title 33 that does concern the security of vessels is section 383, "Resistance of pirates by merchant vessels." That section reads as follows:

> The commander and crew of any merchant vessel of the United States, owned wholly, or in part, by a citizen thereof, may oppose and defend against any aggression, search, restraint, depredation, or seizure, which shall be attempted upon such vessel, or upon any other vessel so owned, by the commander or crew of any armed vessel whatsoever, not being a public armed vessel of some nation in amity with the United States, and may subdue and capture the same; and may also retake any vessel so owned which may have been captured by the commander or crew of any such armed vessel, and send the same into any port of the United States.

This statute clearly authorizes any U.S. flag merchantman, yacht, or other vessel to resist any act of aggression, search, restraint, depredation, or seizure attempted by almost any armed vessel, public or private, and it also allows the seizure of pirate craft and the retaking of any U.S. vessels which may have been seized by pirates. Thus, tankers and freighters in the Phillip Channel have the right to defend themselves against pirate attack, containerships off the west coast of Africa have the right to protect themselves against marauders, yachts in the Caribbean have the right to repel boarders, and U.S.-flagged merchant vessels may defend themselves against attacks by Iranian patrol craft in the Persian Gulf.

Another section in Title 33 which directly affects maritime security is section 1226, "Port, harbor, and coastal facility security." It reads:

(a) General authority. The Secretary may take actions described in subsection (b) to prevent or respond to an act of terrorism against
  (1) an individual, vessel, or public or commercial structure, that is
     (A) subject to the jurisdiction of the United States; and
     (B) located within or adjacent to the marine environment; or
  (2) a vessel of the United States or an individual on board that vessel.
(b) Specific authority. Under subsection (a), the Secretary may
  (1) carry out or require measures, including inspections, port and harbor patrols, the establishment of security and safety zones, and the development of contingency plans and procedures, to prevent or respond to acts of terrorism; and
  (2) recruit members of the Regular Coast Guard and the Coast Guard Reserve and train members of the Regular Coast Guard and the Coast Guard Reserve in the techniques of preventing and responding to acts of terrorism.

This statute grants authority to the U.S. Government and the Coast Guard to respond to acts of terrorism committed against any individual, vessel, or structure subject to the jurisdiction of the United States that is located within or adjacent to the marine environment. It also authorizes the development and enactment of preventive security measures and procedures designed to counter terrorist activity.

Title 33 also contains several sections that address the proper lighting of vessels in various situations, such as underway, at anchor, adrift, and so on. Most of those sections contain language prohibiting the display of lights other than as prescribed by statute *if they can be mistaken for the prescribed lights, or if they impair the visibility or distinctive character of those lights, or if they interfere with the keeping of a proper lookout.* The protective lighting systems to be employed aboard vessels are only affected by such sections in two instances: when a vessel is underway and when she is at anchor. The only time she would employ her protective lighting underway would be to thwart attempted boardings and, under such circumstances, would be entirely within the navigational rules. Section 181 authorizes the use of additional lights when necessary: "Every vessel may, if necessary, in order to attract attention, in addition to the lights which she is required to carry, show a flare-up light or use any detonating signal that can not be mistaken for a distress signal." At anchor, protective lighting may still be used so long as it does not achieve the proscribed effects. The outer-perimeter, glare-projected protective lighting suggested in this book will not. In fact, Rule 30 of the International Regulations (section 1602 of Title 33) requires additional on-deck lighting for vessels at anchor that are 100 meters or more in length.

A number of CFR sections should be mentioned. The relationship between the *Code of Federal Regulations* and the U.S. Code is that the code generally provides the statutory authority for the promulgation of regulations found in the CFR. The CFR section numbers correspond roughly, but not exactly, to the section numbers for the same topics in the code. The CFR volumes are published annually, but not all at the same time, so one should ensure he has the current volume whenever relying upon the regulations found within.

The first set of regulations that should be mentioned appear in Title 33 of the *Code of Federal Regulations,* Part 6 (July 1, 1987, edition). "Protection and Security of Vessels, Harbors, and Waterfront Facilities." This is an important set of regulations, so far as U.S. maritime security is concerned, and is reproduced in its entirety in appendix C to this volume. The regulations are divided into several subparts:

6.01 Definitions.

6.04 General Provisions.

6.10 Identification and Exclusion of Persons From Vessels and
   Waterfront Facilities.

6.12 Supervision and Control of Explosives or Other Dangerous
   Cargo.

6.14 Security of Waterfront Facilities and Vessels in Port.

6.16 Sabotage and Subversive Activity.

6.18 Penalties.

6.19 Responsibility for Security of Vessels and Waterfront
   Facilities.

The Coast Guard is the agency of the U.S. Government responsible
for implementing these regulations. All ship security officers and
port facility security officers should be familiar with them, as
should owners, operators, and agents of vessels and waterfront
facilities, and it should be clearly understood that the *primary*
responsibility for security of a vessel or port facility remains with
the vessel or facility. A homeowner is responsible for locking his
own doors and windows even though the local police may patrol
his neighborhood and offer security suggestions. A vessel is responsible for her own security even though the captain of the port may
implement security procedures and render assistance when necessary. Section 6.19-1 states: "Nothing in this part shall be construed
as relieving the masters, owners, operators, and agents of vessels
or other waterfront facilities from their primary responsibility for
the protection and security of such vessels or waterfront facilities."
This section is important for several reasons. Two of the less obvious ones are that, first of all, if a master is challenged by either
the Coast Guard or the port facility with regard to the security procedures he wishes to implement while in port (such as arming his
security watches), he can point to this section as authority for his
actions. Second, since the master very clearly has the primary
responsibility, under these regulations, for the security of his ship
his security officer should receive all possible cooperation and assistance from the captain of the port in all security matters. Thus,
in addition to making a liaison with the port facility security officer
upon berthing, the ship security officer should also make liaison

with the captain of the port. He should advise the captain of the port of his security intentions and request any information or advice the captain of the port may have. This will certainly be appreciated by the captain of the port, and will ensure everyone understands what everyone else is doing. Furthermore, if a dispute arises with U.S. Customs officials regarding the securing and sealing of firearms while in port (a subject which will be discussed shortly), the captain of the port should assist the master in resolving the dispute in favor of the vessel.

Another section of these regulations that clearly vests primary responsibility for security with the owner and operator of the vessel or facility is section 6.16-3, "Precautions against sabotage." It reads: "The master, owner, agent, or operator of a vessel or waterfront facility shall take all necessary precautions to protect the vessel, waterfront facility, and cargo from sabotage." This section provides more ammunition, if needed, for the master of a vessel to ensure his security measures are allowed. The key words are "all necessary precautions." The determination of what is "necessary" is a judgment call upon which reasonable men might differ, but it is clearly the vessel's responsibility to take such precautions. Consequently, the master of a vessel has every legal right to insist upon posting the security which he believes is necessary for the protection of his vessel and cargo. The captain of the port may, however, disagree with the master with regard to what precautions are necessary. Such disagreement might be based upon a legitimate, professional assessment of the circumstances, founded on current intelligence and years of experience, in which case the ship's master may decide to acquiesce (although from a legal standpoint this is not recommended). On the other hand, the disagreement could just as well be based upon nothing more than bureaucratic inflexibility, in which case the ship's master should definitely not acquiesce without going on record as objecting. In either case, it should be remembered that under these and all other applicable regulations and laws, the legal responsibility for the security of the vessel rests with her master, owners, and operators. These regulations, however, also empower the captain of the port to place guards on any vessel, waterfront facility, or security zone (which may be established in accordance with the regulations), and he may enlist the aid of federal, local, and private security agencies in order to do so. Section 6.04-7 states:

The Captain of the Port may cause to be inspected and searched at any time any vessel, waterfront facility, or security zone, or any person, article, or thing thereon or therein, within the jurisdiction of the United States, may place guards upon any such vessel, waterfront facility, or security zone and may remove therefrom any and all persons, articles, or things not specifically authorized by him to go or remain thereon or therein.

Section 6.04-11 states: "The Captain of the Port may enlist the aid and cooperation of Federal, State, county, municipal, and private agencies to assist in the enforcement of regulations issued pursuant to this part." Consequently, if the captain of the port refuses to allow a master to establish the security he as master deems necessary, regardless of the reasons, certain precautions should be taken by that master to help ensure any liability for negligent security that might arise is shifted to the captain of the port and the U.S. Government. This can be done relatively easily, and should be in every such instance.

The procedure that should be followed is this: First, upon the vessel's arrival at the port facility the ship's security officer should make his liaison with both the port facility's security officer and the captain of the port. At both meetings he should advise those present of the ship's intended security procedures and ask them if they have any objections. If they have no objections he should present them with a "vessel security procedures authorization form" which briefly but accurately describes the intended shipboard security procedures and contains a designated space for approval and authorization. He should obtain the necessary signatures on the form and retain it for the ship's records. The document should be treated as a controlled document and copies left with the signatories only if they insist. One possible format the form might take is as follows:

VESSEL SECURITY PROCEDURES AUTHORIZATION FORM

Port of: Date:
Vessel:
To Whom It May Concern:
    The above-named vessel arrived at the above-named port on or about the   day of   , 19   , and berthed at on or about the   day of   , 19   , at   hours. As

soon as was thereafter practical, a meeting was had between the ship's representatives and   for the expressed purpose of discussing the security conditions present in the port facility and at the assigned berth. At that meeting the ship's representatives advised those present of the ship's intended security procedures during her stay, which shall consist of the following:

(brief description of security procedures)

There being no objection to the stated intended shipboard security procedures they have been approved and authorized by the below-listed persons who expressly warrant they are authorized and empowered to do so.

signature/position   *date*
signature/position   *date*

If, however, approval of the intended shipboard security procedures is refused, the second thing the ship's security officer should do is deliver to the captain of the port a second document. The purpose of this document is to formally request the captain of the port to provide the security services deemed necessary by the ship's master and which he has not been allowed to establish, although he is willing and able to do so. One format could be:

NOTICE OF REQUEST FOR SECURITY

I,   , master of the M/V   ,
do herewith specifically request the captain of the port of   to provide to the above-named vessel, her crew, and cargo the following security precautions pursuant to Part 6 of Title 33 of the *Code of Federal Regulations* (1987):

(describe security procedures)

Said security precautions are deemed by me to be necessary to protect the said vessel and her cargo from sabotage or other threat. I fully understand my security responsibilities pursuant to 33 C.F.R. 6.16-3 and 6.19-1 (1987) and have this date requested permission from the captain of the port to establish the above-requested security precautions on board employing ship's personnel, weapons, and equipment, and have been denied that permission. Accordingly, I herewith serve NOTICE of my request that said security precautions be provided to the vessel by the captain of the port.

signature of vessel's master   *date*

It should be emphasized that in all cases either the vessel security procedures authorization form should be signed or the notice of request for security should be delivered to the captain of the port. The ship can have such forms prepared and a good supply kept on board. In instances where the ship is not capable of providing the proper security a notice of request for security should also be delivered to the captain of the port that describes the security desired. It can either be a second version of the form or simply a modified version of the same form. Thus, armed guards can always be requested of the captain of the port for whatever port at which the vessel calls. This doesn't mean that the request will be granted, or that the services requested will be provided without cost (although the cost might well be argued as being a responsibility of either the port facility or the captain of the port), but it does tend to show a reasonable attempt on the part of the vessel to provide herself with adequate security. The request will also most likely take the captain of the port quite by surprise.

Two other portions of Title 33 should be mentioned before moving on to other CFR volumes. These are Subchapter K, "Security of Vessels," and Subchapter L, "Waterfront Facilities." Subchapter K is very short and merely supplements 33 C.F.R. 6.14-1. It requires that placards containing atomic attack instructions for merchant vessels in port be posted in conspicuous places, when such placards are given to a vessel's master. Subchapter L concerns the issuing and maintaining of Coast Guard port security cards, and is considerably longer. It is reproduced in appendix D to this book. The use of Coast Guard port security cards is a convenient and efficient way of controlling access both to and within a port facility. The cards are issued by the Coast Guard, through a well-established administrative and investigative system maintained at the expense of the government, and are available to all port facilities that choose to utilize it. Why most port facilities do not take full advantage of such an access control system is a deep mystery. It is, in essence, available for the asking and should form the foundation for any access controls implemented by a port facility. *Every* port facility employee should have a port security card, and obtaining and maintaining one should be a condition of employment. Captains of the ports around the country may cringe at the thought of the administrative burden this suggestion may cause their offices, but that is irrelevant. The regulations were enacted to help provide security for the ports of the nation, and it is about time they were utilized as they were intended. A port security card access control system, standing alone, is certainly not foolproof. No access control system is foolproof. It provides, however, a place to start. It also provides some defense to any negligent security/access-control claim that might be made, as well as a possible third-party defendant (the government) if the cause can be attributed to a negligently issued port security card. The eligibility standards, investigative processes, and acceptability requirements are supposed to be stringent, which is the way Congress intended them to be. Section 125.17 states:

> (a) Only the following persons may be issued Coast Guard Security Cards:
>   (1) Persons regularly employed on vessels or on waterfront facilities.
>   (2) Persons having regular public or private business connected with the operation, maintenance, or administration of vessels, their cargoes, or waterfront facilities.
> (b) A holder of a Merchant Mariner's Document shall not be issued a Port Security Card, unless his Merchant Mariner's Document is surrendered to the Coast Guard. In this connection, see § 125.09.

The key word for eligibility under this section is "regular." For persons to be eligible for a Coast Guard port security card they must be *regularly* employed on vessels or waterfront facilities or have *regular* business connected with vessels, cargoes, or port facilities. Absolutely no one else qualifies. So, what does "regular" mean in the context of these regulations? They don't say. Must the employment or business be on a daily basis? Is weekly allowable? What about monthly? Does regular, annual business qualify as "regular" business so far as the issuance of a Coast Guard port security card? Whatever the standard is, is it the same for each issuing authority across the country, or is it easier to get a card in one place than another? The only standards defined in the regulations appear in section 125.19 and relate to the character and habits of the applicant:

Information concerning an applicant for a Coast Guard Port Security Card, or a holder of such card, which may preclude a determination that his character and habits of life are such as to warrant the belief that his presence on waterfront facilities, and port and harbor areas, including vessels and harbor craft therein, would not be inimical to the security of the United States, shall relate to the following:

(a) Advocacy of the overthrow or alteration of the Government of the United States by unconstitutional means.

(b) Commission of, or attempts or preparations to commit, an act of espionage, sabotage, sedition or treason, or conspiring with, or aiding or abetting another to commit such act.

(c) Performing, or attempting to perform, duties or otherwise acting so as to serve the interests of another government to the detriment of the United States.

(d) Deliberate unauthorized disclosure of classified defense information.

(e) [Reserved]

(f) Having been adjudged insane, having been legally committed to an insane asylum, or treated for serious mental or neurological disorder, without evidence of cure.

(g) Having been convicted of any of the following offenses, indicative of a criminal tendency potentially dangerous to the security of such waterfront facilities and port and harbor areas, including vessels and harbor craft therein; arson, unlawful trafficking in drugs, espionage, sabotage, or treason.

(h) Drunkenness on the job or addiction to the use of narcotic drugs, without adequate evidence of rehabilitation.

(i) Illegal presence in the United States, its territories or possessions; having been found finally subject to deportation order by the United States Immigration and Naturalization Service.

According to the regulations these standards, which are in reality negative standards, are the only ones allowed in the determination of fitness for a port security card. Presumably, therefore, if an applicant can show regular employment or business relating to vessels or port facilities, and there is no evidence that he meets any of the negative standards set forth in section 125.19, a card should be issued. There may be a question as to the legality of some of these standards, particularly if a large number of cards begin being issued or revoked, but for the time being the regulations establish at least some sort of control over who should be issued a port security card.

The next CFR sections to be discussed are those that relate to firearms carried aboard vessels for protection and not as cargo. The management of firearms is specifically treated in chapter 7, but the regulatory considerations should be discussed here. The important thing to remember is that *there is absolutely no prohibition under U.S. law against carrying protective firearms on board any commercial vessel.* In fact, the need to carry firearms and ammunition in order to preserve the good order and discipline aboard ship has been recognized for hundreds of years, and is still recognized in the CFR today. Footnote 1 to 46 C.F.R. 147.05-100 (October 1, 1987) states: "A vessel may carry such ammunition for small arms as the master deems indispensable for the preservation of discipline on board the vessel. No person shall bring or have in his possession or use on board a vessel any ammunition for small arms except by express permission of the master or other person in charge of the vessel." This footnote is to a classification table (table S) of ship's stores and supplies of a dangerous nature and specifically relates to the requirements for small arms ammunition, of which there are none except for the footnote. The firearms themselves, rather than their ammunition, are only mentioned once in the CFR and this is in 46 C.F.R. 146.20-3: "The offering of the following explosives for transportation, carriage, conveyance, storage, stowage, or use on board vessels is forbidden: . . . Loaded firearms." The operative word, in the first instance, is "loaded." There is no prohibition against unloaded firearms, which is the way protective firearms would be carried aboard and stowed in the ship's armory or small arms locker. The phrase "use on board" however, appears to be in direct conflict with footnote 1 to 46 C.F.R. 147.05-100 quoted above. Clearly, if a vessel may carry such ammunition for small arms as the master deems indispensable for the preservation of discipline,

Congress must have envisioned the possibility of that ammunition being *loaded* at some time into the small arms for which it is intended. The apparent difficulty is resolved, however, if one takes a second look at the introductory paragraph to section 146.20-3. What it really states is that the *offering* of such items for transportation, stowage, use on board, etc., is forbidden and *not* the actual transportation, stowage, and use on board. Is this splitting hairs? Perhaps, but statutes that are ambiguous are unconstitutionally vague and therefore unenforceable. Besides, it is a well-established principle of law that statutes must be strictly construed and given only the force of law they clearly require. If Congress had intended that loaded firearms not be used on board it would have specifically said so in no uncertain terms, without the use of the word "offering" and without drafting footnote 1. What all this means is that *unloaded* firearms, stowed in the ship's armory, or carried on watch, are absolutely legal in any port in the United States. Loading those firearms may be considered by some as illegal, although this would more than likely be an incorrect interpretation of the law. *Using* those firearms against armed intruders might also be considered by some to be illegal, but again, such an interpretation is not likely to be considered valid, particularly where the vessel's self-defense is involved. Of course, if armed security watches are approved by the port facility security officer and the captain of the port upon the ship's arrival, there should be no complaints. Furthermore, the ship's master has a number of alternatives open to him even if he is denied permission to arm his security watches with loaded weapons. First, he can simply ignore the denial knowing that no one will probably notice that his security watches' weapons are loaded, and that, if someone does, nothing is likely to come of it anyway. Second, if he truly believes the security of his vessel requires loaded weapons, he can make so much fuss over the issue that the denial will be rescinded or additional security provided by the port facility. Third, he can arm his security watches with *unloaded* firearms (perfectly legal) and provide them with *loaded* magazines (clips) which would allow them to load their weapons in a matter of seconds. This is the way they ought to carry them anyway, unless an attack in imminent. Finally, if an attack *is* imminent, the legality of the loaded firearm issue is immaterial, as it is far better to be tried in a court of law than buried in a box of wood.

The last CFR section that will be mentioned is 19 CFR 4.11, which involves the sealing of ship's stores by Customs officials. It is men-

tioned in connection with the practice common to Customs officials
of sealing the ship's small arms locker when she berths, a practice that
the master should vigorously resist. The regulation reads as follows:

> Upon the arrival of a vessel from a foreign port, or a vessel
> engaged in the foreign trade from a domestic port, sea stores
> and ship's stores not required for immediate use or consump-
> tion on board while the vessel is in port and articles acquired
> abroad by officers and members of the crew, for which no per-
> mit to land has been issued, shall be placed under seal, unless
> the Customs officer is of the opinion that the circumstances do
> not require such action. Customs inspectors in charge of the ves-
> sel, from time to time, as in their judgment the necessity of the
> case requires, may issue stores from under seal for consumption
> on board the vessel by its passengers and crew.

There are several things that should be remembered if Customs attempts to seal a vessel's small arms locker. First, the master, not Customs, is responsible by law for the security of his ship, and if he
requires the availability of his small arms for such purpose Customs
may arguably not have the authority to oppose him. Second, small
arms are clearly not consumable ship's stores, they are items of the
vessel's equipment. Third, the small arms *are* required for immediate
use, just as soon as the security watches are posted (the gangway watch
should be posted as soon as the gangway is rigged). Finally, Customs
officials are not responsible for the security of either the vessel or the
port facility. The vessel's master, the port facility security officer, and
the captain of the port are the security experts, and a Customs official's
"opinion" as to what action is either required or not required so far as
security is concerned is not important nor should it be dispositive. If
Customs insists on sealing the small arms locker, the vessel's master
should appeal to the captain of the port. If he does not get satisfaction
from that quarter he has about the same options available to him as
just mentioned regarding loaded weapons.

After discussing the U.S. Code and the *Code of Federal Regulations,* a few words should be said about the *Federal Register.* The
Federal Register is the vehicle used by the U.S. Government to pub-
lish official notices and announcements that are related to all manner
of federal regulatory matters, but do not have the force of law that

rules, regulations, and statutes do. Massive amounts of information are disseminated by the *Federal Register* but, unless one is a professional *Federal Register* watcher, most of it goes unnoticed. The *Federal Register* notice important to this particular discussion has already been mentioned. It is Coast Guard Notice CGD 87-019, dated March 31, 1987, "Measures to Prevent Unlawful Acts Against Passengers and Crew On Board Ships." It appears in the *Federal Register,* volume 52, number 68, on pages 11,587 through 11,594 under the date of Thursday, April 9, 1987, and is reproduced in appendix E of this book.

Maritime commerce, of course, is international in nature and therefore the laws and regulations of other nations besides the United States are of significance to the maritime operator who operates within the jurisdiction of those other nations. The nature and extent of those laws and regulations, as they pertain to the maritime security measures and procedures advocated in this book, as well as their possible application to the particular enterprise in question, must necessarily be ascertained by the maritime operator before he implements his security program. There are a vast number of international treaties, conventions, and agreements concerning maritime commerce and the use of the oceans, some of which may also apply to maritime security. As indicated previously, however, treaties and conventions do not affect private individuals but the laws of the jurisdiction in which an individual finds himself may codify particular treaties and agreements into rules and regulations by which he must abide. Treaties may also be recognized in civil litigation where an action is brought against a signatory nation by a private individual, as was the situation in the 1987 case of *Amerada Hess Shipping Corp. v. Argentine Republic.* (Argentina bombed and destroyed an oil tanker owned and operated by Amerada Hess during the Falklands conflict when the vessel was on the high seas and in neutral waters. Amerada Hess sued Argentina in the U.S. District Court for the Southern District of New York for damages and, on appeal, it was held that certain treaties to which both the United States and Argentina are signatories controlled the issue of jurisdiction and that not only could the suit be maintained in the United States, but Argentina was liable for the damages under maritime tort principles subscribed to in the treaties.) It is not, however, the intent of this book to discuss foreign law or public international law. The subjects are mentioned here merely to alert the maritime security manager to their existence. There have been numerous books and articles written in recent years on international terrorism and the governmental responses to it. The object of this book is to show the security manager how to fight those terrorists, as well as how to handle other maritime security matters, and it is more concerned with security policies and operating procedures than intergovernmental relationships. Suggestions regarding such security policies and operating procedures are also made from time to time by certain international organizations (such as the Baltic and International Maritime Conference, the International Shipping Federation, and the International Maritime Organization), usually in the form of resolutions like the previously mentioned IMO Resolution A.584(14). Such resolutions may or may not concern themselves with actual tactics or have an effect on an individual security manager's policies and procedures but, again, one should be aware that they exist.

The legal discussion concerning maritime security could be considerably longer than it has been presented here. It could form the subject of an entire book, in fact. The purpose of this book, however, is not to discuss only the legal ramifications of maritime security. Its purpose is to raise the security awareness within the maritime industry such that it begins to implement the security measures that are needed to protect both the industry and the public. Consequently, an understanding of legal liabilities and restraints is necessary for security management to be performed with any degree of success, but so is an understanding of tactics and weapons.

CHAPTER SEVEN

WEAPONS, WEAPONS SYSTEMS, AND OTHER CONSIDERATIONS

Maritime security, which must include counterterrorism and anti-piracy, is truly urban and naval warfare and the security manager should consider most aspects of his maritime security operations as military, rather than law enforcement, in nature. This includes the weapons chosen, the tactics employed, and the training conducted. The days of arming security guards with six-shot revolvers and nightsticks are over. The days are over, too, of employing aging retirees or unqualified, low-end-of-the-wage-scale workers. Today's terrorists and pirates are armed with automatic weapons, military explosives, and sophisticated equipment, all of which they know how to use. Terrorists are trained in physical conditioning, weaponry, electronics, communications, explosives, camouflage, first aid, document forgery, martial arts, and military tactics. Only truly professional security forces can expect to succeed against them, and even then the terrorists will have the initial advantage. In order that the security manager may understand the magnitude of the security threats facing his organization, and realize the security options available to him, the first part of this chapter will explore the weapons presently available to, and used by, known international terrorists. Following this, the weapons presently used by the elite counterterrorist units around the world will be discussed. Finally, a brief explanation will be offered of naval weapons systems and their possible employment within the maritime industry.

It must be stressed from the beginning that terrorists, pirates, and mercenaries cannot be underestimated. Most terrorists are fanatics, and some have even been mentally deranged (during the 1970s in a mental hospital in Heidelberg Dr. Wolfgang Huber and his wife Ursula trained their mental patients in bomb-making as others would have trained them in handicrafts). The pirates in the South China Sea are absolutely fearless because they have never had anything to fear. Mercenaries who might undertake an extortion operation against a multimillion-dollar oil platform will be hardened, trained professionals. All of them will be well armed. The 12 Italian Red Brigade terrorists who participated in the kidnapping and murder of Aldo Moro spent $20,000 on firearms and ammunition. Southeast Asian pirates are armed with extensive military weaponry left over from the Vietnam War. Mercenaries know how and where to obtain whatever weapons their mission requires.

In general, the firearms used in any maritime assault by terrorists, pirates, or mercenaries will be compact, lightweight, and capable of delivering substantial firepower. In many cases they may also be concealable. In addition, the ammunition fired will most often be of a type that is readily available. This narrows the firearms likely to be used against a maritime installation down to certain submachine guns, machine pistols, assault rifles, shotguns, and handguns.

The submachine gun is probably the most widely used terrorist weapon, next to the bomb. It meets all the requirements, being compact, lightweight, concealable, and capable of delivering a high rate of fire for short periods of time. Submachine guns characteristically fire pistol ammunition, the most common calibres being .22, .32, 9mm, and .45. Of these, by far the most common and widely used calibre is 9mm, which is easily obtainable, delivers little recoil, has effective penetration, and is utilized in most of the world's military and police side arms. Two of the deadliest submachine guns available today are the Heckler & Koch MP5K and the Beretta M12. The Heckler & Koch MP5K is an exceptionally well made West German automatic firearm. It is standard-issue equipment for many police and security forces around the world, and is favored by terrorists and counterterrorists alike. The MP5K in its most compact version is less than 13 inches long and weighs about 4.5 pounds. It has a cyclic rate of fire of 840 rounds per minute, which translates into a maximum rate of fire of about 200 rounds per minute, and has so little recoil it can be fired with one hand. Because of its size and handleability, it is extremely effective where space is limited (such as aboard ship), and it can easily

Beretta M12 submachine gun. Courtesy: Beretta.

Heckler & Koch MP5A2 submachine gun.
Courtesy: Heckler & Koch.

be carried concealed. Its magazines come in 15- and 30-round varieties. It is particularly favored by West German terrorists because it can be stolen from police armories, and several were used in the kidnapping of Hans-Martin Schleyer in 1977. The Beretta M12 is slightly larger and heavier than the Heckler & Koch MP5K, being about 16.5 inches long with its stock folded and weighing 6.5 pounds. Its maximum rate of fire is about 140 rounds per minute (550 rpm cyclic rate), and it utilizes 20-, 30-, or 40-round magazines. It is issued to elite units of the Italian army, and has been sold to numerous nations in Africa, South America, and the Middle East. Two of these were used in the raid on OPEC headquarters in 1975. The Israeli-made Uzi is another dependable 9mm submachine gun that has gained a following throughout the western world. In fact, it can be said that the MP5K, the Beretta M12, and the Uzi are the "big three" so far as western submachine guns are concerned. The Uzi is the largest of the three and also the oldest, having been in production since 1949. Its overall length is 17 inches and it weighs almost 8 pounds. Its maximum rate of fire is between 140 and 150 rounds per minute, and its various magazines can hold 25, 32, or 40 rounds. It is extremely dependable and, for this reason, is a favorite of the U.S. Secret Service and other security forces throughout the world. It is also prized by any terrorist who manages to obtain one. More than likely, however, terrorists will acquire Czechoslovakian-made Vz23 or Vz25 submachine guns instead. These are similar to Uzis but are more readily available. Their maximum rate of fire is approximately 150 rounds per minute and they weigh about 7 pounds.

Machine pistols are almost as favored among terrorists as submachine guns. These weapons might be considered a cross between a pistol and a submachine gun. They are larger than most pistols but smaller than the submachine guns just discussed, and generally fire 9mm, 9mm short (.380), or .32-calibre ammunition. Probably the most popular machine pistol among terrorists is the Czechoslovakian cousin to the Vz23 and Vz25, the Skorpion Vz61. It has been used in numerous terrorists attacks including the murders of Aldo Moro and the chief prosecutor of Genoa, Francesco Coco, both of whom were killed with the same Skorpion Vz61. It weighs about 3.5 pounds, fires .32 calibre (7.65mm) ammunition, has a maximum rate of fire of 210 rounds per minute, and can be fitted with a silencer. Another well-known machine pistol, the U.S.-made Ingraham MAC 11, also weighs

Micro-Uzi machine pistol. Courtesy: Action Arms, Ltd.

about 3.5 pounds, is less than 9 inches long, and can be silenced. If one includes its slightly larger predecessor, the MAC 10, three different calibre versions are available: .45 ACP, 9mm, and .380, ammunition for all of which is commercially easier to obtain than for the Skorpion Vz61.

Assault rifles are generally not preferred by terrorists because of their inconcealability. However, where submachine guns or machine pistols are not available, automatic assault rifles are preferable to mere pistols. Furthermore, they are perfectly effective in operations that do not require concealability or that require a longer-range capability. Assault rifles are characterized by a relatively short, carbine style design, are magazine-fed, and are capable of being fired in either semi-automatic or fully automatic mode. Many come in buttless or folding-stock versions. A number of nations produce their own assault rifles which, in one form or another, have become the standard infantryman's weapon. The modern assault rifle is manufactured in two primary calibres, 7.62mm and 5.56mm, with the trend being toward the smaller calibre. Two of the most well known assault rifles are the Russian-made Kalashnikov AK-47 and the U.S.-made M-16.

AK-47s were used in the assassination of Anwar Sadat, and were also used by some of the Black September terrorists in Munich in 1972. A close cousin, the Czechoslovakian-made Vz58V, was used by Japanese Red Army terrorists when they committed the massacre at Lod Airport the same year. The Kalashnikovs and their progeny are all 7.62mm weapons. The M-16 is a 5.56mm weapon with a maximum rate of fire on full automatic of between 150 and 200 rounds per minute. There were so many M-16s left behind in Vietnam that a glut has occurred on the international arms market, and any terrorist, pirate, or insurgent can purchase one on the streets of Bangkok for about $100 (less than 20 percent of what the non-fully-automatic version costs in the United States). Heckler & Koch has also produced a new, lightweight assault rifle that may revolutionize assault arms entirely. It is designated the G11, and is chambered for the new 4.7mm caseless round. The weapon is shorter than other assault rifles, carries 50 rounds in its magazine, and is capable of a high rate of fire. An infantryman (or terrorist) equipped with this weapon can carry four times the ammunition he could otherwise carry for a 5.56mm assault rifle. It may soon be adopted by West Germany and, if so, West German and other European terrorists may try to "adopt" it as well.

In certain circumstances combat shotguns wielded by terrorists can be as effective as, if not more effective than, submachine guns. They have the same concealability problem as assault rifles, but their firepower can be absolutely devastating. Like submachine guns, they are primarily short-range weapons. They do have a certain amount of versatility, however. With rifled slug ammunition their effective range is about 100 yards. With No. 00 buckshot it is about 50 yards, and as the size of the shot decreases so does the effective range (00 is the largest shot available in shotgun shells, the shot progressing to No. 1, No. 2, No. 3, down to No. 9). For terrorist applications the shotgun barrel will probably be sawed off, thereby shortening the range even more but increasing the deadly effect of the weapon. One 12-gauge, No. 4 buckshot round contains 27 .22-calibre shot (each roughly equivalent in diameter to a 5.56mm bullet), and thus, at a range where the shot has adequately dispersed, is almost equal in firepower to an entire 30-round magazine fired from an M-16. Seven rounds fired as fast as one can pull the trigger (about 5 seconds for a semiautomatic) will put 189 shot in the air, or the equivalent of more than twelve M-16s firing simultaneously on full automatic for the same amount of time. This is truly awesome firepower, the destructive potential of which will certainly not be overlooked by terrorists. The disadvantage of a shotgun is that it is slow to reload, but if the entire opposition is taken out with the first magazine it doesn't matter.

In addition to being armed with any of the above weapons, every serious adversary will also carry a personal side arm. The number of different designs and calibres of pistols manufactured throughout the world is absolutely phenomenal. Basically, however, pistols are either revolvers or automatics. The term "automatic" is a slight misnomer, for unless the pistol is really a machine pistol, the automatic functioning refers to the ejection and chambering of rounds and not the firing. In other words, "automatic" when used in connection with a pistol usually means "semiautomatic." For this reason automatics are sometimes more accurately referred to as "autoloaders." Most modern military units and security/police forces now arm their personnel with automatics, which are far superior to revolvers in firepower and reloadability. Even in the United States, where the revolver has held an almost revered position among law enforcement tacticians, the change to automatics is finally beginning to occur. The U.S. military, of course, was one of the first to adopt an automatic as its service pistol back in 1911 when it adopted John Browning's .45 auto (manufactured by Colt). Today, service automatics are almost exclusively 9mm (although some European police forces carry .380s) and have magazine capacities of between 13 and 17 rounds. Some of the models and their advantages for security forces are discussed a little later in this section. So far as the terrorist arsenal is concerned, however, one can expect just about anything in the way of a pistol. An Astra .357 magnum revolver was used to kill Ross McWhirter, the publisher of *The Guinness Book of Records,* in 1975 and London businessman Alan Quartermaine in 1974. The Soviet-made Makarov 9mm automatic is the Eastern Bloc's military service pistol and is in general use throughout the world. It is easily obtainable and is a favorite among terrorist organizations. Another Soviet-made 9mm automatic, the Tokarev (TT-33), was in service before the Makarov and has now been replaced by it. The Tokarev can still be found in use, though, in many Asian communist countries as well as among Arab terrorist groups. The Walther P-38 is a German-made 9mm which enjoys both military and commercial popularity. It is the favorite pistol of the Italian Red Brigades, who find it well suited for the knee-capping maiming of their victims for which the Red Brigades are famous. Finally, the Browning Hi-Power is yet another 9mm automatic, produced in Belgium, that is very popular among many terrorist groups and counterterrorist, military, and police units. It is an easily handled and reliable weapon, has been around for a long time, and is less bulky than some of the newer 9mm.

There are other weapons in the terrorist arsenal besides the firearms just discussed. Terrorists are trained to be masters of disguise, and what they disguise besides themselves are their weapons. Firearms have been hidden in, or disguised as, toys, packages, books, umbrellas, attache cases, pens, cigarette packages, cameras, and walking sticks. They can be secreted in clothing, footwear, and headgear. Checkpoint security personnel must be constantly alert for *anything* out of the ordinary, and hand-held magnetometers should be used where the gate variety is not practical. Of course, firearms are not the only dangerous items terrorists may attempt to conceal or utilize. Grenades, both Russian- and U.S.-made are obtainable by terrorists. The modern Soviet grenade, which may be manufactured in China and elsewhere, is the RGD-5. It is a light grenade, capable of being thrown 35 to 40 yards. Green-colored and egg-shaped, its killing radius is

Browning Hi-Power. Courtesy: Browning.

about 30 yards. The U.S. equivalent antipersonnel grenade is the M26 fragmentation hand grenade. It has a smooth sheet metal body shaped like a lemon, with a flange at its base. It is filled with 5.5 ounces of composition B (an explosive) and weighs 16 ounces overall. It can be thrown approximately 45 yards, and has an effective casualty-producing radius of 15 to 20 yards. However, fragments can be thrown as far as 200 yards from the point of detonation. A variation of the M26 is the M26A2 with an impact-detonating fuse. This grenade detonates on impact or, if impact is insufficient, within 3 to 7 seconds after the safety lever is released. M26 hand grenades were used by terrorists in a number of incidents in the 1970s after a large number were stolen from the U.S. Army base at Miesau, West Germany, in 1971. Of course, since the fall of Vietnam every conceivable type of U.S. armament has become available to those who wish to purchase it. The Russian-made RPG-7 portable rocket launcher was used extensively in Vietnam and has found its way throughout the Third World since. Its most notable use recently has been by the Iranians against Persian Gulf shipping. It is not a very accurate weapon, particularly at long range or in high winds, which is why the Iranians deploy them from fast patrol boats at close range to the ships they attack. Of course, when they needn't worry about receiving suppressing or return fire it makes the delivery of the projectile very easy. The RPG-7 has a range of between 1,000 and 1,650 feet and its 3.7-pound grenade is capable of penetrating 320mm (12.8 inches) of steel plate. The U.S. equivalent to the RPG-7 is the LAW (Light Assault Weapon). It replaced both the M31 high-explosive antitank rifle grenade (fired from an M-14 7.62mm rifle) and the 3.5-inch rocket launcher (descendant of the World War II 2.8-inch bazooka). The LAW, which should not be confused with the similar but more effective armor-piercing British-made LAW-80, is a 66mm, single-shot, disposable, self-contained rocket and rocket launcher. It is lightweight, compact, and simple to use. From a terrorist's viewpoint it can also be concealed relatively easily, and LAWs, like the rest of the munitions left behind in Vietnam, are readily available on the world market. A LAW or LAW-80 is the perfect terrorist weapon with which to destroy an LNG tanker and ignite its cargo, assuming the terrorist is willing to be consumed in the ensuing conflagration. If he is not, a number of longer-range, hand-held, wire-guided or heat-seeking, anti-tank and surface-to-air missiles are available. The U.S.-made Dragon antitank assault weapon is a wire-guided, shoulder-fired, recoilless antitank guided missile with a range of 1,000 meters. It is part of the standard infantry weapons inventory for the United States and is available to a number of other nations. The most notable man-portable, surface-to-air missile systems available today that can be employed against maritime targets are the Soviet-made SA-7 (Grail), the British-made Blowpipe, and the U.S.-made Saber and Stinger. SA-7s have been extensively deployed throughout the Third World and are inexpensive and easy to produce. They have a range of about 10 kilometers and utilize a passive infrared guidance system. A number of terrorist groups are known to possess SA-7s, including the various Palestinian factions, the IRA, and several African revolutionary organizations. Unlike the SA-7, which is designed specifically for air defense, Blowpipe, Saber, and Stinger are all intended for either air defense or surface deployment and therefore utilize other guidance systems besides infrared. Blowpipe and Saber also employ a shaped-charge warhead which provides an antiarmor capability. Blowpipe is in service with some 11 nations and 16 different armed forces.

Missiles are simply remote, airborne, bomb-delivery vehicles. Bombs have always been, and still are, the primary terrorist weapon. They kill and maim indiscriminately, without warning, at any place and any time. Manufactured and emplaced by someone who knows what he is doing, they are considerably safer for the terrorist than any other form of attack since they have the capability of being detonated long after he has left the scene. In its simplest form, a bomb consists of an explosive, a detonator, and some sort of time-delay mechanism. Bombs can be made from various types of explosives. The primary ones are TNT, plastic explosives (C3, C4, and cyclonite), guncotton, picric acid (TNP), and nitroglycerin explosives (gelignite and dynamite). The explosives are detonated in one of four ways. They can be detonated electrically, mechanically, chemically, or thermally, and the delay mechanisms can range from a simple fuse to a complex timing, sensing, or command-activated device. Terrorists obtain their explosives in a number of ways: They can be supplied either directly or indirectly with military explosives from governments that support their cause; they can steal the same ordnance from governments that do not support their cause; they can purchase what they desire on the international arms market (with or without the help of a governmental intermediary); they can steal or purchase commercial explosives used in mining or construction; and, finally, they can manufacture their own explosives from commercially available chemicals and fertilizers. However they obtain their explosives, the net result is the same—a bomb. Bombs are designed to kill people or destroy property. Sometimes the goal is to do both. A bomb secreted in a cruise ship passenger terminal will more than likely be designed to kill as many people as possible. That usually means some sort of fragmentation or shrapnel-producing device. A simple but effective terrorist antipersonnel design involves placing explosives in an athletic bag and packing it with nails, bolts, and other projectile-producing scrap. It can be left inconspicuously in the middle of the waiting area and when the bomb goes off it will kill and injure people in all directions. A bomb placed aboard an offshore oil platform, on the other hand, will be designed to destroy the platform itself. It can be a more compact device but it must be carefully emplaced so that it will cause the intended damage. Bombs can take virtually any form the terrorist or saboteur can imagine, and consequently the best thing security personnel can do is remain alert for anything out of the ordinary or for anything that looks, feels, smells, or sounds suspicious.

There are other weapons available to terrorists and saboteurs, however, besides firearms, grenades, rockets, and bombs, and even though some of them may sound like something out of a James Bond novel the security manager should be aware of them. First of all, solitary guards can be dispatched in any number of ways that do not require the use of any weapons other than properly trained hands and feet. Knives, clubs, and garrotes simply make things that much easier. Most terrorists receive some training in hand-to-hand combat, and solitary security guards should consider any approaching individual as a potentially lethal adversary. Common, everyday articles such as umbrellas, canes, briefcases, and pens or pencils can be turned into deadly weapons. Innocuous-looking chemical substances can be killers. Prussic acid (hydrocyanic acid), for instance, if squirted into someone's face will render him unconscious almost immediately and dead within minutes. A child's water pistol or a turkey baster is all that would be needed. Some years ago Japanese security personnel at the Tokyo International Airport discovered a modified cattle prod and belt power pack that could deliver a 500-volt charge to a victim. This is enough to knock a man down, and possibly kill him. The Taser, an electronic stun gun, works on the same principle and there are now commercially produced, compact and concealable, similar self-defense weapons available to everyone.

The weapons employed by counterterrorist units and security forces around the world are primarily submachine guns and pistols. Sniper rifles and shotguns are used under certain circumstances. Unlike terrorists who obviously aren't concerned with accidentally killing innocent bystanders or hostages, counterterrorist units must select weapons with a high degree of accuracy and controllability. Maritime security personnel, however, differ from counterterrorist units in two very significant ways. First, the elite counterterrorist units of the world, such as the British SAS, West German GSG-9, U.S. Delta, and so on, are trained to *respond* to a terrorist incident once it has occurred. The maritime security measures advocated in this book, which include the training and arming of security personnel, are designed to *prevent* a terrorist incident from occurring. Second, counterterrorist units spend most of their time training and preparing for the few instances when their expertise will be needed. Maritime security personnel, on the other hand, must spend most of their time providing the daily security that is needed, and have much less time to spend perfecting any sophisticated counterterrorist skills. In fact, unless they are in areas that are inaccessible to law enforcement or military assistance, any counterterrorist response should be left entirely up to the authorities. Thus, the weaponry employed by maritime security personnel should be selected with their mission in mind which, in virtually all instances, will be defensive rather than offensive.

In all but a few circumstances, therefore, fully automatic weapons such as submachine guns, machine pistols, and automatic assault rifles are probably not the best weapons with which to arm private maritime security forces. Besides the facts that they require a higher degree of training in order to be effective and present an increased civil liability exposure when used in nonmilitary situations, they create certain legal problems with regard to ownership, training, and deployment. Most nations, including the United States, regard fully automatic weapons as permissible primarily within the purview of military and law enforcement agencies, and while it is not necessarily impossible to arm private security forces with automatic weapons it will certainly be very difficult. Semiautomatic weapons, on the other hand, will generally not raise too many eyebrows, and if employed properly can be almost as effective. With the exception, therefore, of the two shipboard security situations where machine-gun fire is recommended, both of which occur at sea and have already been alluded to (underway boarding by pirates and Iranian patrol boat attacks), semiautomatic weapons should suffice.

The semiautomatic weapons that are available for use by private maritime security forces are pistols, rifles, and shotguns. In the United States, all three types of weapons may presently be owned by private individuals with few or no restrictions (although the antigun agitators continue to lobby for controls and California has outlawed semiautomatic assault rifles). Once the decision has been made to arm private security personnel with firearms, the maritime security manager must decide what firearms, or what types of firearms, should be employed. Concomitant decisions concerning such things as private ownership of individual weapons, the calibre of such weapons, control and training, storage and security, ammunition procurement and allotment, and many others must also be made. The initial decisions, though, involve the weapons themselves, and the first place to start is with the type of individual side arms to be carried by security personnel.

The side arms in all instances should be autoloading pistols. They are available in a wide variety of calibres ranging from .22 to .45, and now even include traditional revolver calibres such as .357 and .44 magnum. For years the debate has raged in the United States as to which calibre is best suited for self-defense, home protection, law enforcement, and military use. Everyone agrees that the *smallest* effective calibre for all of these is the .380 or 9mm short, but a lot of people disagree as to the *most* effective calibre after that. So far as law enforcement and military use is concerned, the debate is being settled in favor of the 9mm. The United States has now joined the rest of its NATO allies in adopting the 9mm auto as its service pistol, relegating to history the .45 Colt automatic that saw service in four wars and numerous conflicts over more than 70 years. The reason for the 9mm pistol's popularity is twofold: it is easily controllable and it can hold a large number of rounds—13 to 17 in standard magazines, depending upon the particular pistol model—substantially more firepower than is available with other automatics or revolvers. Also, most submachine guns are chambered for 9mm, and one-round compatibility with supporting weapons is tactically preferable. The same considerations that make the 9mm preferable for military and law enforcement use make it preferable for maritime security use as well (although .45

and 10mm pistols have some advantages for shipboard or offshore installation use). Consequently, the port facility security manager should decide in favor of 9mm automatics. Shipboard or offshore installation security managers may well decide on 9mm automatics and, if so, the next question is *which* 9mm automatic should be selected. Although there are a large number of varieties on the market, the decision can be made fairly easily. Full-time port facility or offshore installation security personnel should be required to provide their own personal weapons, for several reasons, and therefore the choice should be left to those individuals (so long as they choose a 9mm auto). For shipboard or other security personnel for whom it may be more appropriate to provide personal side arms, the security manager can select the pistol he feels will most adequately meet his budgetary and performance requirements after studying both the commercial market and the weapons chosen by the different military forces and counterterrorist units around the world. A few of the more readily available pistols are described below.

The most popular 9mm automatic among European police and military forces is the Browning Hi-Power, or Browning 9mm Parabellum, as it is sometimes called. It is also a favored pistol among counterterrorist units. Invented in 1923, patented in 1927, and first produced in 1935, it has stood the test of time well, particularly in an age of so many new 9mm pistol designs. Unlike virtually all other modern 9mm it is a single-action auto, which means the hammer must be cocked before the first round can be fired. It weighs 32 ounces, is 7.75 inches long, and has a 13-round magazine.

The new service pistol of the U.S. military is the Beretta Model 92SBF, which is very similar to the commercially produced Model 92F. Slightly larger and heavier than the Browning Hi-Power, it is 9.54 inches long and weighs 34 ounces. It has a 15-round magazine and has proved to be highly reliable and accurate. With its double-action, first-round capability, it is well suited for security and police work. It is, however, fairly expensive in relation to other pistols on the market.

In that regard, the Brazilian-made Taurus Model PT 92 AF is an almost exact copy of the Italian Beretta and sells for a little over one-half its price. The workmanship of the Taurus is excellent and, unlike the Beretta, the pistol can be purchased with adjustable rear sights or corrosion-resistant nickel finish (Model PT 99 AF).

Taurus PT 92 AFB. Courtesy: Taurus
International Manufacturing, Inc.

Several excellent 9mm autos are available from Germany and
Switzerland, the most notable of which are the Sig Sauer P 226, Heckler & Koch VP-70Z, and Glock 17. The Sig Sauer P 226 was designed
to compete for U.S. military acceptance when the intended change
from .45 to 9mm was announced. Although it did not win such acceptance, it is a fine weapon, preferred by many over the Beretta 92. Like
the Beretta it has a 15-round magazine. It weighs only 26.5 ounces
and is 7.7 inches long. The Heckler & Koch VP-70Z and the Glock
17 are both unusual pistols with marked differences in appearance and
operation from the more traditional automatics just discussed. They
also have higher magazine capacities (18 and 17 respectively). The
Glock 17 was adopted by the Austrian armed forces in 1983 and approved by NATO in 1984.

The Czechoslovakian-made CZ75 has gained a reasonable following among pistol experts. Its design incorporates many of the best features of the Browning and Sig Sauer pistols, and it can now be
purchased commercially as the Brno CZ75. It is 8 inches long, weighs
35 ounces, and has a 15-shot magazine. An Italian-made copy, the

Tanarmi TA90, claims to be an improved version of the CZ75 and is available in a weather-resistant matte chrome finish.

Two U.S.-made comparable 9mm automatics should be mentioned. The newest is the Ruger P-85. It weighs 32 ounces, is 7.84 inches long, and has a 15-round magazine, all of which make it not much different from most of the other pistols discussed so far. However, its lightweight, aluminum alloy frame and 4140 chrome-moly steel slide make it well suited for service in the marine environment. Ruger firearms also have an excellent reputation so far as craftsmanship and value are concerned. Another U.S.-made 9mm well suited for the marine environment is the Smith and Wesson Model 659. This is the stainless steel version of the Model 459 that is 7.63 inches long, weighs 30 ounces, and has a 14-round magazine. Both the 459 and the 659 are favored by U.S. law enforcement agencies that have switched to 9mm autos, more perhaps for the name than anything else. However, they are well made and dependable firearms.

Several other commercially available autoloaders should be mentioned that are available in calibres other than 9mm but can serve useful purposes within the maritime security context. Specifically, these calibres are 10mm, .357 magnum, .44 magnum, and .45 ACP. The 10mm cartridge was developed in an effort to combine the best attributes of both the 9mm and the .45 ACP cartridges and, to some degree, it has succeeded. Whether or not the round will ever achieve enough acceptance to keep it commercially viable remains questionable. It is, however, definitely more effective than the 9mm and supposedly more manageable than the .45. Several pistols have been introduced that are chambered for this round, the most notable being Colt's 10mm Delta Elite. It is similar in appearance to the Colt Government Model MK IV/Series 80 and its magazine holds 10 rounds. In properly trained hands it might be more effective for shipboard use than either the 9mm or .45 autos. On the other hand, the .45 ACP round has some fine attributes. First, it has been around for a long time and is readily available. Second, it is an extremely effective round so far as stopping power is concerned (although arguments are still waged as to whether it is better to shoot someone twice with a 9mm or once with a .45). Finally, though, it is a slow-moving round with relatively little penetration capability, which makes it well suited for use aboard ship, or inside or below deck, where high-speed ricochets can be lethal. A number of excellent stainless steel .45 autos are manufactured in the

United States, the most notable manufacturers being Colt, Smith and Wesson, and Detonics. In recent years a number of automatic pistols have been developed and chambered for magnum revolver cartridges. The .357 magnum cartridge has been favored by law enforcement and counterterrorist personnel alike for its power and accuracy. It is, however, best reserved for self-defense or one-shot-kill situations rather than military firefights. Two notable .357 magnum automatics are presently on the market: the U.S.-made Coonan .357 Magnum Pistol and the Israeli-made Desert Eagle. The Coonan is manufactured in stainless steel and resembles the Colt Government Model automatic pistol. It is 8.3 inches long, weighs 42 ounces, and has a 7-round magazine. The Desert Eagle, on the other hand, is 10.25 inches long, weighs 62 ounces (in its stainless steel version), and has a 9-round magazine. It can also be purchased in .41 magnum and .44 magnum versions with 6-, 10-, or 14-inch interchangeable barrels.

Before discussing rifles and shotguns a few words should be said about pistol marksmanship training, because once the security manager has decided on the calibre and types of side arms his security personnel will carry he must consider the training those weapons will demand. No matter what pistols they carry, security personnel should feel absolutely confident in their abilities to handle and fire them. This requires continuous marksmanship training on at least a biweekly basis. Many law enforcement personnel spend one or two hours every Saturday (or whatever their day off is) on the pistol range. Competitive pistol shooters practice three or four days per week. There are basically two types of pistol marksmanship training, and security personnel should engage in both. The first type is what is generally referred to as bull's-eye shooting. This is stationary target shooting, usually at 15 or 25 yards, utilizing bull's-eye (or concentric-ring) targets. This type of shooting develops consistency, accuracy, and self-confidence. The second type of marksmanship training is combat shooting, and should only be practiced once an individual has demonstrated his proficiency at bull's-eye shooting. In this type of marksmanship training the shooter is required to move from one position to another, utilizing one shooting stance after another, in simulated combat situations. He may be required to fire from around corners, over and under barriers, at multiple targets, in different body positions, and so on. Combat shooting should also be conducted regularly at night, without lights. This will allow security personnel to develop fire and

Sig Sauer P 226. Courtesy: Sig-Arms, Inc.

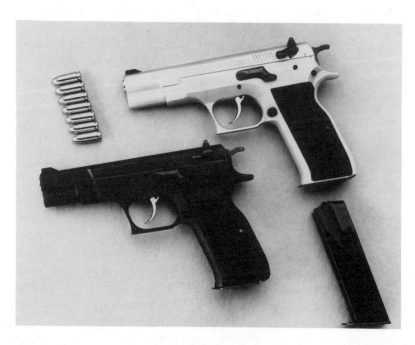

Tanarmi TA90. Courtesy: Excam, Inc.

Glock 19, a compact version of the Glock 17. Courtesy: Glock, Inc.

Ruger P-85. Courtesy: Sturm, Ruger & Co.

Smith & Wesson Model 659 (stainless).
Courtesy: Smith & Wesson.

maneuver skills as well as the technique of night firing, which is a pointing method as opposed to an aiming method of firing. Combat shooting is dangerous and physically demanding. It need not be practiced as often as bull's-eye shooting, but it should be done on a regular basis. It must also be carefully supervised, and the shooters should be rewarded for good performances.

Since, for the purposes of this discussion, it is assumed that private security personnel will not have automatic weapons available to them, the next important firearm that should be considered by the security manager is the shotgun. In the right hands, combat shotguns can be almost as effective as, if not more effective than, submachine guns. Unlike submachine guns, however, shotguns are legal virtually everywhere (with the exception of those that have been illegally modified), and they should be available to all maritime security forces. The best way to ensure their availability is to maintain them in the organization's armory and issue them in accordance with security SOPs. The size of the security force will determine the number of shotguns the organization should have, and this is one of the planning items the security manager must consider. He must also consider which shot-

Coonan .357 Magnum Auto. Courtesy: Coonan Arms, Inc.

Desert Eagle .44 Magnum Auto. Courtesy:
Magnum Research, Inc.

Bull's-eye shooters

guns he wishes to use. Combat shotguns, in all cases, are either semi-automatic or pump 12-gauge shotguns, with extended tubular magazines (7- to 9-round capacity) and 18- to 22-inch barrels. Most law enforcement personnel refer to them as "riot guns" and in the United States they are almost always pump shotguns. It is supposed that police departments have shunned automatic shotguns for the same reason they have until recently shunned automatic pistols: Automatics are allegedly less reliable than manually operated weapons like pump shotguns and revolvers. An automatic shotgun, however, is no more likely to malfunction than an automatic pistol, and neither will malfunction if properly handled and maintained. Another argument, which has more credibility, is that a person armed with an automatic shotgun might have a tendency to exhaust the magazine too quickly in a firefight and, because of its slow reloadability, be left with a useless weapon. The solution to that problem is fire discipline, which is gained through proper training. In any event, whether he chooses automatic or pump shotguns, the security manager needs to know what is available.

In recent years a revived interest in the military shotgun has caused a number of new and improved designs to come on the market. Many of these are no more than traditional pump or automatic shotguns with added extended magazines and pistol grips. Others, however, are truly modern fighting shotguns. Two of these are the Holmes Model 88 and the Mossberg 500 Bullpup, both of which are pump shotguns. At first glance, the Holmes Model 88 has the appearance of an assault rifle complete with forward-curving magazine in front of the trigger guard. In fact, it is the detachable box magazine that makes this shotgun unique among combat shotguns and eliminates the main drawback to the shotgun as a combat arm—slow reloadability. With 10-round magazines the Holmes Model 88 has more magazine capacity than any other shotgun, and it can be reloaded as fast as any assault rifle. If only it were semiautomatic it would be a truly awesome weapon. As it is, however, it is still an impressive firearm. It has an overall length of 38.25 inches (with an 18.25-inch barrel) and weighs 9 pounds. The Mossberg 500 Bullpup utilizes the proven Mossberg 500 pump shotgun action found in the Model 590 Military and Model 500 Security shotguns, but employs it in a bullpup design that allows for an extremely compact weapon. The Mossberg Bullpup is only 28.5 inches long, is available with either a 6- or 8-round tubular magazine, and weighs about 10 pounds. Because of its short overall length, it is well suited for use aboard ship or anywhere else space is at a premium. Like the Holmes 88, however, it would be more effective in an automatic version. Another true combat shotgun is the Italian-made Franchi SPAS 12, imported into the United States by F.I.E. Corporation. It functions as *either* a pump or an automatic, has an 8-round magazine, and weighs a little over 9.5 pounds. It comes with a folding or optional fixed stock, and with its stock folded has on overall length of 31.75 inches. There is also a lightweight variation, designated the Franchi LAW 12 Auto Shotgun that is available only in automatic form and without the folding stock. Its overall length is 41.5 inches and it weighs 7.5 pounds. The Benelli M1 Super 90 is another fine combat autoloader, imported by Heckler & Koch. It comes with a carrier for speed loading and has a 7-round magazine. It is 39.25 inches long and weighs 7.25 pounds. Finally, Mossberg, Remington, Savage, and Winchester have all had police type pump shotguns on the market for years, and all have several models to choose from. Winchester and Mossberg also have marine versions whose alloys and finishes are designed to withstand the rust and corrosion inherent in the marine environment.

Holmes Model 88. Courtesy: Holmes Firearms Corp.

Pistols and shotguns are designed for short-range fighting, as are submachine guns. In most shoreside security emergencies a long-range killing capability is not needed, except perhaps in hostage situations where snipers are employed. If snipers are needed they will most likely be provided by the law enforcement or military authority that responds to the emergency. Thus, so far as port facilities are concerned, rifles are not necessary. The security situation aboard ships and offshore installations, however, is considerably different and a long-range killing capability is definitely needed. Rifle (or preferably machine-gun) fire is the only thing that will keep prospective boarders such as pirates and hijackers at bay. There are a number of light infantry machine guns that could be carried aboard commercial vessels and, under certain circumstances, should be. For the moment, however, it is assumed such weapons are either not authorized or not available and the security manager must therefore consider what rifles, if any, he wishes to employ. Fully automatic rifles, like machine guns and submachine guns, are generally only available to military and law enforcement agencies. Semiautomatic rifles, however, are currently available to anyone in the United States, with the exception of California residents, and may be procured and stowed aboard ships and offshore installations. Only military style weapons with detachable, high-capacity box magazines should be considered and, like automatic pistols, there are a reasonably large number available from which to choose (although, as this book goes to print, a federal ban on the importation of foreign-made assault rifles is in effect).

The first thing the security manager needs to decide is the calibre

Franchi SPAS-12. Courtesy: F.I.E. Corp.

Benelli M1 Super 90. Courtesy: Heckler & Koch.

of the rifles he wishes to employ. While there are semiautomatic rifles available that are chambered for any number of different rounds, the only two real contenders so far as effectiveness is concerned are the 5.56mm and 7.62mm weapons. Of these, the larger and heavier bullet will be most effective against small boats and helicopters. It also has a longer effective range than the 5.56mm. On the other hand, the 5.56mm round is much easier to handle. There are superb weapons available for either, and the security manager will simply need to decide which he prefers.

Commercially produced military style autoloaders are expensive, averaging around $900 each at this writing, and a few of these will be discussed. Before doing so, however, it should be pointed out that many military weapons, particularly rifles, can be purchased by private individuals and companies on the open arms market and through various surplus agencies. The M-16s mentioned earlier are a good example. Until recently, the commercial version, available only as a semiautomatic, cost about $800 in the United States. Colt, its manufacturer, has ceased commercial sales within the United States, however, and this has increased its value in the used arms market. The military version, which is both semi- and fully automatic, costs about $100 in Southeast Asia and it can be modified easily to fire only in semiautomatic mode. Of course, if the security manager is only concerned with providing his organization with a handful of rifles he might just as well purchase them on the commercial market. On the other hand, if he must procure rifles for a fleet of 100 ships or so the alternatives should possibly be considered. That raises the question of the number of rifles that should be provided the security force, and to make that determination the security manager will need to review his security SOPs and envision the most he will need at any one time. By and large, ships and offshore installations can probably get by with between two and four rifles on board, if the number is matched with the same number of shotguns. Thus, a ship's armory might contain six to eight pistols, four rifles, and four shotguns. An offshore installation's armory might contain only two rifles and two shotguns.

The commercial versions of the M-16 are the Colt AR-15A2, AR-15A2 H-BAR, and AR-15A2 Delta H-BAR. They are all slightly different variations of the same weapon, which has a 16-inch barrel, weighs 5.8 pounds, and is 35 inches long. They are all chambered for the .223 Remington round which is, again, the commercial version of the military 5.56mm. The weapons come with a 5-round detachable box magazine but 20-, 30-, and 40-round magazines are available.

Another U.S.-made .223 rifle, and probably the best value of any around, is the Ruger Mini-14. It has an 18.5-inch barrel, is 37.24 inches long, and weighs 6.4 pounds. It is an accurate and dependable rifle, and it is available in a stainless steel version that is particularly well suited for marine use. Like the AR-15, it comes with a 5-round magazine but 20-, 30-, and 40-round magazines are available. This rifle can be purchased for about half the cost of an AR-15.

The Heckler & Koch HK-93 is a .223 German-made rifle of exceptional quality comparable in price to the Colt AR-15. It has a 16.13-inch barrel, is 35.5 inches long, and weighs 7.75 pounds. Twenty-round magazines are available. The HK-91 is roughly the same rifle in .308 Winchester, which is the commercial version of the military 7.62mm. It weighs 9.5 pounds and is 40.25 inches long. Both rifles are the same price, and are commercial versions of the Heckler & Koch 33A2 and G3A3 military rifles that have been purchased by more than 45 countries around the world.

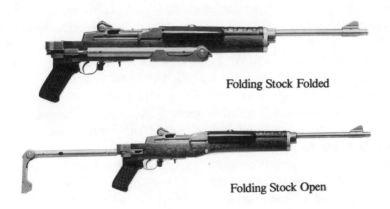

Folding Stock Folded

Folding Stock Open

Ruger Mini-14 in stainless steel with folding stock.
Courtesy: Sturm, Ruger & Co.

Heckler & Koch 93A2. Courtesy: Heckler & Koch.

The Springfield Armory SAR-48 is a U.S.-made 7.62mm rifle that bears a close resemblance to the Fabrique Nationale LAR (Light Automatic Rifle). It is slightly less expensive than the HK-91, but less than one-third the cost of the commercialized version of the FN LAR. It is 43.3 inches long and weighs 9.9 pounds. The Springfield Armory also produces a commercialized version of the M-14 (the 7.62mm predecessor to the 5.56mm M-16), which sells for about $100 less than the SAR-48. Both weapons, the SAR-48 and the M-14, are fine 7.62mm rifles.

The FN LAR, however, is the Cadillac of the 7.62mm rifles and has continued as the leading design in modern infantry long arms for over twenty years. It has been adopted by many countries including Austria, Belgium, Canada, Chile, Ecuador, Ireland, Israel, Libya, the Netherlands, Paraguay, Peru, Portugal, South Africa, the United Kingdom, Venezuela, and West Germany. Its commercial versions all sell for over $3,000 apiece. It has a length of 44.5 inches, a barrel length of 21 inches, and a weight of about 9.5 pounds.

Before moving on to naval weapons systems and how they can be employed aboard commercial vessels and offshore installations, a few words should be said about machine guns. In various places throughout this work the use of machine guns has been advocated, specifically to repel boarders and attacking small craft. There is nothing illegal under international law in the use of such weapons in self-defense of the vessel. Specific jurisdictions may have laws concerning the ownership of automatic weapons, but those laws should not apply unless the flag of the vessel corresponds to that jurisdiction. In the United States, private ownership of automatic weapons is allowed under federal law so long as they are properly transferred and the state in which they are owned allows private ownership. Therefore, the owner of a U.S.-flag vessel who lawfully purchases an automatic weapon may carry it aboard no matter where the vessel sails. As has already been noted, there is no prohibition under U.S. law for vessels to carry firearms. Therefore, there is no prohibition under U.S. law for vessels to carry automatic firearms, so long as they are properly owned. One M-60 machine gun and two men who are trained to use it can prevent *any* pirate attack. It can also keep Iranian patrol boats beyond the limit of their RPGs' effective range and thereby substantially reduce the likelihood of a hit. There are many available belt-fed light machine guns such as the M-60 (which is a 7.62mm weapon),

SAR-48 Std Model (.308 Cal.)
and
SAR-48 Model 22 (.22 LR)

SAR-48. Courtesy: Springfield Armory.

M1A Rifle
(Shown with optional sling.)

Springfield Armory's commercial version of the M-14
(designated M1A). Courtesy: Springfield Armory.

and one of these carried in the ship's armory could add an entirely new dimension to her security capabilities. There are also larger-calibre machine guns available, but these require either temporary or permanent gun mounts and more elaborate ammunition delivery systems which, at some point, turn them into a naval weapons system.

The term "naval weapons system" encompasses a broad spectrum of defensive and offensive devices and weapons that, in the maritime security context, are designed to protect commercial vessels and offshore installations. The electronic detection and guidance systems and the weapons that rely on them, normally associated with naval combatants, are certainly adaptable to commercial maritime usage when the circumstances call for it. The Persian Gulf war and other conflicts where neutral commercial shipping is indiscriminately attacked certainly call for such adaptation. If a vessel owner knows his vessel faces possible attack from surface combatants and surface-to-surface or air-to-surface missiles, and takes no precautions whatsoever to counter such threats, he is not only grossly negligent but morally contemptible. A merchant ship need not be a fully armed naval combatant to be able to defend herself and her crew. She can be fitted with relatively modest electronic countermeasure equipment and automatic weapons systems that will afford a reasonable degree of protection. Only those vessels that face reasonably foreseeable threats of the magnitude that requires such protective measures need be so equipped in order to avoid liability, and once the threats have diminished the weapons and equipment may be removed. This is not much to ask of those who would benefit from voluntarily placing their vessels, cargoes, and employees in danger, but the law demands what little it is. In order to understand what protective measures can be employed, the vessel owner needs to know something about how naval weapons systems work. Consequently, before discussing some of the various available weapons systems that can be effectively installed aboard commercial vessels, a few rudimentary concepts should be mentioned.

Any weapons system must be able to detect a threat, track it as a target, and employ defensive or offensive measures to eliminate it (by either hiding from it or destroying it). Radar is the primary tool by which all of this is accomplished. The term "radar" is an acronym for RAdio Detection And Ranging and the concept is about 100 years old. In 1886 Heinrich Hertz demonstrated that radio waves could be bounced off metallic objects. In 1904 a German engineer patented an obstacle detector and ship navigation device that operated on the principle of radio wave reflection, and in 1922 engineers at the U.S. Naval Research Laboratory detected a wooden ship using a rudimentary continuous-wave radar. With the advent of World War II vast strides were made in military radar development, and have continued to be made ever since. Radar systems utilize two basic types of radio transmission: pulse and continuous wave. Pulsed radar transmits radio waves in short pulses, and target echoes are interpreted during the nontransmission intervals. Range to the target is determined by the elapsed travel time for the pulse/echo, but the target's velocity cannot be determined. Continuous wave radar differs in that it sends out a continuous radio signal and relies upon the change in frequency of the reflected signal to detect moving objects. If both the target and the radar are stationary no target will be detected, but if either one or both are moving, the target can be detected and its velocity determined. Virtually all navigation radars are pulse radars because they have the ability to determine range. Continuous wave radars are valuable, however, because they can display or select targets that meet certain velocity requirements (like incoming missiles). Automatic target tracking systems must be capable of continuously monitoring target parameters in order to predict the collision point between the target and whatever projectile is launched against it. These parameters are azimuth, elevation, range, and relative velocity. This tracking information is then used by fire control or weapons guidance systems to employ the weapon that will destroy the target. Of course, this assumes there are weapons onboard that are capable of engaging the target. If there are not, then the tracking systems can be employed in connection with possible electronic countermeasures (ECM) that are designed to interfere with the incoming target's guidance systems. There are three basic ways this can be done if the target is radar-guided. First, the ship can radiate active signals that interfere with the hostile radar (jamming). Second, it can change the electrical properties of the space between the ship and the radar (chaff dispersion). Third, it can change the reflective properties of the ship itself (deception repeaters). If the target utilizes an infrared heat-seeking guidance system instead of or in conjunction with radar, certain infrared countermeasures can be employed: infrared shielding of high-heat sources, using special nonreflective paints to reduce the radiated levels of infrared, and deploying infrared decoys such as rockets and flares.

At dawn, just off the Kuwaiti coast in the Persian Gulf on October 16, 1987, the Kuwaiti-owned, U.S.-flagged tanker *Sea Isle City* was struck by an Iranian Silkworm missile. The warhead exploded in the accommodations area of the vessel, blasting a jagged hole in her starboard side and injuring 18 crew members. The attack came only 24 hours after another Iranian-launched Silkworm had struck the U.S.-owned, Liberian-registered supertanker *Sungari*. Both hits might have been prevented had the vessels been properly protected with anti-air defense systems or electronic countermeasures.

There are a number of lightweight, fully automatic, and completely autonomous naval weapons systems that may be easily installed and employed aboard commercial vessels to provide a reasonable degree of protection from surface or air attack. One such is the Italian-made Breda Compact Twin 40mm L/70 Naval Mounting Type 70 that is in service with more than 20 navies. This is a twin 40mm naval gun mounting developed by Breda Meccanica Bresciana in close cooperation with Bofors in Sweden. It is claimed to be the lightest and smallest twin 40mm gun mounting currently available, and it is specifically designed to defend against aircraft and antiship missiles. It is fully automatic and comes in two versions, Type A and Type B, the difference being the magazine capacity. Type A has a magazine capacity of 736 rounds while Type B holds 444 rounds. The gun fires at a rate of 2 × 300 rounds per minute. This same system is also available as a mobile field unit that, arguably, could be placed on board and utilized as it would be in the field without any modification to the vessel at all. Another automatic twin antiaircraft naval weapons system specifically designed for commercial convoy protection or vessel self-defense is the Swiss-made 35mm Twin Anti-Aircraft Gun Type GDM-A. It is an all-weather weapon system that can be operated in any one of three modes: automatic operation (electrically controlled from fire control equipment), local operation (electrically controlled through the use of a joystick), and emergency operation (controlled mechanically). It carries 336 rounds of ammunition in two magazines, a ready-to-use magazine and a standby magazine. A number of smaller Gatling guns and machine guns in various calibres are also available that can be easily mounted on deck to provide a certain measure of protection from surface and air attack. The U.S.-made Sea Vulcan 20 Naval Mount and Sea Vulcan 20mm Three-Barrel Deck Mount Mk 10 are examples of this type of weapon system. Both are built around a three-barrel 20mm Gatling gun and are designed to provide lightweight, low-profile firepower for small naval craft. The Sea Vulcan 20 is an autonomous, remotely controlled gun mount with four main elements: a microprocessor-based fire control module, mount electronics, ammunition storage and feed system, and the mount structure itself with its guns. The mount's magazine capacity is 500 rounds, and it fires at rates of 750 and 1,500 rounds per minute. Of course, an old-fashioned .50-calibre M-2 machine gun can be very effective against small surface craft and helicopters, and is easily installed. Also, a number of fully contained gun pods designed to be attached to helicopters and other slow-flying aircraft can be placed aboard and used effectively.

The object of placing any weapons system aboard commercial vessels is not to make them invincible or turn them into surface combatants. The object is merely to (a) provide some means of protection for the vessel and (b) take action that, in court, can be said to have been reasonable under the circumstances. Just as an individual, under any legal system, may defend himself against an unprovoked attack, so may any commercial vessel or offshore installation, when not acting as an instrument of some nation. However, even if a shipowner or off-shore operator believes the installation of a weapons system is not necessary under the circumstances, he should still be prepared to employ electronic countermeasures anywhere a missile attack is reasonably foreseeable.

As with offensive naval weapons systems, there is a vast array of automatic, passive self-defense systems available to the commercial maritime operator. One example is the French-made Dagaie Naval Countermeasures Equipment, an automatic dispenser of infrared (IR) decoy flares and chaff grenades designed to protect vessels from heat-seeking, radar-homing, and dual-mode antiship missiles. The Dagaie launcher comprises 10 replaceable containers, each of which is loaded with chaff or infrared rockets. The firing sequence runs automatically, and is triggered by a variety of sources. Similar systems by the same manufacturer include the Magaie Lightweight AntiMissile Decoy System and the Sagaie Naval Countermeasures Decoy System. Some 15 navies throughout the world utilize these systems. Another IR/chaff dispenser decoy system that might be readily employed aboard merchant vessels is the German-made Buck-Wegmann Decoy System. Known as the hot dog/silver dog decoy system, it consists of a 12- or 24-tube launcher with multiple carrier mountings of 3 tubes each designed to be installed on both the port and starboard sides of the vessel. The launcher tubes may be loaded with IR decoys (hot dogs), chaff grenades (silver dogs), or a combination of both, and can be fired in single or multiple shots. The compact design of this system, and the small physical dimensions of the tubes, make it ideal for use aboard vessels of all types, including merchantmen with limited deck space.

The weapons and weapons systems described in this section are naturally not all-encompassing. Those that have been mentioned have been so for demonstrative purposes only. The intent is to ensure the security manager understands at least something about the weapons that might be used against his organization, and what types of weapons are available to him. Should he, for instance, decide to install chaff grenade and IR decoy launchers aboard those ships of his fleet he believes could face foreseeable missile attacks, he would certainly research the market thoroughly before deciding what system or systems to employ. So far as employing naval weapons systems aboard either commercial vessels or offshore installations, it should be reiterated that the standard that must be applied is one of reasonableness. If the threat of missile or pirate attack is reasonably foreseeable, and a defensive system reasonably available, it is negligence not to utilize it. If the threat is not reasonably foreseeable, or a defensive system is not reasonably available, then of course it is not negligence. Reasonableness, however, is not something that is always easily ascertained. If the security manager has any doubt as to what is reasonable, he should mentally place himself in the position of a juror who lacks any maritime experience whatever and then decide.

Besides knowing what types of weapons are available, the security manager should be aware of the types of security equipment that may also be utilized by him and his organization, since the use of such equipment may very well determine the security measures he employs. The next section, therefore, addresses equipment.

EQUIPMENT

Within the past 10 or 15 years an entire international industry has developed in an attempt to satisfy security needs around the globe. It is indeed ironic that a relatively few terrorists bent upon destroying or disrupting what they view as a decadent, capitalistic society have in essence spawned a multibillion-dollar industry. The security equipment available today wasn't dreamed of 20 years ago. In some cases there are now so many manufacturers and models to choose from one feels almost like a shopper trying to decide on a particular VCR. The security manager needs to know what types of equipment are available so that he may more effectively plan for the security of his organization, and it is this awareness more than anything else that is the purpose of this section. Once he knows, for instance, that a variety of night vision optics are available and how they can be used, he can research the market and determine which, if any, he wishes to utilize. The security equipment field is far too large to cover in its entirety here. Whole books have been written on the subject. However, some of the major areas will be discussed, and a few of the products mentioned, so that an idea may be gained as to the scope of the market. But it is the existence of this market, not the extent of it, that is important at this time.

One area that has developed from virtually nothing before the 1970s is the design and manufacture of internal security vehicles

(ISVs). Before then, armored vehicles were employed by military forces only, with the exception perhaps of police bomb disposal vans and bank armored cars. ISVs are now manufactured in numerous countries and look more like combat tanks and armored personnel carriers than anything else. Many of them are designed strictly for riot control or counterinsurgency operations and for that reason are not particularly applicable to maritime security. However, port facilities may well require ISVs in one form or another for a number of reasons, not the least of which is the delivery of reinforcement security personnel to areas under attack, or for use as command vehicles in hostage or hijacking situations. Surveillance vans may also be utilized to great advantage in parking lots adjacent to cruise ship passenger terminals and cargo storage areas. These vehicles, a type of ISV, are usually referred to as discreet operational vehicles (DOVs). One new and very impressive ISV is the Transaif Multi-Role Armoured Vehicle, designed and marketed by Transac International Ltd. of Great Britain and manufactured by Thiele of Bremen, West Germany. It has the advantage of not looking like a military vehicle, and thus may be better suited for airport and port facility security. In fact it is available in three versions, one of which is specifically designed for airport security use, which makes it well suited for port facility use as well.

X-ray and bomb detection equipment has become very sophisticated over the last 20 years, primarily as a result of increased airport security requirements. There are all sorts of weapons and explosives detectors on the market that can be used in any number of different applications. Some of them are very compact, hand-held or portable units suitable for use aboard ship or offshore installations, and others are larger pieces of equipment more suited for passenger terminal use. Anyone in the free world today who has taken an airplane flight has more than likely passed through a metal detector gate of some sort on his way to the departure area. What many don't realize is that some of these detectors are also capable of "sniffing" various types of explosives. One such dual-purpose detector used in airports throughout the world is the Explosives Detector Model 85 Entry Scan II manufactured by A.I. Security of Great Britain. A.I. Security also manufactures an entire line of portable explosives detectors, including a truly remarkable pocket-sized model (Model 35), powered by small radio batteries. It will detect very small quantities of explosives, and is ideally suited for shipboard and offshore installation use. Two other

Typical metal detector gate and X-ray machine used at airports

hand-held explosives detectors not quite as small but still easily carried are the HED Explosives Detector Type L3A1 and the Thorn EMI Simtec Portable Explosives Detector. Both detectors are manufactured and marketed in Great Britain. The HED will detect explosives within closed metalwork and inside walls, ceilings, and floors. It can also be used to detect concealed drugs. The Simtec Portable Explosives Detector is slightly larger than the HED, with everything other than the probe carried in a backpack worn by the operator. It is capable of detecting very small quantities of nitroglycerine- and nitrobenzene-based explosives, and can also be calibrated to detect TNT. Its manufacturers claim it is the world's most sensitive portable explosives detector. Hand-held metal detectors are much more common than hand-held explosives detectors, and are manufactured by any number of companies. One popular unit is manufactured by the Swiss firm of Riwosa (Zurich) and is designated the Model MD-12. It operates on three 9-volt batteries and is used throughout the world. A new and improved version has been designated the Model MD-15, which is even smaller and detects both ferrous and nonferrous metals. The German-made Vallon Metal Detector Models MH 1603, MH 1604, and MH 1607 are other examples of compact but effective metal detectors used by police and security personnel. As far as baggage inspection machines are concerned, there are a variety of manufacturers and models to choose from as well. Several, like the British-made Tri-Scan Airport Security System and the Rapidex Hand Baggage Screening System, combine X-ray and explosives detection capabilities in one machine. Others, like the Pantax X-Checker 30 (also made in Britain), combine check-in desk, weigh unit, and X-ray machine.

Riot control equipment can be effectively employed in the maritime security context primarily aboard ship, in the darkened and confining passageways of a vessel whose outer perimeter and secondary perimeter defenses have failed. With intruders aboard and inside, security personnel will be forced to either retreat behind the inner perimeter barriers and hope for rescue, or fight a pitched battle within the passageways of the vessel. Unless assistance is definitely imminent the only logical decision is to fight, particularly since the intruders will be at their most vulnerable at that point. First, they will have had to fight their way (hopefully) on board and across the deck to the ship's superstructure, which they will have had to breech to get inside, and so they may very well be injured and exhausted. Second, once inside they will be faced with unfamiliar darkened and deserted passageways perfectly suited for booby traps and ambushes; and it is here they should be dealt with by security personnel equipped with night vision goggles, stun grenades, and CS (tear gas) fog dispensers or grenades. Night vision goggles will be discussed shortly. Stun grenades, sometimes referred to as "flash-bangs," can be effective in temporarily shocking intruders into inactivity by blinding and disorienting them. The grenades explode with a blinding flash (2 million-plus candlepower) and deafening concussion (200-plus decibels), which are made even more effective by a confined and darkened space. They should be employed by security personnel immediately prior to launching an ambush from around a passageway junction. In such an ambush, it is hard to imagine any intruders surviving. Stun grenades are available from manufacturers in the United States, United Kingdom, France, and Germany. There are also mechanical versions available that, while possibly not as effective, reduce the chance of fire and injury. Besides lending themselves to the effective use of stun grenades, ship passageways also provide wonderful places to use CS gas. In all likelihood the intruders will not be prepared for gas, and a darkened and gas-filled passageway will present a formidable obstacle (particularly if security personnel are lurking around a corner equipped with night vision goggles and gas masks waiting to eliminate the intruders). Since passageways are essentially sealed containers, CS dispensed into them will remain heavily concentrated for extended periods. Thus, as the security force retreats deeper into the vessel (once it becomes apparent the intruders intend to breech the superstructure), a heavy concentration of CS can be laid down through the use of either CS grenades or a fog dispenser. A number of manufacturers market CS grenades. Two of the more notable are Smith and Wesson in the United States and Fabrique Nationale in Belgium. Both produce an entire line of grenades. Two excellent compact CS fog dispensers are the French-made Alsatex Gas Grenade Equipment (a backpack dispenser) and the Israeli-made Projectojet CS Fog Projector. A slightly larger, U.S.-made dispenser is the Smith and Wesson Mark XII-C Pepper Fog Smoke Generator, which can produce 100,000 cubic feet of gas in only 26 seconds. It is in the service inventory of many police departments throughout the United States.

Perimeter protection equipment has become big business in the United States and elsewhere in recent years. Fencing, lights, surveillance cameras, radars, access control equipment, and intrusion detection devices of all kinds are manufactured and marketed by hundreds of companies around the world. In every major city in the United States one can find security firms willing to recommend and install all manner of physical security systems, from relatively simple fencing and lighting to complex, state-of-the-art electronics. The only delimiting factor is the amount of money one wishes to spend. Obviously, much of the available equipment has a maritime security application and the security manager should be aware of the extent of the market.

Starting with the outer perimeter fencing, there are a number of fence intrusion detection systems available. The Yael-5 fence intrusion detection system was developed by Yael Electrical Instruments and Control Company of Beersheba, Israel. It may be installed on any type of existing fencing, and will detect an attempt by an intruder to climb or crawl under the fence, cut the fence or interfere with the system in any way. Another perimeter protection system is the Euro-Med Perim-Alert system, manufactured in the Netherlands by Euro-Med Bv. This is a vibration-sensing system that incorporates fence-mounted sensors and a computerized monitor can be adjusted to various levels of sensitivity. It has been selected for NATO nuclear site security, and is utilized at various private corporate installations around the world. In the United States it is employed by IBM, Exxon, and DuPont. Geophone systems are available from a number of manufacturers (as a result of technology developed during the Vietnam War) and are capable of detecting vibrations created by human movement. Geophones can be installed either below the surface of the ground (about 12 inches) or on the sides of buildings or fences, and the monitoring system can be designed to display the intrusion both visually and audibly. Other systems that utilize buried coaxial cables and microwave generators are also available.

Night vision equipment has also developed commercially as a result of first-generation passive image intensifiers (known as starlight scopes) and infrared lighting devices developed during the Vietnam War. Light, rugged, and compact night vision goggles and rifle scopes are now available that can enhance security capabilities in various ways. Javelin Electronics of Los Angeles, California, markets several models of night vision equipment based upon image intensification. Their Model 223 is adaptable to almost any rifle and is in use in many countries. Smith and Wesson also markets a night vision rifle scope, designated the Mk 700 Series 1, that is extremely compact and light-weight. Pilkington Electro Optical Systems in the United Kingdom manufactures an entire line of night vision devices, including rifle sights, laser target indicators, and personal hand-held devices. One particularly useful product is the Nova General-Purpose Night Vision Goggles, that allow a hands-free operation while maintaining a night vision capability. Of course, *some* light must be present for such passive night vision devices to function. If no light is present, as would be the case inside a darkened ship, then infrared lighting must be used. As with the passive systems, there are a number of IR rifle scopes and goggles available. The disadvantage to almost all of these is the fact that they require a much larger power source than the image intensifiers and are generally bulkier. Also, in a very dark environment, the IR bulb's glowing filament (not the light itself) may be visible to those who are being illuminated.

There are, of course, many other types of equipment that have not been mentioned, such as body armor, riot batons and electric wands, special ammunition, boots and clothing, and communications equipment. All are designed for specific use, and may or may not be something the maritime security manager needs to consider. One thing he does need to consider, however, in relation to all the weapons and equipment that are available, is what his security personnel are capable of *without* those weapons or equipment. In other words, he must consider the subject of unarmed combat or martial arts training.

THE MARTIAL ARTS

International terrorists, military personnel, and law enforcement individuals all receive training in unarmed combat. Professional security forces should as well, and for the same reasons. First, there may come a time when a guard is subjected to a surprise attack while he is either unarmed or unable to employ his weapon. Second, in law enforcement and security work the use of deadly force is not always authorized, in fact most of the time it is specifically not authorized, even when apprehending a suspect. Security personnel must therefore be able to employ that amount of force that is reasonably necessary to apprehend the suspect *without* using deadly force. (In Florida it is now illegal for law enforcement personnel to use deadly force to prevent or apprehend a suspect in *any* crime of property. Thus, a fleeing felon who has not committed rape or murder can be fairly well assured he is not going to receive a bullet between the shoulder blades. If he can outrun or outfight the apprehending policeman he will get away.) A port facility security guard who must apprehend an unarmed, or even an armed, suspect without using deadly force must be able to do so. He cannot, however, if he has not been trained in the proper techniques. Third, martial arts training develops an individual's self-confidence, which is something all security personnel must have to remain effective.

There are some subtle differences between "unarmed combat," "hand-to-hand combat," and "martial arts." Unarmed combat is precisely what the term implies: combat without arms. In combat the primary objective is to kill the enemy, and in unarmed combat the objective is still the same. Thus, unarmed combat concentrates on killing techniques that are effected primarily with one's hands and feet. Nonlethal restraints and "come-alongs" play no part in such training. Recreational sports activities play no part in such training. It is a deadly serious business in which one learns the quickest and most effective methods of dispatching an opponent. Hand-to-hand combat, like unarmed combat, is still combat and the objective remains the same, but it may be either unarmed or armed combat. Knife fighting is hand-to-hand combat, so is stick fighting, and so is garroting. Martial arts, on the other hand, can encompass hand-to-hand and unarmed combat. It can also be a recreational sport, like judo or arm-wrestling. In the United States martial arts are taught primarily as a recreational sport and form of physical conditioning. Demonstrations are performed, tournaments are held, and trophies are given. Self-defense techniques are taught and weight-reduction accomplished. All of these have the effect of developing self-confidence in the participants, many of whom would otherwise never develop it. Killing techniques are not taught and, by and large, should not be, since the participants don't need to know such things. Some forms of nonlethal restraint may be learned, particularly by practitioners of judo and aikido, but by and large come-alongs and nonlethal restraints are not needed in self-defense situations and are therefore not taught.

Security personnel should certainly receive training in police restraint techniques, for without such training they may very well not be able to perform their jobs. They should also receive some martial arts instruction, if for no other reason than to build self-confidence, but it is also an enjoyable form of physical conditioning. Hand-to-hand and unarmed combat, however, probably need not be taught. Instead, training with regard to staying alert, being prepared for any eventuality, and knowing when to unholster a weapon ought to be conducted. The security manager should therefore consider such training and how he can best arrange for it. Because he will be working closely with the local law enforcement agencies, the security manager may well be able to arrange for a police instructor to teach nonlethal restraint techniques to his security personnel on a part-time basis. He may have accomplished martial artists in his security force who can provide some instruction, or he may have some reserve police officers who can do the same. Finally, he can arrange for private instruction by an established martial arts instructor who may have a school in the area. If he chooses this option, however, he should know something about the various martial arts in order to find the right instructor.

The most well known forms of martial arts in the United States are boxing, judo, karate, Tae Kwon Do, and kung fu, probably in that order. There are many other forms of martial arts, none of which the security manager need worry much about, with the possible exception of aikido. Of all of them, only boxing developed in the western world and it is unique in that just the fists are used as weapons. It is also the least scientific of the pugilistic forms, because it developed more as a sport than a means of killing or incapacitating. Since the days of Queen Victoria young men have been taught to box, in prep schools and service academies, as a form of "manly" self-expression and defense. One was not, however, expected to kill one's opponent. Judo is a highly developed form of wrestling. It too developed as a sport, and therefore does not concentrate on deadly or incapacitating blows. What it does concentrate on is nonlethal forms of restraint—just what law enforcement and security personnel need to know in order to apprehend suspects without doing serious bodily injury. Judo focuses on foot-sweeps and body-throws, using leverage and the opponent's inertia to accomplish the desired result. In that respect, it is similar to aikido, which also utilizes leverage and inertia. Judo however, because it is a form of wrestling, depends upon one being grabbed for it to work, whereas aikido concentrates on not allowing oneself to be grabbed. The difference in significant. Both forms are true self-defense styles; that is, their nature is more defensive than offensive, but aikido is further along the evolutionary path to actual unarmed combat. Karate, Tae Kwon Do, and kung fu are representatives of real unarmed combat. Every part of the human body that can be used as a weapon is, and it is applied to the most vulnerable parts of the opponent's body in a scientific and calculated manner most likely to kill or incapacitate. A seriously trained and hardened Tae Kwon Do practitioner is a fearsome killing machine, but one doesn't come along too often. What the public sees instead are tournament fighters, demonstration board-breakers, and movie actors, none of whom are truly representative of the art. Karate, Tae Kwon Do, and kung fu all developed as fighting forms about 2,000 years ago. Karate is Japanese, Tae Kwon Do is Korean, and kung fu is Chinese. The three major forms, each of which is subdivided into numerous styles, have significant differences in technique and philosophy, and proponents of each claim their particular form and style is the most effective. Since perfectly matched individuals trained in the different forms will never be found, the question most likely will remain unanswered. However, in open tournaments (open to all styles) around the country, Tae Kwon Doists repeatedly defeat everyone else. Furthermore, for what it is worth, the U.S. Marine Corps teaches basic Tae Kwon Do techniques in its hand-to-hand combat training of its individual marines.

Effective maritime security requires enlightened security management. The topics discussed in this and the previous chapter—negligent security, risk management, legal concerns, weapons and weapons systems, equipment, and martial arts—are only some of the things a good security manager must consider. His is a leadership role, both in relation to the security force he manages and the security policies he must advocate; and he, more than anyone else in his organization, must realize the awesome responsibilities that come with the job. Of course, it would be nice if his superiors realized it as well. Hopefully, this and the preceding chapter will have helped them do so.

CONCLUSION

Contrary to what most Americans know or believe, the world is not a safe place. It is, in fact, a very dangerous place that has become more dangerous with the advent of international terrorism, the development of a multibillion-dollar ocean resources industry, and an international maritime community that persists in refusing to seriously consider its own security. Combined, the three present a potential for catastrophe and extortion to a degree previously unknown in the course of human development. Terrorists and common criminals alike now have the ability to disrupt hundreds of lives and place entire communities at risk by seizing or sabotaging commercial vessels, port facilities, and offshore installations. Ransoms in the tens of millions of dollars are now realistically demandable in return for refraining from destroying a $400 million drilling platform, creating a $2 billion oil spill, or incinerating an entire port city.

Acts of terrorism and sabotage can be prevented, however, through the implementation of proper maritime security. Maritime security is what this book has been all about, but it has also been about liabilities, legal judgments, and staying in business. Acts of piracy, so long allowed to continue unchecked because it was easiest to do so, must now be reasonably resisted if liabilities are to be avoided. LNG and crude oil carriers must now be reasonably protected if catastrophes and liabilities are to be avoided. Offshore oil platforms must be reasonably secured from sabotage if liabilities are to be avoided. Commercial vessels may no longer sail into war-torn waters without taking reasonable precautions, if liabilities are to be avoided.

The law does not require an absolute standard of maritime security. It does, however, require a reasonable one. The security measures and procedures presented in this book are reasonable. They are not difficult to implement, nor are they particularly expensive. They are, however, necessary.

The maritime industry is on the brink of a new era. Enormous technological advances in ocean resources recovery are at hand that will benefit all of mankind and, in doing so, the entire spectrum of ocean commerce. On the other hand, Third-World social unrest is greater now than it has ever been. Weapons and explosives are more available now than they have ever been. Maritime targets are more attractive now than they have ever been, and the maritime industry is consequently more at risk now than it has ever been. Whether it moves into an era of expansion and prosperity or one of destruction and terror is up to the industry.

REPORT ON AN UNLAWFUL ACT

Date _____

1. Ship or port area description _____

   Name of ship _____

   Flag _____ Master _____

   Port facility security officer _____

2. Brief description of incident or threat

   _____

   _____

   _____

   _____

   Date, time, and place of incident or threat

   _____

3. Number of alleged offenders:

   Passenger _____ Crew _____ Other _____

4. Method utilized to introduce dangerous substances
   or devices into the port facility or ship:

   Persons _____ Baggage _____ Cargo _____

   Ship's Stores _____ Other _____

5. Type of dangerous substances or devices used, with
   full description:

   Weapon _____ Explosives _____ Other _____

Description ——————————————————————————

6(a). Where were the items described in section 5 above concealed, if known?

——

6(b). How were the items described in section 5 above Used and where?

——

6(c). How were the security measures circumvented?

——

——

——

7. What measures and procedures are recommended to prevent recurrence of a similar event?

——

——

——

8. Other pertinent details

——

——

——

Submitted by ——————————————————————————————

APPENDIX B

INTERNATIONAL MARITIME AND PORT SECURITY

46 U.S.C. app. §§ 1801 – 1809 (1986)

§ 1801. International measures for seaport and shipboard security
The Congress encourages the President to continue to seek agreement through the International Maritime Organization on matters of international seaport and shipboard security, and commends him on his efforts to date. In developing such agreement, each member country of the International Maritime Organization should consult with appropriate private sector interests in that country. Such agreement would establish seaport and vessel security measures and could include—
(1) seaport screening of cargo and baggage similar to that done at airports;
(2) security measures to restrict access to cargo, vessels, and dockside property to authorized personnel only;
(3) additional security on board vessels;
(4) licensing or certification of compliance with appropriate security standards; and
(5) other appropriate measures to prevent unlawful acts against passengers and crews on board vessels.

§ 1802. Threat of terrorism to United States ports and vessels
Not later than February 28, 1987, and annually thereafter, the Secretary of Transportation shall report to the Congress on the threat from acts of terrorism to United States ports and vessels operating from those ports.

§ 1803. Security standards at foreign ports
(a) Assessment of security measures. The Secretary of Transportation shall develop and implement a plan to assess the effectiveness of the security measures maintained at those foreign ports which the Secretary, in consultation with the Secretary of State, determines pose a high risk of acts of terrorism directed against passenger vessels.

(b) Consultation with the Secretary of State. In carrying out subsection (a), the Secretary of Transportation shall consult the Secretary of State with

respect to the terrorist threat which exists in each country and poses a high risk of acts of terrorism directed against passenger vessels.

(c) Report of assessments. Not later than 6 months after the date of enactment of this Act [enacted Aug. 27, 1986], the Secretary of Transportation shall report to the Congress on the plan developed pursuant to subsection (a) and how the Secretary will implement the plan.

(d) Determination and notification to foreign country. If, after implementing the plan in accordance with subsection (a), the Secretary of Transportation determines that a port does not maintain and administer effective security measures, the Secretary of State (after being informed by the Secretary of Transportation) shall notify the appropriate government authorities of the country in which the port is located of such determination, and shall recommend the steps necessary to bring the security measures in use at that port up to the standard used by the Secretary of Transportation in making such assessment.

(e) Antiterrorism assistance related to maritime security. The President is encouraged to provide antiterrorism assistance related to maritime security under chapter 8 of part II of the Foreign Assistance Act of 1961 to foreign countries, especially with respect to a port which the Secretary of Transportation determines under subsection (d) does not maintain and administer effective security measures.

§ 1804.   Travel advisories concerning security at foreign ports

(a) Travel advisory. Upon being notified by the Secretary of Transportation that the Secretary has determined that a condition exists that threatens the safety or security of passengers, passenger vessels, or crew traveling to or from a foreign port which the Secretary of Transportation has determined pursuant to section 907(d) to be a port which does not maintain and administer effective security measures, the Secretary of State shall immediately issue a travel advisory with respect to that port. Any travel advisory issued pursuant to this subsection shall be published in the Federal Register. The Secretary of State shall take the necessary steps to widely publicize that travel advisory.

(b) Lifting of travel advisory. The travel advisory required to be issued under subsection (a) may be lifted only if the Secretary of Transportation, in consultation with the Secretary of State, has determined that effective security measures are maintained and administered at the port with respect to which the Secretary of Transportation had made the determination described in section 907(d).

(c) Notification to Congress. The Secretary of State shall immediately notify

the Congress of any change in the status of a travel advisory imposed pursuant to this section.

§ 1805. Suspension of passenger services

(a) President's determination. Whenever the President determines that a foreign nation permits the use of territory under its jurisdiction as a base of operations or training for, or as a sanctuary for, or in any way arms, aids, or abets, any terrorist or terrorist group which knowingly uses the illegal seizure of passenger vessels or the threat thereof as an instrument of policy, the President may, without notice or hearing and for as long as the President determines necessary to assure the security of passenger vessels against unlawful seizure, suspend the right of any passenger vessel common carrier to operate to and from, and the right of any passenger vessel of the United States to utilize, any port in that foreign nation for passenger service.

(b) Prohibition. It shall be unlawful for any passenger vessel common carrier, or any passenger vessel of the United States, to operate in violation of the suspension of rights by the President under this section.

(c) Penalty. (1) If a person operates a vessel in violation of this section, the Secretary of the department in which the Coast Guard is operating may deny the vessels of that person entry to United States ports.

(2) A person violating this section is liable to the United States Government for a civil penalty of not more than $50,000. Each day a vessel utilizes a prohibited port shall be a separate violation of this section.

§ 1806. Sanctions for the seizure of vessels by terrorists

The Congress encourages the President—

(1) to review the adequacy of domestic and international sanctions against terrorists who seize or attempt to seize vessels; and

(2) to strengthen where necessary, through bilateral and multilateral efforts, the effectiveness of such sanctions.

Not later than one year after the date of enactment of this Act [enacted Aug. 27, 1986], the President shall submit a report to the Congress which includes the review of such sanctions and the efforts to improve such sanctions.

§ 1807. Definitions

For purposes of this title—

(1) the term "common carrier" has the same meaning given such term in section 3(6) of the Shipping Act of 1984 (46 U.S.C. App. 1702(6)); and

(2) the terms "passenger vessel" and "vessel of the United States" have the same meaning given such terms in section 2101 of title 46, United States Code.

§ 1808. Authorization of appropriations

There are authorized to be appropriated $12,500,000 for each of the fiscal years 1987 through 1991, to be available to the Secretary of Transportation to carry out this title.

§ 1809. Reports

(a) Consolidation. To the extent practicable, the reports required under sections 903, 905, and 907 shall be consolidated into a single document before being submitted to the Congress. Any classified material in those reports shall be submitted separately as an addendum to the consolidated report.

(b) Submission to committees. The reports required to be submitted to the Congress under this title shall be submitted to the Committee on Foreign Affairs and the Committee on Merchant Marine and Fisheries of the House of Representatives and the Committee on Foreign Relations and the Committee on Commerce, Science and Transportation of the Senate.

PROTECTION AND SECURITY OF VESSELS, HARBORS, AND WATERFRONT FACILITIES

33 C.F.R. 6.01-1–6.19-1

Subpart 6.01—Definitions

§ 6.01-1 Commandant.

"Commandant" as used in this part, means the Commandant of the United States Coast Guard.

§ 6.01-2 District Commander.

"District Commander" as used in this part, means the officer of the Coast Guard designated by the Commandant to command a Coast Guard District.

§ 6.01-3 Captain of the Port.

"Captain of the Port" as used in this part, means the officer of the Coast Guard, under the command of a District Commander, so designated by the Commandant for the purpose of giving immediate direction to Coast Guard law enforcement activities within his assigned area. In addition, the District Commander shall be Captain of the Port with respect to remaining areas in his District not assigned to officers designated by the Commandant as Captain of the Port.

[EO 11249, 30 FR 13001, Oct. 13, 1965]

§ 6.01-4 Waterfront facility.

"Waterfront facility" as used in this part, means all piers, wharves, docks, and similar structures to which vessels may be secured; areas of land, water, or land and water under and in immediate proximity to them; buildings on such structures or contiguous to them and equipment and materials on such structures or in such buildings.

[EO 11249, 30 FR 13001, Oct. 13, 1965]

§ 6.01-5 Security zone.

"Security zone" as used in this part, means all areas of land, water, or land and water, which are so designated by the Captain of the Port for such time as he deems necessary to prevent damage or injury to any vessel or waterfront facility, to safeguard ports, harbors, territories, or waters of the United States or to secure the observance of the rights and obligations of the United States.

[EO 11249, 30 FR 13001, Oct. 13, 1965]

Subpart 6.04—General Provisions

§ 6.04-1 Enforcement.

(a) The rules and regulations in this part shall be enforced by the captain of the port under the supervision and general direction of the District Commander and the Commandant, and all authority and power vested in the captain of the port by the regulations in this part shall be deemed vested in and may be exercised by the District Commander and the Commandant.

(b) The rules and regulations in this part may be enforced by any other officer of the Coast Guard designated by the Commandant or the District Commander.

[EO 10173, 15 FR 7012, Oct. 20, 1950, as amended by EO 10277, 16 FR 7541, Aug. 2, 1951]

§ 6.04–5 Preventing access of persons, articles or things to vessels, or waterfront facilities.

The Captain of the Port may prevent any person, article, or thing from boarding or being taken or placed on board any vessel or entering or being taken into or upon or placed in or upon any waterfront facility whenever it appears to him that such action is necessary in order to secure such vessel from damage or injury or to prevent damage or injury to any vessel, or waterfront facility or waters of the United States, or to secure the observances of rights and obligations of the United States.

[EO 11249, 30 FR 13001, Oct. 13, 1965]

§ 6.04–6 Establishing security zones; prohibitions with respect thereto.

The Captain of a Port may establish security zones subject to the terms and conditions specified in § 6.01–5. No person or vessel shall enter a security zone without the permission of the Captain of the Port. No person shall board or take or place any article or thing on board any vessel in a security zone without the permission of the Captain of the Port. No person shall take or place any article or thing upon any waterfront facility in any such zone without such permission.

[EO 11249, 30 FR 13001, Oct. 13, 1965]

§ 6.04–7 Visitation, search, and removal.

The Captain of the Port may cause to be inspected and searched at any time any vessel, waterfront facility, or security zone, or any person, article, or thing thereon or therein, within the jurisdiction of the United States, may place guards upon any such vessel, waterfront facility, or security zone and may remove therefrom any and all persons, articles, or things not specifically authorized by him to go or remain thereon or therein.

[EO 11249, 30 FR 13002, Oct. 13, 1965]

§ 6.04–8 Possession and control of vessels.

The Captain of the port may supervise and control the movement of any vessel and shall take full or partial possession or control of any vessel or any part thereof, within the territorial waters of the United States under his jurisdiction, whenever it appears to him that such action is necessary in order to secure such vessel from damage or injury, or to prevent damage or injury to any vessel or waterfront facility or waters of the United States, or to secure the observance of rights and obligations of the United States.

§ 6.04–11 Assistance of other agencies.

The Captain of the port may enlist the aid and cooperation of Federal, State, county, municipal, and private agencies to assist in the enforcement of regulations issued pursuant to this part.

Subpart 6.10—Identification and Exclusion of Persons From Vessels and Waterfront Facilities

§ 6.10–1 Issuance of documents and employment of persons aboard vessels.

No person shall be issued a document required for employment on a merchant vessel of the United States nor shall any person be employed on a merchant vessel of the United States unless the Commandant is satisfied that the character and habits of life of such person are such as to authorize the belief that the presence of the individual on board would not be inimical to the security of the United States: *Provided,* That the Commandant may designate categories of merchant vessels to which the foregoing shall not apply.

[EO 10352, 17 FR 4624, May 21, 1952]

§ 6.10–5 Access to vessels and waterfront facilities.

Any person on board any vessel or any person seeking access to any vessel or any waterfront facility within the jurisdiction of the United States may be required to carry identification credentials issued by or otherwise satisfactory to the Commandant. The Commandant may define and designate those categories of vessels and areas of the waterfront wherein such credentials are required.

§ 6.10–7 Identification credentials.

The identification credential to be issued by the Commandant shall be known as the Coast Guard Port Security Card, and the form of such credential, and the conditions and the manner of its issuance shall be as prescribed by the Commandant after consultation with the Secretary of Labor.

The Commandant shall not issue a Coast Guard Port Security Card unless he is satisfied that the character and habits of life of the applicant therefor are such as to authorize the belief that the presence of such individual on board a vessel or within a waterfront facility would not be inimical to the security of the United States. The Commandant shall revoke and require the surrender of a Coast Guard Port Security Card when he is no longer satisfied that the holder is entitled thereto. The Commandant may recognize for the same purpose such other credentials as he may designate in lieu of the Coast Guard Port Security Card.

[EO 10277, 16 FR 7541, Aug. 2, 1951]

§ 6.10-9 Appeals.

Persons who are refused employment or who are refused the issuance of documents or who are required to surrender such documents, under this subpart, shall have the right of appeal, and the Commandant shall appoint Boards for acting on such appeals. Each such Board shall, so far as practicable, be composed of one Coast Guard officer, one member drawn from management, and one member drawn from labor. The members drawn from management and labor shall, upon suitable security clearance, be nominated by the Secretary of Labor. Such members shall be deemed to be employees of the United States and shall be entitled to compensation under the provisions of section 15 of the act of August 2, 1946 (5 U.S.C. 55a) while performing duties incident to such employment. The Board shall consider each appeal brought before it and, in recommending final action to the Commandant, shall insure the appellant all fairness consistent with the safeguarding of the national security.

Subpart 6.12—Supervision and Control of Explosives or Other Dangerous Cargo

§ 6.12-1 General supervision and control

The Captain of the Port may supervise and control the transportation, handling, loading, discharging, stowage, or storage of hazardous materials on board vessels as covered by the regulations in 49 CFR Parts 170-189, 46 CFR Parts 150-156, 46 CFR Parts 146-148 and the regulations governing

tank vessels (46 CFR Parts 30-39).

[CGD 77-228, 43 FR 53427, Nov. 16, 1978]

§ 6.12-3 Approval of facility for dangerous cargo.

The Commandant may designate waterfront facilities for the handling and storage of, and for vessel loading and discharging, explosives, inflammable or combustible liquids in bulk, or other dangerous articles or cargo covered by the regulations referred to in § 6.12-1, and may require the owners, operators, masters, and others concerned to secure permits for such handling, storage, loading, and unloading from the Captain of the Port, conditioned upon the fulfillment of such requirements for the safeguarding of such waterfront facilities and vessels as the Commandant may prescribe.

Subpart 6.14—Security of Waterfront Facilities and Vessels in Port

§ 6.14-1 Safety measures.

The Commandant, in order to achieve the purposes of this part, may prescribe such conditions and restrictions relating to the safety of waterfront facilities and vessels in port as he finds to be necessary under existing circumstances. Such conditions and restrictions may extend, but shall not be limited to, the inspection, operation, maintenance, guarding, and manning of, and fire-prevention measures for, such vessels and waterfront facilities.

[EO 10277, 16 FR 7541, Aug. 2, 1951]

§ 6.14-2 Condition of waterfront facility a danger to vessel.

Whenever the captain of the port finds that the mooring of any vessel to a wharf, dock, pier, or other waterfront structure would endanger such vessel, or any other vessel, or the harbor or any facility therein by reason of conditions existing on or about such wharf, dock, pier, or other waterfront structure, including, but not limited to, inadequate guard service, insufficient lighting, fire hazards, inadequate fire protection, unsafe machinery, internal disturbance, or unsatisfactory operation, the captain of the port may prevent the mooring of any vessel to such wharf, dock, pier, or other waterfront structure until the unsatisfactory condition or conditions so found are corrected, and he may, for the same reasons, after any vessel has been moored, compel the shifting of such vessel from any such wharf, dock, pier, or other waterfront structure.

[EO 10277, 16 FR 7541, Aug. 2, 1951]

Subpart 6.16—Sabotage and Subversive Activity

§ 6.16-1   Reporting of sabotage and subversive activity.

Evidence of sabotage or subversive activity involving or endangering any vessel, harbor, port, or waterfront facility shall be reported immediately to the Federal Bureau of Investigation and to the captain of the port, or to their respective representatives.

§ 6.16-3   Precautions against sabotage.

The master, owner, agent, or operator of a vessel or waterfront facility shall take all necessary precautions to protect the vessel, waterfront facility, and cargo from sabotage.

Subpart 6.18—Penalties

§ 6.18-1   Violations.

Section 2, Title II of the act of June 15, 1917, as amended, 50 U.S.C. 192, provides as follows:

If any owner, agent, master, officer, or person in charge, or any member of the crew of any such vessel fails to comply with any regulation or rule issued or order given

under the provisions of this title, or obstructs or interferes with the exercise of any power conferred by this title, together with her tackle, apparel, furniture, and equipment, shall be subject to seizure and forfeiture to the United States in the same manner as merchandise is forfeited for violation of the customs revenue laws; and the person guilty of such failure, obstruction, or interference shall be punished by imprisonment for not more than ten years and may, in the discretion of the court, be fined not more than $10,000.

(a) If any other person knowingly fails to comply with any regulation or rule issued or order given under the provisions of this title, or knowingly obstructs or interferes with the exercise of any power conferred by this title, he shall be punished by imprisonment for not more than ten years and may, at the discretion of the court, be fined not more than $10,000.

Subpart 6.19—Responsibility for Security of Vessels and Waterfront Facilities

§ 6.19-1   Primary responsibility.

Nothing contained in this part shall be construed as relieving the masters, owners, operators, and agents of vessels or other waterfront facilities from their primary responsibility for the protection and security of such vessels or waterfront facilities.

[EO 10277, 16 FR 7541, Aug. 2, 1951]

IDENTIFICATION CREDENTIALS FOR PERSONS REQUIRING ACCESS TO WATERFRONT FACILITIES OR VESSELS

33 C.F.R. 125.01–125.57

§ 125.01 Commandant.

The term "Commandant" means Commandant of the Coast Guard.

§ 125.03 District Commander.

The term "District Commander" means the officer of the Coast Guard designated by the Commandant to command a Coast Guard District.

§ 125.05 Captain of the Port.

The term "Captain of the Port" means the officer of the Coast Guard, under the command of a District Commander, so designated by the Commandant for the purpose of giving immediate direction to Coast Guard law enforcement activities within the general proximity of the port in which he is situated.

§ 125.06 Western rivers.

The term "western rivers" as used in the regulations in this subchapter shall include only the Red River of the North, the Mississippi River and its tributaries above the Huey P. Long Bridge, and that part of the Atchafalaya River above its junction with the Plaquemine-Morgan City alternate waterway.

[CGFR 57-52, 22 FR 10301, Dec. 20, 1957]

§ 125.07 Waterfront facility.

The term "waterfront facility," as used in this subchapter, means all piers, wharves, docks, and similar structures to which vessels may be secured, buildings on such structures or contiguous to them, and equipment and materials on such structures or in such buildings.

§ 125.08 Great Lakes.

The term "Great Lakes" as used in the regulations in this subchapter shall include the Great Lakes and their connecting and tributary waters.

[CGFR 57-52, 22 FR 10301, Dec. 20, 1957]

§ 125.09 Identification credentials.

The term "Identification credentials," as used in this subchapter, means any of the following:

(a) Coast Guard Port Security Card (Form CG 2514).

(b) Merchant Mariner's Document.

(c) Armed Forces Identification Card.

(d) Identification credentials issued by Federal Law enforcement and intelligence agencies to their officers and employees (e. g., Department of the Treasury, Department of Justice, Federal Communications Commission).

(e) Identification credentials issued to public safety officials (e. g., police, firemen) when acting within the scope of their employment.

(f) Such other identification as may be approved by the Commandant from time to time.

[CGD 56-15, 21 FR 2940, May 3, 1956, as

315

amended by CGD 77-228, 43 FR 53427, Nov. 16, 1978]

§ 125.11 Form of Coast Guard Port Security Card.

The Coast Guard Port Security Card issued by the Coast Guard under the provisions of this subchapter shall be a laminated card bearing photograph, signature, fingerprint, and personal description of the holder, and other pertinent data.

§ 125.12 Period of validity of Coast Guard Port Security Cards.

(a) The Coast Guard Port Security Card (Form CG-2514) shall be valid for a period of eight years from the date of issuance thereof unless sooner suspended or revoked by proper authority. On the first day after eight years from the date of issuance, the Coast Guard Port Security Card (Form CG-2514) is hereby declared invalid and shall be considered null and void for all purposes.

(b) The holder of a Coast Guard Port Security Card, which is about to expire or has expired, may apply for a new Coast Guard Port Security Card in accordance with the procedures set forth in § 125.21. In the event the applicant's Coast Guard Port Security Card has expired, such card shall accompany the application for a new Coast Guard Port Security Card. In the event the applicant is holding a valid Coast Guard Port Security Card at the time he submits his application for a new card, such person shall surrender the old or expired Coast Guard Port Security Card at the time he is issued a new Coast Guard Port Security Card. In the event the old Coast Guard Port Security Card was lost, stolen, or destroyed, then the applicant shall comply with the provisions in § 125.51, regarding the replacement of a lost Coast Guard Port Security Card and the new card issued as a replacement for a lost card which has expired or is about to expire shall bear a current issuance date.

[CGFR 58-52, 23 FR 9751, Dec. 18, 1958]

§ 125.13 Captain of the Port Identification Cards.

Captain of the Port Identification Cards issued under the form designation "Form CG 2514" prior to the revision of August 1950 were declared invalid by a notice published in the FEDERAL REGISTER on September 11, 1946

(11 FR 10103), which declaration is hereby reaffirmed.

§ 125.15 Access to waterfront facilities, and port and harbor areas, including vessels and harbor craft therein.

(a) The Commandant will, from time to time, direct Captains of the Port of certain ports to prevent access of persons who do not possess one or more of the identification credentials listed in § 125.09 to those waterfront facilities, and port and harbor areas, including vessels and harbor craft therein, where the following shipping activities are conducted:

(1) Those vital to the Military Defense Assistance Program.

(2) Those pertaining to the support of U.S. military operations.

(3) Those pertaining to loading and unloading explosives and other dangerous cargo.

(4) Those essential to the interests of national security and defense, to prevent loss, damage or injury, or to insure the observance of rights and obligations of the United States.

(b) No person who does not possess one of the identification credentials aforesaid shall enter or remain in such facilities, or port or harbor areas, including vessels and harbor craft therein.

(c) The Captain of the Port shall give local public notice of the restriction of access to waterfront facilities, and port and harbor areas, including vessels and harbor craft therein, as far in advance as practicable, and shall cause such facilities and areas to be suitably marked as to such restriction.

[CGFR 56-15, 21 FR 2940, May 3, 1956, as amended by CGFR 58-43, 23 FR 8542, Nov. 1, 1958]

§ 125.17 Persons eligible for Coast Guard Port Security Cards.

(a) Only the following persons may be issued Coast Guard Port Security Cards:

(1) Persons regularly employed on vessels or on waterfront facilities.

(2) Persons having regular public or private business connected with the operation, maintenance, or administration of vessels, their cargoes, or waterfront facilities.

(b) A holder of a Merchant Mariner's Document shall not be issued a Port Security Card, unless his Merchant Mariner's Document is surrendered to the Coast Guard. In this connection, see § 125.09.

[CGFR 62-39, 27 FR 11259, Nov. 15, 1962, as amended by CGD 77-228, 43 FR 53427, Nov. 16, 1978]

§ 125.19 Standards.

Information concerning an applicant for a Coast Guard Port Security Card, or a holder of such card, which may preclude a determination that his character and habits of life are such as to warrant the belief that his presence on waterfront facilities, and port and harbor areas, including vessels and harbor craft therein, would not be inimical to the security of the United States, shall relate to the following:

(a) Advocacy of the overthrow or alteration of the Government of the United States by unconstitutional means.

(b) Commission of, or attempts or preparations to commit, an act of espionage, sabotage, sedition or treason, or conspiring with, or aiding or abetting another to commit such an act.

(c) Performing, or attempting to perform, duties or otherwise acting so as to serve the interests of another government to the detriment of the United States.

(d) Deliberate unauthorized disclosure of classified defense information.

(e) [Reserved]

(f) Having been adjudged insane, having been legally committed to an insane asylum, or treated for serious mental or neurological disorder, without evidence of cure.

(g) Having been convicted of any of the following offenses, indicative of a criminal tendency potentially dangerous to the security of such waterfront facilities and port and harbor areas, including vessels and harbor craft therein; arson, unlawful trafficking in drugs, espionage, sabotage, or treason.

(h) Drunkenness on the job or addiction to the use of narcotic drugs, without adequate evidence of rehabilitation.

(i) Illegal presence in the United States, its territories or possessions; having been found finally subject to deportation order by the United States Immigration and Naturalization Service.

[CGFR 56-15, 21 FR 2940, May 3, 1956, as amended by 37 FR 23422, Nov. 3, 1972]

§ 125.21 Applications.

(a)(1) Application for a Coast Guard Port Security Card shall be made under oath in writing and shall include applicant's answers in full to inquiries with respect to such matters as are deemed by the Commandant to be pertinent to the standards set forth in § 125.19, and to be necessary for a determination whether the character and habits of life of the applicant are such as to warrant the belief that his presence on waterfront facilities, and port and harbor areas, including vessels and harbor craft therein, would not be inimical to the security of the United States.

(2) The application also shall include applicant's complete identification, citizenship record, personal description, military record, if any, and a statement of the applicant's sponsor certifying the applicant's employment or union membership and that applicant's statements are true and correct to the best of sponsor's knowledge.

(3) The application shall be accompanied by two unmounted, dull finish photographs, 1 inch x 1 15/16 inches, of passport type, taken within one year of the date of application. The photograph shall show the full face with the head uncovered and shall be a clear and satisfactory likeness of the applicant. It shall portray the largest image of the head and upper shoulders possible within the dimensions specified.

(4) Fingerprint records on each applicant shall be taken by the Coast Guard at the time application is submitted.

(5) The applicant shall present satisfactory proof of his citizenship.

(6) The applicant shall indicate the address to which his Coast Guard Port Security Card can be delivered to him by mail. Under special circumstances the applicant may arrange to call in person for the Coast Guard Port Security Card.

(7) The applicant shall present his application, in person, to a Coast Guard Port Security Unit designated to receive such applications. Such units will be located in or near each port where Coast Guard Port Security Cards are required. Each Captain of the Port shall forward promptly to the Commandant each application for a Coast Guard Port Security Card received by him.

(b) If an applicant fails or refuses to furnish the required information or to make full and complete answer with respect to all matters of inquiry, the Commandant shall hold in abeyance further consideration of the application, and shall notify the applicant that further action will not be taken unless and until the applicant furnishes the required information and fully and completely answers all inquiries directed to him.

[CGFR 59-63, 25 FR 1589, Feb. 24, 1960]

§ 125.23 United States citizens.

Acceptable evidence of United States citizenship is described in this section in the order of its desirability; however, the Coast Guard will reject any evidence not believed to be authentic;

(a) Birth certificate or certified copy thereof.

(b) Certificate of naturalization. This shall be presented by all persons claiming citizenship through naturalization.

(c) Baptismal certificate or parish record recorded within one year after birth.

(d) Statement of a practicing physician certifying that he attended the birth and that he has a record in his possession showing the date and place of birth.

(e) United States passport.

(f) A commission in one of the armed forces of the United States, either regular or reserve; or satisfactory documentary evidence of having been commissioned in one of the armed forces subsequent to January 1, 1936, provided such commission or evidence shows the holder to be a citizen.

(g) A continuous discharge book, or Merchant Mariner's Document issued by the Coast Guard which shows the holder to be a citizen of the United States.

(h) If an applicant claiming to be a citizen of the United States submits a delayed certificate of birth issued under a State's seal, it may be accepted as prima facie evidence of citizenship if no one of the requirements in paragraphs (a) through (g) of this section can be met by the applicant and in the absence of any collateral facts indicating fraud in its procurement.

(i) If no one of the requirements in paragraphs (a) through (h) of this section can be met by the applicant, he should make a statement to that effect, and in an attempt to establish citizenship, he may submit for consideration data of the following character:

(1) Report of the Census Bureau showing the earliest record of age or birth available. Request for such information should be addressed to the Director of the Census, Suitland, Md. 20233. In making such request, definite information must be furnished the Census Bureau as to the place of residence when the first census was taken after the birth of the applicant, giving the name of the street and the number of the house, or other identification of place where living, etc.; also names of parents or the names of other persons with whom residing on the date specified.

(2) School records, immigration records, or insurance policies (the latter must be at least 10 years old).

§ 125.25 Aliens.

Alien registration records together with other papers and documents which indicated the country of which the applicant is a citizen shall be accepted as evidence of citizenship in a foreign nation.

§ 125.27 Sponsorship of applicant.

Applications for a Coast Guard Port Security Card shall not be accepted unless sponsored. The applicant shall be sponsored by an authorized official of applicant's employer or by an authorized official of applicant's labor union. Each company and each labor union concerned shall file with the appropriate Captain of the Port a list of officials of the company or union who are authorized to sponsor applicants. Other sponsorship may be accepted where the circumstances warrant.

§ 125.29 Insufficient information.

(a)(1) If, in the judgment of the Commandant, an application does not contain sufficient information to enable him to satisfy himself that the character and habits of life of the applicant are such as to warrant the belief that his presence on waterfront facilities, and port and harbor areas, including vessels and harbor craft herein, would not be inimical to the security of the United States, the Commandant may require the applicant to furnish, under oath in writing or orally, such further information as he deems pertinent to the standards set forth in § 125.19 and necessary to enable him to make such a determination.

(2) If an applicant fails or refuses to furnish such additional information, the Commandant shall hold in abeyance further consideration of the application, and shall notify the applicant that further action will not be taken unless and until the applicant furnishes such information.

(b) Upon receipt, the application and such further information as the Commandant may have required shall be referred, except in those instances where action on an application is held in abeyance pursuant to § 125.21(b) or to paragraph (a)(2) of this section, to a committee composed of a representative of the Legal Division, of the Merchant Vessel Personnel Division and of the Intelligence Division, Coast Guard Headquarters. The committee shall prepare an analysis of the available information and shall make recommendations for action by the Commandant.

[CGFR 59-63, 25 FR 1589, Feb. 24, 1960]

§ 125.31 Approval of applicant by Commandant.

(a) If the Commandant is satisfied that the character and habits of life of the applicant are not such as to warrant the belief that his presence on waterfront facilities, and port and harbor areas, including vessels and harbor craft therein, would be inimical to the security of the United States, he will direct that a Coast Guard Port Security Card be issued to the applicant.

(b) If the Commandant is not satisfied that the character and habits of life of the applicant are such as to warrant the belief that his presence on waterfront facilities, and port and harbor areas, including vessels and harbor craft therein, would not be inimical to the security of the United States, he will notify the applicant in writing as provided for in § 125.35.

§ 125.33 Holders of Coast Guard Port Security Cards.

(a) Whenever the Commandant is not satisfied that the character and habits of life of a holder of a Coast Guard Port Security Card are such as to warrant the belief that his presence on waterfront facilities and port and harbor areas, including vessels and harbor craft therein, would not be inimical to the security of the United States, he will request the holder to furnish, under oath in writing, such information as he deems pertinent and necessary for a determination on this issue.

(b) If the holder fails or refuses to furnish such information within thirty (30) days after receipt of the Commandant's request, the Commandant may issue the written notice provided for in § 125.35(a).

(c) The holder's failure or refusal to furnish such information shall preclude a determination that the holder's character and habits of life are such as to warrant the belief that his presence on waterfront facilities, and port and harbor areas, including vessels and harbor craft therein, would not be inimical to the security of the United States.

(d) Upon receipt of such information as the Commandant may have required, the procedure prescribed in § 125.29(b) shall be followed.

(e) If the Commandant is satisfied that the character and habits of life of the holder are such as to warrant the belief that his presence on waterfront facilities, and port and harbor areas, including vessels and harbor craft therein, would not be inimical to the security of the United States, he shall notify the holder accordingly.

(f) If the Commandant is not satisfied that the character and habits of life of the holder are such as to warrant the belief that his presence on waterfront facilities, and port and harbor areas, including vessels and harbor craft therein, would not be inimical to the security of the United States, he shall notify the holder in writing as provided for in § 125.35.

[CGFR 59-63, 25 FR 1589, Feb. 24, 1960]

§ 125.35 Notice by Commandant.

(a) The notice provided for in §§ 125.31 and 125.33 shall contain a statement of the reasons why the Commandant is not satisfied that the character and habits of life of the applicant or holder are such as to warrant the belief that his presence on waterfront facilities, and port and harbor areas, including vessels and harbor craft therein, would not be inimical to the security of the United States. Such notice shall be as specific and detailed as the interests of national security shall permit and shall include pertinent information such as names, dates, and places in such detail as to permit reasonable answer.

(b) The applicant or holder shall have 20 days from the date of receipt of the notice of reasons to file written answer thereto. Such answer may include statements or affidavits by third parties or such other documents or evidence as the applicant or holder deems pertinent to the matters in question.

(c) Upon receipt of such answer the procedure prescribed in § 125.29(b) shall be followed.

(d) If the Commandant is satisfied that the character and habits of life of the applicant or holder are such as to warrant the belief that his presence on waterfront facilities, and port and harbor areas, including vessels and harbor craft therein, would not be inimical to the security of the United States, he shall, in the case of an applicant, direct that a Coast Guard Port Security Card be issued to the applicant, or, in the case of a holder, notify him accordingly.

(e) If the Commandant is not satisfied that the applicant's or holder's character and habits of life are such as to warrant the belief that his presence on waterfront facilities, and port and harbor areas, including vessels and harbor craft therein, would not be inimical to the security of the United States, the Commandant shall refer the matter to a Hearing Board for hearing and recommendation in accordance with the provisions of this part.

§ 125.37 Hearing Boards.

The Commandant may establish a Hearing Board in each Coast Guard District. The Commandant shall designate for each Hearing Board a Chairman, who shall be, so far as practicable, an officer of the Coast Guard. The Commandant shall designate, so far as practicable, a second member from a panel of persons representing labor named by the Secretary of Labor, and a third member from a panel of persons representing management named by the Secretary of Labor.

§ 125.39 Notice by Hearing Board.

Whenever the Commandant refers a matter to a Hearing Board, the Chairman shall:

(a) Fix the time and place of the hearing;

(b) Inform the applicant or holder of the names of the members of the Hearing Board, their occupations, and the businesses or organizations with which they are affiliated, of his privilege of challenge, and of the time and place of the hearing;

(c) Inform the applicant or holder of his privilege to appear before the Hearing Board in person or by counsel or representative of his choice, and to present testimonial and documentary evidence in his behalf, and to cross-examine any witnesses appearing before the Board; and

(d) Inform the applicant or holder that if within 10 days after receipt of the notice he does not request an opportunity to appear before the Hearing Board, either in person or by counsel or representative, the Hearing Board will proceed without further notice to him.

§ 125.41 Challenges.

Within five days after receipt of the notice described in § 125.39 the applicant or holder may request disqualification of any member of the Hearing Board on the grounds of personal bias or other cause. The request shall be accompanied by an affidavit setting forth in detail the facts alleged to constitute grounds for disqualification. The affidavit may be supplemented by an oral presentation if desired. If after due consideration the Chairman believes a challenged member is qualified notwithstanding the challenge, he shall notify the person who made the challenge and arrange to proceed with the hearing. If the person who made the challenge takes exception to the ruling of the Chairman, the exception and data relating to the claim of disqualification shall be made a matter of record. If the Chairman finds that there is reasonable ground for disqualification he shall furnish the person who made the challenge with the name of an alternate in lieu of the challenged member and arrange to proceed with the hearing. In the event the Chairman is challenged, he shall forthwith notify the Commandant, furnishing the grounds for the claim of disqualification, and the Commandant shall act upon the challenge in accordance with the foregoing procedure. In addition to the right to challenge for cause, a person who has requested a hearing shall have two peremptory challenges, one challenge for the management member and one challenge for the labor member of the Hearing Board. Should the management member be so challenged, the person who made the challenge may elect to have the management member replaced by another management member or by a member not representing either management or labor; if the member peremptorily challenged represents labor, the person who made the challenge may elect to have the labor member replaced by another labor member or by a member not representing either management or labor.

§ 125.43 Hearing procedure.

(a) Hearings shall be conducted in an orderly manner and in a serious, businesslike atmosphere of dignity and decorum and shall be expedited as much as possible.

(b) The hearing shall be in open or closed session at the option of the applicant or holder.

(c) Testimony before the Hearing Board shall be given under oath or affirmation.

(d) The Chairman of the Hearing Board shall inform the applicant or holder of his right to:

(1) Participate in the hearing;

(2) Be represented by counsel of his choice;

(3) Present witnesses and offer other evidence in his own behalf and in refutation of the reasons set forth in the Notice of the Commandant; and

(4) Cross-examine any witnesses offered in support of such reasons.

(e) Hearings shall be opened by the reading of the Notice of the Commandant and the answer thereto. Any statement and affidavits filed by the applicant or holder may be incorporated in the record by reference.

(f) The Hearing Board may, in its discretion, invite any person to appear at the hearing and testify. However, the Board shall not be bound by the testimony of such witness by reason of having called him and shall have full right to cross-examine the witness. Every effort shall be made to produce material witnesses to testify in support of the reasons set forth in the Notice of the Commandant, in order that such witnesses may be confronted and cross-examined by the applicant or holder.

(g) The applicant or holder may introduce such evidence as may be relevant and pertinent. Rules of evidence shall not be binding on the Hearing Board, but reasonable restrictions may be imposed as to the relevancy, competency and materiality of matters considered. If the applicant or holder is, or may be, handicapped by the nondisclosure to him of confidential sources, or by the failure of witnesses to appear, the Hearing Board shall take the fact into consideration.

(h) The applicant or holder or his counsel or representative shall have the right to control the sequence of witnesses called by him.

(i) The Hearing Board shall give due consideration to documentary evidence developed by investigation, including membership cards, petitions bearing the applicant's or holder's signature, books, treatises or articles written by the applicant or holder and testimony by the applicant or holder before duly constituted authority.

(j) Complete verbatim stenographic transcription shall be made of the hearing by qualified reporters and the transcript shall constitute a permanent part of the record. Upon request, the applicant or holder or his counsel or representative shall be furnished, without cost, a copy of the transcript of the hearing.

(k) The Board shall reach its conclusion and base its determination on information presented at the hearing, together with such other information as may have been developed through investigation and inquiries or made available by the applicant or holder.

(l) If the applicant or holder fails, without good cause shown to the satisfaction of the chairman, to appear personally or to be represented before the Hearing Board, the Board shall proceed with consideration of the matter.

(m) The recommendation of the Hearing Board shall be in writing and shall be signed by all members of the Board. The Board shall forward to the Commandant, with its recommendation, a memorandum of reasons in support thereof. Should any member be in disagreement with the majority a dissent should be noted setting forth the reasons therefor. The recommendation of the Board, together with the complete record of the case, shall be sent to the Commandant as expeditiously as possible.

§ 125.45 Action by Commandant.

(a) If, upon receipt of the Board's recommendation, the Commandant is satisfied that the character and habits of life of the applicant or holder are such as to warrant the belief that his presence on waterfront facilities, and port and harbor areas, including vessels and harbor craft therein, would not be inimical to the security of the United States, he shall, in the case of an applicant, direct that a Coast Guard Port Security Card be issued to the applicant, or, in the case of a holder, notify him accordingly.

(b) If, upon receipt of the Board's recommendation, the Commandant is not satisfied that the character and habits of life of the applicant or holder are such as to warrant the belief that his presence on waterfront facilities, and port and harbor areas, including vessels and harbor craft therein, would not be inimical to the security of the United States, the Commandant shall:

(1) In the case of an applicant, notify him that a Coast Guard Port Security Card will not be issued to the applicant, or,

(2) In the case of a holder, revoke and require the surrender of his Coast Guard Port Security Card.

(c) Such applicant or holder shall be notified of his right, and shall have 20 days from the receipt of such notice within which, to appeal under this part.

§ 125.47 Appeals.

(a) The Commandant shall establish at Coast Guard Headquarters, Washington, D.C., an Appeal Board to hear appeals provided for in this part. The Commandant shall designate for the Appeal Board a Chairman, who shall be so far as practicable, an officer of the Coast Guard. The Commandant shall designate, so far as practicable, a member from a panel of persons representing management nominated by the Secretary of Labor, and a member from a panel of persons representing labor nominated by the Secretary of Labor. The Commandant shall insure that persons designated as Appeal Board members have suitable security clearance. The Chairman of the Appeal Board shall make all arrangements incident to the business of the Appeal Board.

(b) If an applicant or holder appeals to the Appeal Board within 20 days after receipt of notice of his right to appeal under this part, his appeal shall be handled under the same procedure as that specified in § 125.39, and the privilege of challenge may be exercised through the same procedure as that specified in § 125.41.

(c) Appeal Board proceedings shall be conducted in the same manner as that specified in § 125.43.

§ 125.49 Action by Commandant after appeal.

(a) If, upon receipt of the Appeal Board's recommendation, the Commandant is satisfied that the character and habits of life of the applicant or holder are such as to warrant the belief that his presence on waterfront facilities, and port and harbor areas, including vessels and harbor craft therein, would not be inimical to the security of the United States, he shall, in the case of an applicant, direct that a Coast Guard Port Security Card be issued to the applicant, or in the case of a holder, notify him accordingly.

(b) If, upon receipt of the Appeal Board's recommendation, the Commandant is not satisfied that the character and habits of life of the applicant or holder are such as to warrant the belief that his presence on waterfront facilities, and port and harbor areas, including vessels and harbor craft therein, would not be inimical to the security of the United States, the Commandant shall notify the applicant or holder that his appeal is denied.

§ 125.51 Replacement of lost Coast Guard Port Security Card.

(a) Any person whose Coast Guard Port Security Card has been stolen, lost, or destroyed shall report that fact to a Coast Guard Port Security Unit or Captain of the Port as soon thereafter as possible.

(b) A person who has lost a Coast Guard Port Security Card may apply for a replacement card by submitting "An Application for Replacement of Lost Port Security Card" (Form CG 2685A) to a Coast Guard Port Security Unit. A replacement will be issued only after a full explanation of the loss of the Coast Guard Port Security Card is made in writing to the Coast Guard and after a full check is made and authorization is granted by the Commandant.

(c) Any person to whom a Coast Guard Port Security Card has been issued as a replacement for a lost card, shall immediately surrender the original card to the nearest Coast Guard Port Security Unit or Captain of the Port if the original card should be recovered.

§ 125.53 Requirements for credentials; certain vessels operating on navigable waters of the United States (including the Great Lakes and Western Rivers).

(a) Every person desiring access to vessels, except public vessels, falling within any of the categories listed below, as a master, person in charge, or member of the crew thereof, shall be required to be in possession of one of the identification credentials listed in § 125.09.

(1) Towing vessels, barges, and lighters operating in the navigable waters of the continental United States other than the Great Lakes and Western Rivers.

(2) Harbor craft, such as water taxis, junk boats, garbage disposal boats, bum boats, supply boats, repair boats, and ship cleaning boats, which in the course of their normal operations service or contact vessels, foreign or domestic, public or merchant, in the navigable waters of the continental United States other than the Great Lakes and Western Rivers.

(b) The term "master, person in charge, or member of the crew" shall be deemed to include any person who serves on board in any capacity concerned with the operation, maintenance, or administration of the vessel or its cargo.

(c) Where the Coast Guard Port Security Card (Form CG 2514) is to be used as the identification required by paragraph (a) of this section, application for such card may be made immediately by the persons concerned. The issuance of the Coast Guard Port Security Card shall be in the form and manner prescribed by § 125.11.

(d) At the discretion of the District Commander any person desiring access to vessels of the categories named in this section, who may be required by the provisions hereof to possess identification credentials, may be furnished a letter signed by the District Commander or the Captain of the Port and this letter shall serve in lieu of a Coast Guard Port Security Card and will authorize such access for a period not to exceed 60 days, and such a letter issued shall be deemed to be satisfactory identification within the meaning of § 125.09. The issuance of the letter shall be subject to the following conditions:

(1) The services of the person are necessary to avoid delay in the operation of the vessel;

(2) The person does not possess one of the identification credentials listed in § 125.09.

(3) The person has filed his application for a Coast Guard Port Security Card or submits his application before the letter is issued; and,

(4) The person has been screened by the District Commander or Captain of the Port and such officer is satisfied concerning the eligibility of the applicant to receive a temporary letter.

[CGFR 56-15, 21 FR 2940, May 3, 1956, as amended by CGFR 58-51, 21 FR 9339, Nov. 30, 1956]

§ 125.55 Outstanding Port Security Card Applications.

A person who has filed an application for a Coast Guard Port Security Card and who did not receive such a document prior to May 1, 1956, shall submit a new application in accordance with the requirements of this part.

[CGFR 61-54, 26 FR 11862, Dec. 12, 1961]

§ 125.57 Applications previously denied.

A person who has been denied a Coast Guard Port Security Card before May 1, 1956, may file a new application for such a document in accordance with the requirements of this part.

MEASURES TO PREVENT UNLAWFUL ACTS AGAINST PASSENGERS AND CREWS ON BOARD SHIPS

52 Fed. Reg. 11,587–11,594 (1987)

SUMMARY: This Notice publishes the International Maritime Organization Circular 443, 1986, on Measures to Prevent Unlawful Acts Against Passengers and Crews On Board Ships. Circular 443 contains a set of recommended preventative security measures which should be utilized by both passenger vessels and the facilities which serve them, to increase the safety and security of passengers and crews. Adoption of these guidelines, in coordination with increased emphasis on passenger terminal and vessel security by Coast Guard Captain of the Port offices, will provide improved levels of security for passenger vessel operations in U.S. ports.

FOR FURTHER INFORMATION CONTACT: LT Patrick T. KEANE, Project Manager, Office of Marine Safety, Security and Environmental Protection (G-MPS-2) at (202) 267-0475.

DRAFTING INFORMATION: The principal person involved in drafting this Notice is Lieutenant Patrick T. Keane, Project Manager, Office of Marine Safety, Security and Environment Protection (G-MPS-2).

Background

The October 7th, 1985 hijacking of the ACHILLE LAURO and the murder of a U.S. citizen, resulted in the Coast Guard and State Department drafting a resolution for submission to the International Maritime Organization (IMO) Assembly in London in November 1985 on measures to protect passengers and crews onboard ships. The measures were reviewed and endorsed by both the Facilitation and Legal Committees of the IMO in March and April 1986, respectively. On September 12, 1986 the IMO unanimously adopted recommended preventative security measures. The measures are published in IMO Circular 443 dated 26 SEP 86.

The purpose of the IMO measures is to assist member governments in reviewing and strengthening port and vessel security. They include detailed and practical technical measures which may be employed to ensure the security of passengers and crews on board ships by reducing the vulnerability to unlawful acts.

Concurrently, the Omnibus Diplomatic Security and Antiterrorism Act of 1986, Pub. L. 99-399, August 26, 1986, was enacted. This legislation specifically recognizes the international aspects of terrorism and the desirability of internationally coordinated action. Title IX of this law, the International Maritime And Port Security Act addresses maritime terrorism and is codified in Title 46, U.S. Code at 46 U.S.C. App. 1801 et seq. and 33 U.S.C. 1226. In addition to promoting efforts of the International Maritime Organization to develop measures to improve international seaport and shipboard security, it requires the Secretary of Transportation to evaluate the security meas-res and the threat of terrorism at U.S. and foreign ports. It amends existing legislation (Ports And Waterways Safety Act of 1972) to allow the Secretary of Transportation to take action to prevent or respond to an act of terrorism, which includes the authority to carry out or require specific measures and procedures.

The Secretary of Transportation, in consultation with the Secretary of State must implement a plan to assess the effectiveness of security at foreign ports. The Secretary of State is required to issue travel advisories with respect to those ports which the Secretary of Transportation finds have inadequate security. The President may suspend the right of any passenger vessel common carrier to operate to and from, and the right of any U.S. passenger vessel to utilize, any port in a foreign nation which permits the use of territory under its jurisdiction for terrorists or terrorist groups which knowingly use the illegal seizure of passenger vessels or threat thereof as an instrument of policy.

The IMO Measures are intended to be applicable to passenger ships making international voyages of 24 hours or more and the facilities which service them, however, they provide guidance on measures that could be applicable to all port and vessel operations. They address measures and equipment to prevent weapons or other dangerous devices being taken aboard ships, use of restricted access on terminals and on board ships, designation of security personnel, their evaluation and training, and detailed survey and inspection procedures and planning.

Implementation Strategy

Since all U.S. ports and passenger vessels are unique, the Coast Guard feels that an antiterrorism preventative security program can best be implemented on a port-by-port and ship-by-ship basis, utilizing the IMO approved measures as guidelines. The local Coast Guard Captains of the Port have excellent rapport and liaison with the local port officials and vessel owners and are therefore in a position to coordinate voluntary compliance with the IMO measures. Internal Coast Guard program guidelines and policy are being established and promulgated by the Port Safety and Security Program Director in U.S. Coast Guard Headquarters. A program of mandatory regulatory requirements under the authority of 33 U.S.C. 1226 is not considered necessary or appropriate at this time.

Recognizing the need for implementation of preventative security measures on a local basis, the Coast Guard is assisting the cooperative efforts of vessel operators and port authority/terminal operators. The Coast Guard has established local Port Readiness Committees (PRCs), for liaison with the participating agencies concerning the issues of port security. The PRC's include a Security Sub-Committee, with members from the maritime industry, to coordinate security and security operations including waterside security, shoreside security, personnel access control, physical security, onboard vessel security, and intelligence.

Through these committees, Coast Guard Captains of the Port are tasked with assisting industry in implementing the procedures and equipment outlined in the IMO Measures. Periodic security assessments are being conducted to evaluate existing procedures and equipment and identify potential improvements.

The maritime industry has been cooperating in the Coast Guard's efforts to reduce the risk of terrorism in U.S. ports. Many U.S. cruise ship terminals and the passenger vessels using them have already designated security personnel and are developing contingency plans in accordance with the Measures and it is expected that the remaining ships and terminals will be doing so in the near future.

Ports and vessels should now be conducting a Security Survey as outlined in the Measures (Annex 1), or an appropriate equivalent. Action then needs to be taken utilizing Security Measures and Procedures (Annex 2) of the IMO Measures to identify and correct those deficiencies discovered by the surveys.

It is anticipated that voluntary action by ports and vessels to reduce vulnerability to terrorist acts will preclude the need for development of mandatory regulations to meet this threat. To facilitate these voluntary actions and to provide information to the travel industry and public on the measures being taken, IMO Circular 443 is reprinted as an attachment to this notice.

Dated: April 3, 1987.

J.W. Kime,

Rear Admiral, U.S. Coast Guard, Chief, Office of Marine Safety, Security and Environmental Protection.

Measures to Prevent Unlawful Acts Against Passengers and Crews on Board Ships

1. Introduction

1.1   Assembly resolution A.584(14) directed that internationally agreed measures should be developed, on a priority basis, by the Maritime Safety Committee to ensure the security of passengers and crews on board ships and authorized the Maritime Safety Committee to request the Secretary-General to issue a circular containing information on the agreed measures to governments, organizations concerned and interested parties for their consideration and adoption.

1.2   The text of Assembly resolution A.584(14) is attached at appendix 1.

2. Definitions

For the purpose of these measures:

.1   *Designated Authority* means the organization or organizations or the administration or administrations identified by or within the Government as responsible for ensuring the development, implementation and maintenance of port facility security plans or flag State ship security plans, or both.

.2   *Port Facility* means a location within a port at which commercial maritime activities occur affecting ships covered by these measures.

.3   *Passenger Terminal* means any area within the port facility which is used for the assembling, processing, embarking and disembarking of passengers and baggage.

.4   *Port Facility Security Plan* means a comprehensive written plan for a port facility which identifies, *inter alia,* regulations, programmes, measures and procedures necessary to prevent unlawful acts which threaten the passengers and crews on board ships.

.5   *Port Facility Security Officer* means the person in a port responsible for the development, implementation and maintenance of the port facility security plan and for liaison with the ships' security officers.

.6 *Operator* means the company or representative of the company which maintains operational control over the ship while at sea or dockside.

.7 *Ship Security Plan* means a written plan developed under the authority of the operator to ensure the application of measures on board ship which are designed to prevent unlawful acts which threaten passengers and crews on board ships.

.8 *Operational Security Officer*[1] means the person designated by the operator to develop and maintain the ship security plan and liaise with the port facility security officer.

.9 *Ship Security Officer*[1] means the master or the person on board the ship responsible to the master and operator for on-board security, including implementation and maintenance of the ship security plan and for liaison with the port facility security officer.

3. General Provisions

3.1 Governments, port authorities, administrations, shipowners, operators, shipmasters and crews should take all appropriate measures against unlawful acts threatening passengers and crews on board ships. The measures implemented should take into account the current assessment of the likely threat together with local conditions and circumstances.

3.2 It is desirable that there be appropriate legislation or regulations which, *inter alia,* could provide penalties for persons gaining or

attempting to gain unauthorized access to the port facility and persons committing unlawful acts against passengers or crews on board ships. Governments should review their national legislation, regulations and guidance to determine their adequacy to maintain security on board ships.

3.3 The measures contained in this document are intended for application to passenger ships engaged on international voyages[2] of 24 hours or more and the port facilities which serve them. Certain of these measures may, however, also be appropriate for application to other ships or port facilities if the circumstances so warrant.

3.4 Governments should identify a designated authority responsible to ensure the development, implementation and maintenance of ship and port facility security plans. The designated authority should co-ordinate with other relevant domestic agencies to ensure that specific roles and functions of other agencies and departments are agreed and implemented.

3.5 Governments should notify the Secretary General of progress made in the implementation of security measures. Any useful information, which might assist other governments in their implementation of measures, on any difficulties and problems which arose and were overcome during implementation of the security measures, should be forwarded with the notification. The designated authority should cooperate with similar authorities of other governments in the exchange of appropriate information.

3.6 Governments concerned with an act of unlawful interference should provide the Organization with all pertinent information concerning the

---

[1]The operator security officer functions may be assigned to the ship security officer on board the ship

[1]The operator security officer functions may be assigned to the ship security officer on board the ship

[2]Voyages include all segmented voyages.

security aspects of the act of unlawful interference as soon as practicable after the act is resolved. Further information and a reporting format is given in appendix 2.

3.7   In the process of implementing these measures, all efforts should be made to avoid undue interference with passenger services and take into account applicable international conventions.

3.8   Governments and port authorities should ensure the application of these measures to ships in a fair manner.

4. Port Facility Security Plan

4.1   Each port facility should develop and maintain an appropriate port facility security plan adequate for local circumstances and conditions and adequate for the anticipated maritime traffic and the number of passengers likely to be involved.

4.2   The port facility security plan should provide for measures and equipment as necessary to prevent weapons or any other dangerous devices, the carriage of which is not authorized, from being introduced by any means whatsoever on board ships.

4.3   The port facility security plan should establish measures for the prevention of unauthorized access to the ship and to restricted areas of the passenger terminal.

4.4   The port facility security plan should provide for the evaluation, before they are employed, of all persons responsible for any aspect of security.

4.5   A port facility security officer should be appointed for each port facility. The port facility security plan should identify the security officer for that port facility.

4.6   The responsibilities of the port facility security officer should include, but not be limited to:

.1   Conducting an initial comprehensive security survey in order to prepare a port facility security plan, and thereafter regular subsequent security inspections of the port facility to ensure continuation of appropriate security measures;

.2   Implementing the port facility security plan;

.3   Recommending modifications to the port facility security plan to correct deficiencies and satisfy the security requirements of the individual port facility;

.4   Encouraging security awareness and vigilance;

.5   Ensuring adequate training for personnel responsible for security;

.6   Maintaining records of occurrences of unlawful acts which affect the operations of the port facility;

.7   Coordinating implementation of the port facility security plan with the competent operator security officers; and

.8   Coordinating with other national and international security services, as appropriate.

4.7   Security measures and procedures should be applied at passenger terminals in such a manner as to cause a minimum of interference with, or delay to, passenger services, taking into account the ship security plan.

5. Ship Security Plan

5.1   A ship security plan should be developed for each ship. The plan should be sufficiently flexible to take into account the level of security reflected in the port facility security plan for each port at which the ship intends to call.

5.2   The ship security plan should include measures and equipment as necessary to prevent weapons or any other dangerous devices, the carriage of which is not authorized, from being introduced by any means whatsoever on board a ship.

5.3   The ship security plan should establish measures for the prevention of unauthorized access to the ship and to restricted areas on board.

5.4   A ship security officer should be appointed on each ship. The ship security plan should identify the ship security officer.

5.5   The operator security officer should be responsible for, but not be limited to:

.1   Conducting an initial comprehensive security survey and thereafter regular subsequent inspections of the ship;

.2   Developing and maintaining the ship security plan;

.3   Modifying the ship security plan to correct deficiencies and satisfy the security requirements of the individual ship;

.4   Encouraging security awareness and vigilance;

.5   Ensuring adequate training for personnel responsible for security; and

.6   Co-ordinating implementation of the ship security plan with the competent port facility security officer.

5.6   The ship security officer should be responsible for, but not limited to:

.1   Regular inspections of the ship;

.2   Implementing and maintaining the ship security plan;

.3   Proposing modifications to the ship security plan to correct deficiencies and satisfy the security requirements of the ship;

.4   Encouraging security awareness and vigilance on board;

.5   Ensuring that adequate training has been provided for personnel responsible for security;

.6   Reporting all occurrences or suspected occurrences of unlawful acts to the port facility security officer and ensuring that the report is forwarded, through the master, to the operator for submission to the ship's flag State's designated authority; and

.7   Co-ordinating implementation of the ship security plan with the competent port facility security officer.

6. Annexes

The annexes attached hereto contain information which may be useful when developing or improving security measures.

Appendix 1—Resolution A-584(14)

Adopted on 20 November 1985.

Measures to Prevent Unlawful Acts Which Threaten the Safety of Ships and the Security of Their Passengers and Crews

The Assembly,

Recalling Article 1 and Article 15(j) of the Convention on the International Maritime Organization concerning the purposes of the Organization and the functions of the Assembly in relation to regulations and guidelines concerning maritime safety,

Noting with great concern the danger to passengers and crews resulting from the increasing number of incidents involving piracy, armed robbery and other unlawful acts against or on board ships, including small craft, both at anchor and under way,

Recalling resolution A-545(13) which urged action to initiate a series of measures to combat acts of piracy and armed robbery against ships and small craft at sea,

Recognizing the need for the Organization to assist in the formulation of internationally agreed technical measures to improve security and reduce the risk to the lives of passengers and crews on board ships,

1. Calls upon all Governments, port authorities and administrations, shipowners, ship operators, shipmasters and crews to take, as soon as possible, steps to review and, as necessary, strengthen port and on-board security;

2. Directs the Maritime Safety Committee, in co-operation with other committees, as required, to develop, on a priority basis, detailed and practical technical measures, including both shoreside and shipboard measures, which may be employed by Governments, port authorities and administrations, shipowners,

ship operators, shipmasters and crews to ensure the security of passengers and crews on board ships;

3. Invites the Maritime Safety Committee to take note of the work of the International Civil Aviation Organization in the development of standards and recommended practices for airport and aircraft security;

4. Authorizes the Maritime Safety Committee to request the Secretary-General to issue a circular containing information on the measures developed by the Committee to Governments, organizations concerned and interested parties for their consideration and adoption.

Appendix 2.—Reports of Unlawful Acts

1. To safeguard maritime interests against unlawful acts which threaten the security of passengers and crews on board ships, reports on incidents and the measures taken to prevent their recurrence should be provided to the Organization as soon as possible by the flag and port state, as appropriate. This information will be utilized in updating or revising these agreed measures, as necessary.

2. Use of the following report format is recommended for conveying information for such purposes:

REPORT ON AN UNLAWFUL ACT

Date:————

1. Ship or Port Area Description:
Name of Ship————————————
Flag————————————————
Master——————————————
Port Facility Security Officer—————

2. Brief Description of Incident or Threat————————————————
Date, Time and Place of Incident or Threat————————————————

3. Number of Alleged Offenders:
Passenger——Crew——Other——

4. Method Utilized To Introduce Dangerous Substances or Devices Into the Port Facility or Ship
Persons——;
Baggage:——Cargo:——Ship Stores: ——
Other:——

5. Type of Dangerous Substances or Devices Used, With Full Description:
Weapon ——————
Explosives ——————
Other ——————

6. (a) Where Were the Items Described in

Section 5 Above Concealed, if Known?
————————————————

(b) How Were the Items Described in Section 5 Above Used and Where?
————————————————

(c) How Were the Security Measures Circumvented?
————————————————

7. What Measures and Procedures are Recommended To Prevent Recurrence of a Similar Event?
————————————————

8. Other Pertinent Details:
————————————————

Annex 1—Security Surveys

1. General

1.1 In order to prepare security plans, an initial comprehensive security survey should be undertaken to assess the effectiveness of security measures and procedures for the prevention of unlawful acts and determine the vulnerability of the port facility or the ship, or both, to such acts.

1.2 The results of this security survey should be used to determine the security measures necessary to counter the threat both at the port facility and on board ships taking into consideration local conditions.

1.3 The level of security may vary from port to port, from ship to ship and from time to time. Liaison between security officers is important to ensure the best utilization of ship and shore resources.

1.4 The survey should determine what needs to be protected, what security measures are already in effect, and what additional security measures and procedures are required.

1.5 The security survey should be periodically reviewed and the security plans updated as necessary.

2. Port Facility Security Survey

2.1 The port facility security survey may be divided into two parts, the initial preliminary assessment and an on-scene security survey

2.1.1 Preliminary Assessment

2.1.1.1 Prior to commencing the survey the port facility security officer should obtain current information on the assessment of threat for the locality and should be knowledgeable about the port facility and type of ships calling at the port. He should study previous reports on similar security needs and know the general layout and nature of the operations conducted.

2.1.1.2 The port facility security officer should meet with appropriate representatives of the port facility, of the operator, or both of them, to discuss the purpose and methodology of the survey.

2.1.1.3 The port facility security officer should obtain and record the information required to conduct a vulnerability assessment, including:

.1 The general layout of the port facility and terminal including topography, building locations, etc.;

.2 Areas and structures in the vicinity of the port facility such as, fuel storage depots, bridges, locks, etc.;

.3 The degree of dependence on essential services, such as electric power, communications, etc.;

.4 Stand-by equipment to assure continuity of essential services;

.5 Locations and functions of each actual or potential access point;

.6 Numerical strength, reliability and function of staff, permanent labour and casual labour forces;

.7 The details of existing security measures and procedures, including inspection, control and monitoring procedures, identification documents, access control procedures, fencing, lighting, fire hazards, storm drains, etc.;

.8 The equipment in use for protection of passengers, crews and port facility personnel;

.9 All vehicle traffic or services which enter the port facility; and

.10 Availability of other personnel in an emergency.

2.1.2 On-scene Security Survey

2.1.2.1 The port facility security officer should examine and evaluate the methods and procedures used to control access to ships and restricted areas in the port facility, including:

.1 Inspection, control and monitoring of persons and carry-on articles;

.2 Inspection, control and monitoring of cargo, ship stores, and baggage; and

.3 Safeguarding cargo, ship stores and baggage held in storage within the port facility.

2.1.2.2 The port facility security officer should examine each identified point of access to ships and restricted areas in the port facility and evaluate its potential for use by individuals who might be engaged in unlawful acts. This includes persons having legitimate access as well as those who seek to obtain unauthorized entry.

2.1.2.3 The port facility security officer should examine and evaluate existing security measures, procedures and operations under both emergency and routine conditions, including:

.1 Established safety procedures;

.2 Restrictions or limitations on vehicle access to the port facility;

.3 Access of fire and emergency vehicles to restricted areas and availability of parking and marshalling areas;

.4 The level of supervision of personnel;

.5 The frequency and effectiveness of patrols by security personnel;

.6 The security key control system;

.7 Security communications, systems and procedures; and

.8 Security barriers and lighting.

3. Ship Security Survey

3.1 The ship security survey may be divided into two parts, the initial preliminary assessment and an on-scene security survey.

3.1.1 Preliminary Assessment

3.1.1.1 Prior to commencing the ship security survey, the operator security officer should take advantage of such information as is available to him on the assessment of threat for the ports at which the ship will call or at which passengers embark or disembark and about the port facilities and their security measures. He should study previous reports on similar security needs.

3.1.1.2 Where feasible, the operator security officer should meet with appropriate persons on the ship and in the port facilities to discuss the purpose and methodology of the survey.

3.1.1.3 The operator security officer should obtain and record the information required to conduct a vulnerability assessment, including:

.1 The general layout of the ship;

.2 The location of areas which should have restricted access, such as bridge, engine-room, radio-room etc.;

.3 The location and function of each actual or potential access point to the ship;

.4 The open deck arrangement including the height of the deck above the water;

.5 The emergency and stand-by equipment available to maintain essential services;

.6 Numerical strength, reliability and security duties of the ship's crew;

.7 Existing security and safety equipment for protection of passengers and crew; and

.8 Existing security measures and procedures in effect, including inspection, control and monitoring

equipment, personnel identification documents and communication, alarm, lighting, access control and other appropriate systems.

3.1.2 On-scene Security Survey

3.1.2.1 The operator security officer should examine and evaluate the methods and procedures used to control access to ships, including:

.1 Inspection, control and monitoring of persons and carry-on articles; and

.2 Inspection, control and monitoring of cargo, ship's stores and baggage.

3.1.2.2 The operator security officer should examine each identified point of access, including open weather decks, and evaluate its potential for use by individuals who might be engaged in unlawful acts. This includes individuals having legitimate access as well as those who seek to obtain unauthorized entry.

3.1.2.3 The operator security officer should examine and evaluate existing security measures, procedures and operations, under both emergency and routine conditions, including:

.1 Established security procedures;

.2 Response procedures to fire or other emergency conditions;

.3 The level of supervision of the ship's crew, vendors, repair technicians, dock workers, etc.;

.4 The frequency and effectiveness of security patrols;

.5 The security key control system;

.6 Security communications systems and procedures; and

.7 Security doors, barriers and lighting.

4. Periodic Security Inspections

Security inspections should be undertaken on a periodic basis to permit a review and updating of the initial comprehensive security survey and possible modification of the port facility and ship security plans.

5. Report

5.1   From the information obtained during the survey assessment and inspection, the respective security officer should assess the vulnerability of the port facility, ship, or both.

5.2   The report should contain, as appropriate, recommendations for new or revised security measures and procedures.

5.3   The report will form the basis for development or revision of security plans, should be confidential and have limited distribution.

Annex 2—Security Measures and Procedures

1. General

1.1   Port facility security measures and procedures and ship security measures and procedures should take account of the recommendations contained in the report described in paragraph 5 of annex 1.

2. Port Facility Security

2.1   Security measures and procedures reduce port facility vulnerability. Increased levels of threat will have a significant influence on the number and type of security measures used and the degree of measures and procedures adopted. During short periods of heightened threat, increased security can be achieved through the use of additional manpower.

2.2   The following on-scene security measures should be considered.

.1   Restricted areas;
.2   Security barriers;
.3   Security lighting;
.4   Security alarms and communication systems; and
.5   Access control and identification.

2.2.1   Restricted Areas

The establishment of restricted areas helps control and channel access, improves security and increases efficiency by providing degrees of security compatible with the port facility's operational requirements. Restricted areas may be further subdivided depending on the degree of restriction or control required to prevent unauthorized access.

2.2.2   Security Barriers

2.2.2.1   The boundary between restricted and uncontrolled areas should be clearly defined. This can be achieved by security barriers which prevent access except at authorized points. Where permanent security barriers are appropriate, security fences have proven effective.

2.2.2.2   The purpose of security barriers is to:

.1   Delineate the area to be protected;

.2   Create a physical and psychological deterrent to persons attempting unauthorized entry;

.3   Delay intrusion, enabling operating personnel and security guards to detect and, if necessary, apprehend intruders; and

.4   Provide designated and readily identifiable places for entry of personnel and vehicles into areas where access is restricted.

2.2.2.3   Openings in security barriers should be kept to a minimum and secured when not in use.

2.2.2.4   Security fences and other barriers should be located and constructed so as to prevent the introduction of dangerous substances or devices, and should be of sufficient height and durability to deter unauthorized passage.

2.2.2.5   Security fence lines should be kept clear of all obstructions.

2.2.2.6   The effectiveness of a security fence against penetration depends to a large extent on the construction employed. The total height of the security fencing should be not less than 2.50 metres.

2.2.2.7   Natural barriers such as water, ravines, etc., can sometimes be effectively utilized as part of the control boundary. However, they may require supporting safeguards (i.e., fencing, security patrols, surveillance, anti-intrusion devices, lighting) especially during high threat periods.

2.2.2.8   The roofs of buildings may also provide a possible route for unauthorized access to the restricted area. Safeguards should be taken to prevent such access by these routes.

2.2.2.9   Restricted areas partly surrounded by water may require security barriers with sufficient illumination during night hours and, if on navigable waters, frequent and unscheduled patrols by boat or ashore on foot, or both. Illumination of these areas must be of a type and so placed that it does not interfere with safe navigation.

2.2.3   Security Lighting

2.2.3.1   Security lighting with uninterrupted power supply is an important element in a security program.

2.2.3.2   The primary system should consist of a series of lights arranged to illuminate a specific area continuously during the hours of darkness or restricted visibility. In some circumstances, it may be preferable to use such lighting systems only in response to an alarm.

2.2.3.3.   Floodlights may be used to supplement the primary system and may be either portable or fixed. Floodlights when used should have sufficient flexibility to permit examination of the barrier under observation and adjacent unlighted areas.

2.2.3.4   Multiple circuits may be used to advantage in the security lighting system. Circuits should be so arranged that the failure of any one lamp will not affect a series of others.

2.2.3.5   Controls and switches for security lighting should be protected at all times.

2.2.3.6   Where fences and other barriers are to be illuminated, it is important to ensure that the intensity of illumination is adequate for the purpose.

2.2.4   Security Alarms and Communication Systems

2.2.4.1   Intrusion detection systems and alarm devices may be appropriate as a complement to guards and patrols during periods of increased threat.

2.2.4.2   Immediate response capability by guards to an alarm from an intrusion detection system or device is important if its use is to be effective. Alarms may be local, i.e. at the site of the intrusion, provided at a central location or station, or a combination of both.

2.2.4.3   A wide variety of intrusion detection systems and devices are available for possible use. These systems include those which are sensitive to:

.1   Breaking of an electrical circuit;
.2   Interruption of a light beam;
.3   Sound;
.4   Vibration;
.5   Motion; or
.6   Capacitance change in an electrical field.

2.2.4.4   In view of the wide range of technical matters which must be taken into account in deciding upon the device or system best suited for application in each environment and for each task, it is prudent to obtain the advice of a qualified expert before a decision is made on the system or device to be used.

2.2.4.5   A means of transmitting discreet or covert signals by radio, direct-line facilities or other similarly reliable means should be provided at each access point for use by the control and monitoring personnel to contact police, security control, or an emergency operations centre in the event assistance is required. An additional public or overt communications system would be useful to obtain information on advice or routine matters.

2.2.5   Access Control and Identification

2.2.5.1   Persons and their property, before being permitted to proceed beyond access points, should be subject to routine inspection or control and monitoring, or both.

2.2.5.2   It is recommended that port facility employees, vendors, operators' personnel, assigned law enforcement officials and others, whose official duties require them to pass through the access point, should prominently display a tamper resistant identification card. This procedure should be closely monitored and strictly enforced to preserve the integrity of the inspection, control and monitoring processes and the security of the passenger terminal and ships. Approved means of identification and the procedures to be followed should be specifically provided for in the security plan.

2.2.5.3   An effective means of identification is a card which incorporates a photograph of the individual as an integral part. These should show the relevant details of the holder, e.g., name, description, or other pertinent data. The provision of a photograph is recommended in order to prevent misuse of the card by unauthorized persons.

2.2.5.4   To prevent substitution of a photograph and subsequent illegal use, the entire card should be sealed in a plastic container, preferably of a type which will mutilate the photograph and card if tampered with.

2.2.5.5   The number and types of different styles of identification cards in the port area should be limited in order to avoid control problems for security staff and the administration of the identification programme.

2.2.5.6   Identification cards should be issued by an appropriate control authority, such as a port authority or ship operator. Strict card control and accountability procedures should be established and maintained.

2.2.5.7   Persons who refuse to submit to security clearance at an access point must be denied entry.

2.2.5.8   Persons denied entry for refusal to submit to security clearance, or for other security reasons should be, if possible, identified and reported to appropriate security personnel.

2.2.5.9   A booth or other area in which a manual search can be conducted is advisable. The access points should, as appropriate, be equipped with metal detectors to expedite the security clearance of people.

2.2.5.10   All items should be subject to inspection, appropriate to the risk of unlawful acts, prior to being placed on board ships. Such inspection methods may include hand search, electronic screening, the use of dogs, or other means.

2.2.5.11   Tables on which baggage may be searched should be provided at the appropriate access points. Such tables should be high enough to permit inspection without requiring the examiner to bend. They also should be sufficiently wide to provide some measure of separation of the baggage from the passenger. The latter should be able to witness the examination, but should not be in a position to interfere with the examiner.

3. Ship Security

3.1   The master's traditional authority in matters of ship security remains unchanged. Maintaining ship security is an ongoing task. Additional security measures should be implemented to counter increased risks when warranted.

3.2   Ship security should be continually supervised by the ship security officer. A properly trained crew is in itself a strong deterrent to being subjected to unlawful acts.

3.3   Communication and co-operation with the port facility in security matters should be maintained.

3.4   The following on-board security measures should be considered:

.1   Restricted areas;

.2   Deck and overside lighting;

.3   Access control and identification; and

.4   Security alarms and communication systems.

3.4.1   Registered Areas

3.4.1.1   The establishment of restricted areas on board ships (e.g., bridge, engine-room, radio-room etc.) is recommended.

3.4.1.2   The use, number and distribution of master keys on-board ships should be controlled by the master.

3.4.1.3   The ship security plan should provide for immediate corrective action in the event of security being compromised by potential misuse or loss of keys.

3.4.2   Deck and Overside Lighting

3.4.2.1   While in port, at anchor or underway the ship's deck and overside should be illuminated in periods of darkness and restricted visibility, but not so as to interfere with the required navigation lights and safe navigation.

3.4.3   Access Control and Identification

3.4.3.1   Crew members should carry at all times a photo identification document.

3.4.3.2   When visitors to the ship are permitted their embarkation and disembarkation should be closely controlled.

3.4.3.3   All vendors should have an identification document prior to boarding the ship or should be escorted at all times on board the ship.

3.4.4   Security Alarms and Communication Systems

3.4.4.1   Security alarms and devices may be appropriate in restricted areas and at access points to the ship, as a complement to guards and patrols. Immediate appropriate response to an alarm is important if the security alarms and devices are to be effective.

3.4.4.2   In view of the wide range of technical matters which must be taken into account in deciding upon the device or system best suited for application in each environment, it is prudent that the advice of a qualified expert be obtained before a decision is made on the system or device to be used.

3.4.4.3   A means of discreet or covert communications by radio, direct-line facilities or other reliable means should be provided in each restricted zone and at each access point for use by security or operating personnel to contact the ship security officer in the event assistance is required.

Annex 3—Security Training

1. General

A continuous and thorough training programme should support measures taken to safeguard the security of passengers and crews on board ships. Basic guidance for development of security training and education is given in the following paragraphs.

2. Criteria

Security training should meet the following criteria:

.1   Be comprehensive;

.2   Have an adequate number of qualified instructors;

.3   Have an effective system of presentation;

.4   Use adequate training equipment and aids; and

.5   Have a clearly defined objective, i.e. the attainment of an established minimum standard of proficiency, knowledge and skill to be demonstrated by each individual.

3. Port Facility Security Personnel Training

3.1   Security Officer and Appropriate Staff

The port facility security officer and appropriate port facility staff should have knowledge and, as necessary, receive training in some or all of the following, as appropriate:

.1   Security administration;

.2   Relevant international conventions, codes and recommendations;

.3   Responsibilities and functions of other involved organizations;

.4   Relevant government legislation and regulations;

.5   Risk, threat and vulnerability assessments;

.6   Security surveys and inspections;

.7   Ship security measures;

.8   Security training and education;

.9   Recognition of characteristics and behavioral patterns of persons who are likely to commit unlawful acts;

.10   Inspection, control and monitoring techniques;

.11   Techniques used to circumvent security measures;

.12   Dangerous substances and devices and how to recognize them;

.13   Ship and local port operations and conditions; and

.14   Security devices and systems.

3.2   Inspection, Control and Monitoring

Instruction and, where appropriate, training for persons assigned to conduct inspection, control and monitoring at a port facility should take into consideration, as appropriate:

.1   Responsibilities under the port facility plan or ship security plan;

.2   Inspection, control and monitoring regulations or policies and pertinent laws,

.3   Detection and identification of fire-arms, weapons and other dangerous substances and devices;

.4   Operation and testing of security equipment;

.5   Manual search methods of persons, baggage, cargo and ship's stores;

.6   Emergency procedures;

.7   Recognition of characteristics and behavioural patterns of persons who are likely to commit unlawful acts;

.8   Human relations techniques; and

.9   Techniques used to circumvent security measures.

3.3   Guards

Port facility guards who are assigned either to specific fixed locations or to patrols for the purpose of preventing unauthorized access to areas should receive a general briefing on the training subjects recommended for the port facility security officer. Initial and subsequent training should emphasize techniques for:

.1   Entry control;

.2   Patrols, observation and communications;

.3   Inspection, identification and reporting;

.4   Person, building and vehicle searches;

.5   Apprehension of suspects;

.6   Self-defence;
.7   Recognizing dangerous
substances and devices;
.8   Human relations; and
.9   First aid.

4. Ship Security Personnel Training

4.1   Operator Security Officer and Appropriate Staff

The operator security officer and appropriate staff should have knowledge and, as necessary, receive training in some or all of the following, as appropriate:
.1   Security administration;
.2   Relevant international conventions, codes and recommendations;
.3   Responsibilities and functions of other involved organizations;
.6   Operation of technical aids to security, if used;
.7   Recognition of characteristics and behavioural patterns of persons who may be likely to commit unlawful acts;
.8   The detection and recognition of dangerous substances and devices;
.9   Port and ship operations; and
.10   Methods of physical searches of persons and their baggage.

4.3 [sic]   Inspection, Control and Monitoring Personnel

Instruction and training, as appropriate, for persons assigned to conduct inspection, control and monitoring on board ships should take into consideration, as appropriate, the following:
.1   Responsibilities under the port facility or ship security plan;
.2   Inspection, control and monitoring regulations or policies and pertinent laws;
.3   Detection and identification of firearms, weapons and other dangerous substances and devices;
.4   Relevant government legislation

and regulations;
.5   Risk, threat and vulnerability assessments;
.6   Security surveys and inspections;
.7   Ship security measures;
.8   Security training and education;
.9   Recognition of characteristics and behavioural patterns of persons who are likely to commit unlawful acts;
.10   Inspection, control and monitoring techniques;
.11   Techniques used to circumvent security measures;
.12   Dangerous substances and devices and how to recognize them;
.13   Ship and local port operations and conditions; and
.14   Security devices and systems.

4.2[sic]   Ship Security Officer

The ship security officer should have adequate knowledge of and, if necessary, training in the following, as appropriate:
.1   The ship security plan and related emergency procedures;
.2   The layout of the ship;
.3   The assessment of the risk, threat and vulnerability;
.4   Methods of conducting security inspections;
.5   Techniques used to circumvent security measures;
.4   Operation and testing of security equipment, if used;
.5   Physical search methods of persons, baggage, cargo and ship's stores;
.6   Emergency procedures;
.7   Recognition of characteristics and behavioural patterns of persons who are likely to commit unlawful acts;
.8   Human relations techniques; and
.9   Techniques used to circumvent security measures.

4.4   Ship's Crew

Crew members having specific security duties should know their responsibilities for ship security as described in the ship security plan and should have sufficient knowledge and ability to perform their assigned duties.

5. Law Enforcement Personnel

Appropriate law enforcement personnel, when not directly involved in or responsible for port facility security, should receive a general briefing to become familiar with port and ship operations and the training of port facility and ship operator security personnel. They should also be orientated regarding inspection, control and monitoring and the security plans.

Annex 4—Exchange of Information

1. The prompt and continuing dissemination and exchange of information will assist the maintenance of effective port and ship security procedures and will enable States, port facilities, operators and shipmasters to adjust their procedures in response to changing conditions and the specific or general threats.

2. Effective port and ship security requires efficient two-way communications for the exchange of information at all levels both domestic and with the governments and organizations concerned. The prompt, clear and orderly dissemination of such information is vital to the success of the security programme.

DRUG ABUSE PREVENTION
ON BOARD VESSELS

46 U.S.C. app. §§ 1901–1904 (1986)

This Act may be cited as the "Maritime Drug Law Enforcement Act."

§ 1902. Congressional findings and declarations

The Congress finds and declares that trafficking in controlled substances aboard vessels is a serious international problem and is universally condemned. Moreover, such trafficking presents a specific threat to the security and societal well-being of the United States.

§ 1903. Manufacture, distribution, or possession with intent to manufacture or distribute, a controlled substance on board vessels

(a) It is unlawful for any person on board a vessel of the United States, or on board a vessel subject to the jurisdiction of the United States, to knowingly or intentionally manufacture or distribute, or to possess with intent to manufacture or distribute, a controlled substance.

(b) For purposes of this section, a "vessel of the United States" means—

    (1) a vessel documented under chapter 121 of title 46, United States Code, or a vessel numbered as provided in chapter 123 of that title;

    (2) a vessel owned in whole or part by—

        (A) the United States or a territory, commonwealth, or possession of United States;

        (B) a State or political subdivision thereof;

        (C) a citizen or national of the United States; or

        (D) a corporation created under the laws of the United States or any State, the District of Columbia, or any territory, commonwealth, or possession of the United States;

    unless the vessel has been granted the nationality of a foreign nation in accordance with article 5 of the 1958 Convention on the High Seas; and

    (3) a vessel that was once documented under the laws of the United States and, in violation of the laws of the United States, was either sold to a person not a citizen of the United States or placed under foreign registry or

a foreign flag, whether or not the vessel has been granted the nationality of a foreign nation.

(c)(1) For purposes of this section, a "vessel subject to the jurisdiction of the United States" includes—

(A) a vessel without nationality;

(B) a vessel assimilated to a vessel without nationality, in accordance with paragraph (2) of article 6 of the 1958 Convention on the High Seas;

(C) a vessel registered in a foreign nation where the flag nation has consented or waived objection to the enforcement of United States law by the United States;

(D) a vessel located within the customs waters of the United States; and

(E) a vessel located in the territorial waters of another nation, where the nation consents to the enforcement of United States law by the United States.

Consent or waiver of objection by a foreign nation to the enforcement of United States law by the United States under subparagraph (C) or (E) of this paragraph may be obtained by radio, telephone, or similar oral or electronic means, and may be proved by certification of the Secretary of State or the Secretary's designee.

(2) For purposes of this section, a "vessel without nationality" includes—

(A) a vessel aboard which the master or person in charge makes a claim of registry, which claim is denied by the flag nation whose registry is claimed; and

(B) any vessel aboard which the master or person in charge fails, upon request of an officer of the United States empowered to enforce applicable provisions of United States law, to make a claim of nationality or registry for that vessel.

A claim of registry under subparagraph (A) may be verified or denied by radio, telephone, or similar oral or electronic means. The denial of such claim of registry by the claimed flag nation may be proved by certification of the Secretary of State or the Secretary's designee.

(3) For purposes of this section, a claim of nationality or registry only includes:

(A) possession on board the vessel and production of documents evidencing the vessel's nationality in accordance with article 5 of the 1958 Convention on the High Seas;

(B) flying its flag nation's ensign or flag; or

(C) a verbal claim of nationality or registry by the master or person in charge of the vessel.

(d) A claim of failure to comply with international law in the enforcement of this Act may be invoked solely by a foreign nation, and a failure to comply with international law shall not divest a court of jurisdiction or otherwise constitute a defense to any proceeding under this Act.

(e) This section does not apply to a common or contract carrier or an employee thereof, who possesses or distributes a controlled substance in the lawful and usual course of the carrier's business or to a public vessel of the United States, or any person on board such a vessel who possesses or distributes a controlled substance in the lawful course of such person's duties, if the controlled substance is a part of the cargo entered in the vessel's manifest and is intended to be lawfully imported into the country of destination for scientific, medical, or other legitimate purposes. It shall not be necessary for the United States to negative the exception set forth in this subsection in any complaint, information, indictment, or other pleading or in any trial or other proceeding. The burden of going forward with the evidence with respect to this exception is upon the person claiming its benefit.

(f) Any person who violates this section shall be tried in the United States district court at the point of entry where that person enters the United States, or in the United States District Court of the District of Columbia.

(g)(1) Any person who commits an offense defined in this section shall be punished in accordance with the penalties set forth in section 1010 of the Comprehensive Drug Abuse Prevention and Control Act of 1970 (21 U.S.C. 960).

(2) Notwithstanding paragraph (1) of this subsection, any person convicted of an offense under this Act shall be punished in accordance with the penalties set forth in section 1012 of the Comprehensive Drug Abuse Prevention and Control Act of 1970 (21 U.S.C. 962) if such offense is a second or subsequent offense as defined in section 1012(b) of that Act.

(h) This section is intended to reach acts of possession, manufacture, or distribution committed outside the territorial jurisdiction of the United States.

(i) The definitions in the Comprehensive Drug Abuse Prevention and Control Act of 1970 (21 U.S.C. 802) apply to terms used in this Act.

(j) Any person who attempts or conspires to commit any offense defined in this Act is punishable by imprisonment or fine, or both, which may not exceed the maximum punishment prescribed for the offense, the commission of which was the object of the attempt or conspiracy.

§ 1904. Seizure or forfeiture of property

Any property described in section 511(a) of the Comprehensive Drug Abuse Prevention and Control Act of 1970 (21 U.S.C. 881(a)) that is used or intended for use to commit, or to facilitate the commission of, an offense under this Act shall be subject to seizure and forfeiture in the same manner as similar property seized or forfeited under section 511 of the Comprehensive Drug Abuse Prevention and Control Act of 1970 (21 U.S.C. 881).

SELECTED READINGS

Alexander, Yonah, and Kilmarx, Robert A., eds. *Political Terrorism and Business.* New York: Praeger, 1979.

Applegate, Rex. *Riot Control—Materiel and Techniques.* 2d ed. Boulder, Col.: Paladin Press, 1981.

Ayoob, Massad. *The Truth About Self-Protection.* New York: Bantam Books, 1983.

Bolz, Frank A., Jr. *How To Be A Hostage and Live.* Secaucus, N.J.: Lyle Stuart, Inc., 1987.

Bottom, Norman R., Jr. *Security/Loss Control Negligence.* Columbia, Md.: Hanrow Press, 1985.

Braun, Matt. *The Save-Your-Life Defense Handbook.* Old Greenwich, Conn.: The Devin-Adair Co., 1977.

Brittin, Burdick H. *International Law for Seagoing Officers.* 5th ed. Annapolis, Md.: Naval Institute Press, 1986.

Chapman, Robert D., and Chapman, M. Lester. *The Crimson Web of Terror.* Boulder, Col.: Paladin Press, 1980.

Chelminski, Rudolph. *Superwreck.* New York: William Morrow and Company, 1987.

Collins, Patrick. *Living in Troubled Lands.* Boulder, Col.: Paladin Press, 1981.

Couhat, Jean Labayle, and Prezelin, Bernard, eds. *Combat Fleets of the World 1988/89.* Annapolis, Md.: Naval Institute Press, 1988.

Demaris, Ovid. *Brothers in Blood.* New York: Charles Scribner's Sons, 1977.

Dewar, Michael. *Weapons and Equipment of Counter-Terrorism.* London: Arms and Armour Press, 1987.

Dobson, Christopher, and Payne, Ronald. *The Terrorists.* New York: Facts On File, 1979.

Ellen, Eric F., ed. *Violence at Sea: A Review of Terrorism, Acts of War and Piracy, and Coutermeasures to Prevent Terrorism.* Paris: I. C. C. Publishing S.A., 1987.

———. *Piracy at Sea.* London: International Maritime Bureau, in press.

Evans, Alona E., and Murphy, John F., eds. *Legal Aspects of International Terrorism.* Lexington, Mass.: D. C. Heath and Company, 1978.

Friedan, David R., ed. *Principles of Naval Weapons Systems.* Annapolis, Md.: Naval Institute Press, 1985.

Hacker, Frederick J. *Crusaders, Criminals, Crazies.* New York: W. W. Norton & Co., 1976.

Healy, Richard J. *Design for Security.* 2d ed. New York: John Wiley & Sons, 1983.

Herbert, Anthony B. *Complete Security Handbook.* New York: Macmillan Publishing Company, 1983.

Hubbard, David G. *Winning Back the Sky.* Dallas: Saybrook Publishing Company, 1986.

Jane's Weapons Systems 1985–86. New York: Jane's Publishing, Inc.

Janke, Peter, and Sim, Richard. *Guerrilla and Terrorist Organizations: A World Directory and Bibliography.* New York: Macmillan Publishing Company, 1983.

Laqueur, Walter. *Terrorism.* Boston: Little, Brown and Company, 1977.

———. *The Age of Terrorism.* Boston: Little, Brown and Company, 1987.

Laqueur, Walter, and Alexander, Yonah, eds. *The Terrorism Reader.* Rev. ed. New York: NAL Penguin, 1987.

Lesce, Tony. *The Shotgun in Combat.* Cornville, Ariz.: Desert Publications, 1979.

Livingston, Neil C. *The War against Terrorism.* Lexington, Mass.: D. C. Heath and Company, 1982.

Mellman, Yossi. *The Master Terrorist: The True Story of Abu-Nidal.* New York: Avon, 1987.

Menefee, S[amuel] P[yeatt]. "The Salvador and Guatemala Affair: A Nineteenth Century American Response to Maritime Terrorism." *Sea Changes* 6: 80–111.

———. "Maritime Terror in Europe and the Mediterranean." *Marine Policy* (April 1988): 143–52.

———. "Scourges of the Sea: Piracy and Violent Maritime Crime." *Marine Policy Reports* forthcoming (1989).

Mueller, G. O. W., and Adler, Freda. *Outlaws of the Ocean.* New York: William Morrow and Company, 1985.

Netanyahu, Benjamin, ed. *International Terrorism: Challenge and Response.* Jerusalem: The Jonathan Institute, 1981.

Pepper, Curtis Bill. *Kidnapped!* New York: Harmony Books, 1978.

A Report into the Incidence of Piracy and Armed Robbery from Merchant Ships. Barking, Essex: I. C. C.—International Maritime Bureau, May, 1983.

Rivers, Gayle. *The Specialist.* New York: Stein and Day, 1985.

———. *The War against Terrorists: How to Win It.* New York: Stein and Day, 1986.

Ronzitti, Natalino, ed. *The* Achille Lauro *and International Law.* Dordrecht, Netherlands: Martinus Nijhoff, forthcoming.

A Second Report into the Incidence of Piracy and Armed Robbery from Merchant Ships. Barking, Essex: I. C. C.—International Maritime Bureau.

Sterling, Claire. *The Terror Network.* New York: Holt, Rinehart and Winston and Reader's Digest Press, 1981.

Swanson, Charles S., et al. *Police Administration: Structures, Processes and Behaviors.* New York: MacMillan Publishing Company, 1987.

A Third Report into the Incidence of Piracy and Armed Robbery from Merchant Ships. Barking, Essex: I. C. C.—International Maritime Bureau, October, 1985.

Thompson, Leroy. *The Rescuers: The World's Top Anti-Terrorist Units.* Boulder, Col.: Paladin Press, 1986.

Truby, David J. *How Terrorists Kill: The Complete Terrorist Arsenal.* Boulder, Col.: Paladin Press, 1978.

Villar, Roger. *Piracy Today: Robbery and Violence at Sea since 1980.* London: Conway Maritime Press, 1985.

Winter, William D. *Marine Insurance.* New York: McGraw-Hill, 1952.

INDEX

Numbers in italics are references to illustrations.

pilferage, pilferers, 32–33, 67, 144, 146–47, 199
pilots, 30, 132–33, 191, 224
Piper Alpha, 202, 216–17, 232, 235
piracy, pirates, 7, 14, 70–71, 74, 95, 189, 244–45
pistol
automatic (autoloader), 265–66, 271–75
machine, 4, 262–63
plan, planning
contingency, 11
security, 10, 11, 16, 64–94, 146, 154–206; offshore installation, 90–94; port facility, 34–35, 82–90; ship, 18, 28, 29, 127
police (law enforcement agencies), 35, 44, 75, 76, 86, 87, 199, 200
policy, security, 18, 26, 75–76, 86, 92, 166, 208–9, 229–33
polygraph examination, 163–64
precedent, in court cases, 212

R
radar, 97, 150, 151, 288–89; collision prevention alarm, 28
radio
marine, 6
single-sideband, 62
rail transport, 144
reasonableness, doctrine of, 28, 121, 155, 159, 160, 166, 202–3, 215, 216, 217, 218, 224, 229, 231–32, 233, 236, 243, 248, 251, 288, 289, 290–91, 292
registry, ship's, 18

restraint technique(s), nonlethal, 173–74, 299
rifle, 263–64, 282–86

S
sabotage, saboteurs, 32, 69–70, 95, 148–49, 153, 193
Santa Maria, 6
Sea Isle City, 7, 289
search, 135, 147, 153, 162–63, 198
seaworthiness, lack of, 243
self-defense, 159–60; passive weapons systems, 291
sentry, 108–9
settlement, court, 222–23
shotgun, 264–65, 278–81
smoke devices, 194
stores, ship's, 32–33, 48, 66
stowaway(s), 67–68, 74
submachine gun, 260–62, 286–87
submarine, mini-, 6, 91
support organizations, external, 35, 61, 86, 147
surveillance. *See* electronic(s), alarms & surveillance
survey, security
offshore installation, 49–60
port facility, 34–49
ship, 17–34
"survivors," 131–32

T
Tae Kwon Do, 299, 300
Taser, 269–70
tear gas, 194, 295–96
terrorists, 6, 147, 245, 259–60
testimony, 221
training, 109, 155, 164–69, 171, 173–74, 217, 225–27, 299

training (*continued*)
  marksmanship, 275–78, *280*
  offshore installation, 201–4
  port facility, 195–97
  record of, 165–66, 220
  shipboard, 182–83
  See also weapons, training
treaty, 158, 237–38, 257–58
trial, court, 218–23
trucks, 142–44

U
unions, 8, 121, 242
utilities
  public, 45
  self-generated, 62

V
vehicle(s), 46, 85, 124, 142–44, 163; internal security (ISV), 292–93
vendors, 44, 123
"vessel in distress," 126, 240
vision, night, 171–72; goggles (scopes), 292, 295, 297

visitors, 31, 122, 123, 124, 134–35, 152, 162–63

W
walkie-talkie(s), 129, 133, 134
walls, 12, 98, 100, 141
watch, watch standers, 73, 123, 127, 128–30, 131, 133, 134, 184–89, 191, 241–42, 255
water. *See* utilities, public
watercannon, 152
weapons, 11, 29, 63, 74, 75, 86, 160–61, 187–88, 189, 198, 254–56, 259–301
  disguised, 266
  systems, naval, 77, 137–38, 287, 289–90
  training, 172–73, 174–75, 203, 275–78
  See also particular types
whistles, 133

X
X-rays, 141

ABOUT THE AUTHOR

As the son of a career military officer, Mr. Hawkes grew up travel-ing and living overseas. At the age of 18 he went to sea as a commercial fisherman aboard a salmon purse seiner in Alaska. Thereafter he attended the University of Washington, in Seattle, on an N.R.O.T.C. scholarship, and in 1972 was commissioned a second lieutenant in the United States Marine Corps. While in the Marine Corps Mr. Hawkes served as a ship's security officer and nuclear weapons security officer, where he designed and implemented shipboard security procedures. When not serving afloat or in command billets, Mr. Hawkes was an instructor and training supervisor in such areas as infantry tactics, amphibious warfare, small arms marksmanship, weapons employment, riot control, and physical conditioning. He holds a Second Degree Black Belt in the Korean martial art of Tae Kwon Do, and has taught hand-to-hand combat, personal security, and counterterrorist tactics to corporate, civilian, and military personnel.

Mr. Hawkes received his Juris Doctor from the University of Miami in 1979 and was admitted to the Florida Bar the same year. He is admitted to practice before the Supreme Court of the United States, the Fifth and Eleventh U.S. Circuit Courts of Appeal, and federal and state courts in the State of Florida. In 1988 he closed his maritime trial practice in order to devote full-time attention to writing and consulting.